Speech and Phenomena

Northwestern University
STUDIES IN *Phenomenology &*
Existential Philosophy

Jacques Derrida

Translated, with an Introduction, by

Preface by

Speech and Phenomena

And Other Essays on Husserl's Theory of Signs

DAVID B. ALLISON

NEWTON GARVER

NORTHWESTERN UNIVERSITY PRESS

EVANSTON   1973

Speech and Phenomena was originally published in French under the title *La Voix et le Phénomène,* copyright © 1967 by Presses Universitaires de France.

"Form and Meaning" appeared in French under the title "La Forme et le vouloir-dire: Note sur la phénoménologie du langage," in the *Revue internationale de philosophie,* Volume LXXXI (1967).

"Differance" appeared in French under the title "La Différance" in the *Bulletin de la Société française de philosophie,* Volume LXII (1968) and was reprinted in *Théorie d'ensemble,* a collection of essays published by Éditions du Seuil in 1968.

Quotations from the following works of Edmund Husserl are used by permission of the publishers: *Logical Investigations,* translated by J. N. Findlay. Copyright © 1970 by Routledge & Kegan Paul Ltd, London, and Humanities Press, Inc., New York. *Ideas,* translated by W. R. Boyce Gibson. Copyright © 1931 by George Allen & Unwin Ltd, London, and Humanities Press, Inc., New York.

Jacques Derrida is Professor of Philosophy at the Ecole Normale Supérieure of the University of Paris.

David B. Allison is Assistant Professor of Philosophy at the State University of New York at Stony Brook.

Contents

Preface

DERRIDA'S CRITIQUE of Husserl is a first-class piece of
analytical work in the philosophy of language. But since Derrida
belongs to a philosophical tradition which is foreign, both geo-
graphically and intellectually, to most English-speaking philosophers, he is difficult to read. To see the power of his thought, it
is necessary for us to see how the problems that he articulates
and the comments that he makes fit within the framework of
issues in the philosophy of language that are commonly considered in Britain and America—which is difficult to do without
irreparably distorting his thoughts. Surely for this purpose it is
wiser not to try a direct translation from Derrida's Heideggerian
language into the more straightforward prose of American analytic philosophy, but rather to look for a wider framework in
which both these schools can be seen and compared.

Mediaeval thought can give us this wider perspective, if we
take as our starting point its pedagogical division of the study of
language into three parts—grammar, logic, and rhetoric. The
mediaeval trivium is a much sounder approach to the study of
language and gives a much more adequate framework for understanding the philosophy of language than its all too fashionable
neglect might lead one to suppose. The three studies correspond
nicely to three skills, or three sorts of competence, that we expect of a person who uses language. We expect, first, that a
speaker (and *mutatis mutandis* a hearer) will be able to put
together the words of the language in acceptable phrases and will
be able to modify those words as required by their position in
the phrases. The details of this requirement are studied by
grammarians; and though grammatical skill is superficial from

the point of view of philosophical problems, it is nonetheless a prerequisite for the other sorts of competence we expect of language-users. We expect, second, that a language-user will be able to recognize when an expression or a sequence of expressions is absurd or contradictory. The expressions which are recognized as absurd or contradictory will always be somehow complex, rather than simple, and it is in the combination of more simple expressions that this absurdity or contradiction lies. For example, "the colorless green ball," "the shapeless square box," and "the alert response of the dead man" are all noun phrases, but in each one of them there is a combination of more than one expression, and it is the combination of incombinables that makes these noun phrases absurd or illogical. In the case of sequences of expressions, such as "The poet is a penguin" (e. e. cummings) or "All the boys went on a hike, but two of them stayed in their rooms," where we have a predicative sentence or a conjunction of two sentences, it is obvious that more than one expression is involved. In a broad sense logic studies both these sorts of absurdity and proceeds formally, presenting its rules in terms of the expressions themselves without reference to the time or place or circumstances of their use. We expect, third, that a speaker will know how and when to use the linguistic expressions whose grammar and logic he has mastered. We expect that he will know when it is appropriate, and when it is not, to describe his sensations, to offer a definition, to curse, to pray, to utter an imperative, and so on. Traditionally rhetoric, ignoring the details of these common garden-variety uses of language, has concentrated its attention on the more subtle features of public speech and of literature and on the classification of styles and tropes. In spite of the way that the tradition has restricted itself, it has included within its purview a discussion of the proper use of contradictory expressions, such as the logical absurdities that occur in metaphors, and has thereby implicitly claimed a kind of priority over logic. This implicit claim sets the stage for an important controversy that concerns us directly. But the traditional restriction of scope is bothersome, and it is more useful to think of rhetoric as the general study of the aptness and ineptness of the use of various expressions or sorts of expressions in various sorts of circumstances. Rhetoric is thus not a matter of pure form but has to do with the relation of language to the world (to life) through the relation of linguistic expressions to the specific circumstances in which their use makes sense.

In these traditional terms, the central issue of philosophy of language, the issue around which all other issues revolve and to which they all return and in terms of which we can surely see the relation of Derrida to other philosophers, is the issue about the relation of logic and rhetoric. Grammar, having to do with the good order of signs and their relation to one another, is relatively superficial. Logic and rhetoric, on the other hand, both lead us into more profound areas because they both have to do with the use and interpretation of signs. The very fact that logic and rhetoric both have to do with the use and interpretation of signs leads us immediately into the all-important question of their relative priority: Can there be two independent foundations for our theory of meaning? Must there be two irreconcilable criteria for the use and interpretation of signs and hence for linguistic description? Or is one of these two seemingly fundamental disciplines in fact contained in or derivative from the other? When we are able to resolve this fundamental question about the relation of logic to rhetoric, we will then have established a solid vantage point from which to resolve the subsidiary questions about private language, about meaning, about form and use, about *Sinn* and *Bedeutung,* about *Ausdruck* and *Anzeigung,* and about the temporal and the nontemporal aspects of discourse.

In the history of Western philosophy, the philosophy of language—including a great deal of its metaphysics—has almost invariably been based on logic rather than rhetoric. This is certainly true of Plato's theory of forms, of Aristotle's doctrine of predication, of the mediaeval controversy over universals, of Leibniz' grand project for a universal symbolism, and of rationalism and idealism in general. It is also true, though less obviously so, of empiricist philosophy from Hobbes and Locke through to Brentano and James and Russell; for the empiricists have taken it for granted that the ideas represented by our linguistic signs already stand in logical relations to one another before we have signs to represent them. The exceptions that come to mind are on the fringe of the philosophical tradition rather than in its mainstream. Ibn Khaldūn is one: as much a historian and sociologist as a philosopher (he regarded philosophy as frivolous), he characterized language as a "technical habit" (that is, a trait or talent having to do with some art or craft or technique—*malaka ṣināʿiyya*), and for him grammar and logic seem to be refinements of rhetoric, in our broad sense of the term.

Condillac is another, with his view that language began with gestures and that verbal language has retained the essential features of this original "language of action." Rousseau is perhaps the best known of these exceptions; much influenced by Condillac, he saw the origins (and hence the essence) of language in the rhythms and intonations of our passions rather than in the more logical realm of practical affairs—reason enough for Derrida to devote a long section of his *De la grammatologie* to a sympathetic account of Rousseau's *Essay on the Origin of Languages*. But Rousseau's *Essay* remained unpublished during his lifetime, and this typifies how weak a challenge these alternative conceptions of language posed to the mainstream of philosophical tradition.

Twentieth-century philosophy has been dominated by considerations about the nature of language. It was only to be expected that there would be a flurry of activity as the nature and foundations of logic came to be closely investigated in the last part of the nineteenth century and the early part of our century, for the first time in more than two thousand years. In fact there have been two distinct flurries. The first movement was naturally a reinforcement of the philosophy of language based on logic; but the subsequent movement has been an overthrow of that long tradition, the overthrow which Derrida speaks of as the closure of metaphysics. In order to see the significance of Derrida's critique of Husserl, we must look more closely at these two movements.

THE END of the nineteenth century and the first few decades of the present century were a time of profound and far-reaching work on the nature of logic, the foundations of mathematics, and the relation of logic to mathematics. It was inevitable that this surge of new vitality in logical theory should have an impact on the philosophy of language, of one sort or another: on the one hand it was urgent that the new concepts and theories should fit into a general conception of language, and on the other hand the new burst of progress in logic seemed to promise an explanation of the nature of language. Already by the turn of the century it was apparent that the dominant theme was to be the increasing submission of philosophy in general, and of philosophy of language in particular, to the sovereignty of logic. This movement was due primarily to the work of five great men: Frege and Husserl in Germany, Whitehead and Russell in England, and Wittgenstein, who straddled the gap that separates the Continent from its most illustrious island. Though some allowance must be made for the later work of Husserl and Wittgenstein, all five of these powerful figures were logicians, all five associated the problems of logic in some way or other with the problems of mathematics, and the five of them together gave an irresistible impetus to the view that language is basically and primarily logical in character and that the fundamental essential features of language can be determined on the basis of require-ments of logic.

Since Derrida, through his critique of Husserl, is attacking the whole tradition in which language is conceived as founded on logic rather than on rhetoric, it is necessary to try to get a general picture of the common features of this philosophical tradition—in spite of the obvious risk that such generalization will inevitably distort the views that are generalized and may even seem outrageous to some of us who have been brought up to regard the differences between empiricism and rationalism as more fundamental than their common adherence to a philosophy of language that uses logic rather than discourse as the ultimate criterion for meaning. What rationalists and empiricists disagree about is the origin of ideas; what they have in common is the view that signs represent ideas and that an idea is something that can stand in semantic contrast or contradiction to another idea—and can be seen to stand in such contrast or contradiction without reference to contexts of communication, to "voices resounding in the corridors," or to how they figure in the "stream of life." This agreement about language being founded upon signs that represent ideas, which might be called the proximate source of language, has generally been considered less important than the disagreement between rationalism and empiricism about the ultimate source of language, the origin of the ideas that are to be represented by the signs. But it is precisely the common logical presuppositions, based on a common view that the primary purpose of language is epistemological, that need to be re-examined. Working within a Heideggerian framework, Derrida, like the later Wittgenstein, focuses attention on this common tradition in order to question its intelligibility—and hence to challenge the cogency of both schools of philosophy that are based upon it.

One important feature of the ideas that signs represent is that they are timeless, in the sense that they are not to be located and identified spatiotemporally. In this respect they differ from the acts of communication, the actual utterances, that occur in the course of our activities as language-users. That signs represent timeless ideas has a number of direct consequences that set the problems that Derrida considers. The first of these is that since a sign, in at least one prominent sense of that term, is something with physical characteristics and occurs in spatio-temporal contexts, there must be a radical distinction, a distinction in kind, between signs and what they signify. In France this distinction is most commonly known through the work of Saussure as the distinction between *signifiant* and *signifié* (signifier and signified). Derrida assumes familiarity with Saussure's terminology and its implications, and a key point in his attack on metaphysics in Chapter 4 is his attack on the requirement of a logical account of language that a sign be a completely different sort of thing from what it signifies and that the latter not be determined in any manner by the former. He may well seem to be overstating his point, since what he attacks is a distinction between signs and reality, which seems not to be so much a metaphysical distinction as one of the most down-to-earth common sense. But we should bear in mind that what is ultimately real, on the view that he is attacking, is some sort of *ideas,* or things that can stand in *logical* relations to one another; and this conception of the world as fundamentally logical is *not* a common-sense view, nor does the *common-sense* distinction between signs and reality in any way imply that there must be a concomitant *metaphysical* distinction between reality (thus metaphysically conceived) and signs. Indeed, if I have understood Derrida right, his insistence that there cannot be such a metaphysical distinction is both sound and profound.

A second consequence of taking the timelessness of ideas as the foundation of language is that a certain amount of Platonism is inevitable, in that the actual is explained in terms of the ideal. Consider, for example, actual linguistic utterances where speakers mean something or other by uttering some linguistic expression at some specific time and place. How is the speaker's meaning (what he means at that time and place) to be explained? The thought that he is expressing—that is, in Frege's terminology, the sense (*Sinn*) of the sentence he utters or, in Husserl's terminology, its meaning (*Bedeutung*)—must be explicated by means of the ideas that are represented by the constituent words of that sentence. Derrida develops this issue in his final chapter, where the dilemma that he poses for Husserl might be rephrased as the question, "How can language (meaning) ever be used in reference to transient objects and circumstances, given that it is established and constituted independent of them?" It is obvious that this question strikes at the very heart of Husserl's phenomenological account of language. Some idea of the way in which the issue arises in other versions of the logical view of language may be appreciated by comparing this question with one that Wittgenstein asked himself in the *Tractatus:*

> 5552   The "experience" that we need in order to understand logic is not that something or other is the state of things, but that something *is:* that, however, is *not* an experience.
>
> Logic is *prior* to every experience—that something *is so.*
>
> It is prior to the question "How?," not prior to the question "What?"
>
> 55521   And if this were not so, how could we apply logic? We might put it in this way: if there would be a logic even if there were no world, how then could there be a logic given that there is a world? [1]

A third consequence, closely related to the second, is that there must be a radical distinction between what Frege called sense and reference, or between what Husserl called expression and indication. These distinctions are not exactly the same, but they have the same purpose, namely, to distinguish as two separate and independent domains the (timeless, context-free) semantic relations of signs to one another and the (time-dependent, contextually variant) semantic relations of signs to the world. It is now commonplace among British and American philosophers to suppose that the theory of meaning must be divided into at least two parts, a theory of sense and a theory of reference (though those who follow Charles Morris would divide it into three parts: syntax, semantics, and pragmatics). The underlying assumption is that what linguistic expressions *mean* is one sort of question and that how and when they are to be *applied* is a separate and independent question. To the extent that this assumption is part and parcel of the logical conception

1. Ludwig Wittgenstein, *Tractatus Logico-Philosophicus,* trans. D. F. Pears and B. F. McGuiness (New York: Humanities Press, 1961).

of the foundations of language, one challenges the underlying philosophy when one denies that these two domains of meaning can really be kept separate, as Derrida does throughout *Speech and Phenomena* and, in particular, in Chapter 7. The parallel is striking with the later work of Wittgenstein, in which such a denial is one of the first and most prominent themes.

A fourth consequence of basing meaning on timeless ideas is that the analysis and resolution of the nest of issues involved is going to turn on one's conception of time and eternity. Involved in this is the underlying issue of the relation between the finite and the infinite; for the question whether time presupposes eternity or eternity presupposes time is a more specific form of the general question whether the infinite is to be conceived within the finite or the finite within the infinite. All of these questions sound like rather abstract metaphysical issues, unfamiliar as critical considerations within Anglo-American philosophy. Yet in Chapter 6 Derrida explicitly makes *time* the key to his analysis (or what he calls his "deconstruction"). This move will appear less baffling when one realizes that Derrida's deconstruction in terms of *time* is equivalent to analysis of the meaning of linguistic expressions in terms of their *use* or the role that they play in human activities. In both cases the point is to insist that the timeless can be understood only as an aspect of, or as an abstraction from, temporal occasions.

A second feature of the philosophy of language based on logic is just as crucial but can be dealt with more briefly. It is the commitment to what Wittgenstein called a "private language," or to some conception of private understanding or inner speech such that it is possible for linguistic expressions to have meaning for us in "private mental life," quite independent of *any* reference to public objects or external circumstances. Such a commitment to private language or to private understanding cannot be renounced once the criterion for linguistic meaning has been set within the domain of logic. For logical truths and logical considerations are formal and do not vary according to circumstance; so their essence must be independent of any sets of circumstances. What is independent of circumstance in this way I cannot learn by example or by teaching—at any rate its essence cannot be given to me in any such manner. If I learn it at all, it must, so it would seem, be within a realm that lies entirely within me, in my private mental life. This kind of commitment is obvious throughout modern philosophy, beginning with Descartes and Locke, and shows itself with equal vigor and clarity at the turn of the century in the writings of Husserl and Russell. One of the remarkable and rewarding parts of Derrida's book is his forceful rejection (in Chapter 4) of the possibility of private understanding, an interesting parallel to the famous "private-language argument" in Wittgenstein's *Philosophical Investigations* (§ § 243–315).

THE SECOND MOVEMENT in the twentieth-century philosophy of language has lacked the solid foundation that the first enjoyed. Unlike grammar and logic, rhetoric has not been refurbished by new ideas and new vigor but remains a weak and ancillary discipline about which few students of language have strong or clear ideas. As an academic subject, rhetoric remains associated with elocution and literary criticism rather than with linguistics and logic. The development of linguistics in the twentieth century has tended to reinforce the association between meaning and logic rather than to challenge it. It did this from the very beginning in the hands of Saussure, who regarded the elements of language as something ideal rather than empirical and whose distinction between *signifiant* and *signifié* we have already mentioned. The latest developments in linguistics continue the trend. Transformational grammar is based on a distinction between surface structure and deep structure, with deep structure being an idealized abstraction that either contains or interprets the semantic component of language. Behind the rather esoteric controversy in transformational linguistics between generative semantics and interpretive semantics there lies unexamined and almost unnoticed the assumption that linguistic meaning belongs to an abstract realm where logical criteria predominate. This assumption is not altogether unwelcome, since it leads to fruitful collaboration between linguists and logicians; but it does make it difficult to raise and press the fundamental questions in the philosophy of language, the ones that have to do with the ultimate foundation of linguistic meaning.

In spite of the lack of a vigorous discipline of rhetoric, that is, of any hardheaded, detailed study of the rules and regularities and presuppositions of the use of linguistic expressions in the circumstances in which they actually are used, there have been philosophers who have emphasized this aspect of meaning, either as one part of a semantic dualism or as a primary sense of meaning within which the logical aspects of meaning must find a specialized and restricted niche.

In Britain and America semantic dualism undoubtedly rests most prominently on the work of Frege and his distinction between sense and reference. Within the framework of that general distinction or some variation on it, there have developed the ideas of operational definitions and coordinating definitions in science and of recursive definitions in mathematics. It is characteristic of these definitions that they do not really explain the meaning (*Bedeutung* in Husserl's sense) or the sense (*Sinn* in Frege's sense) of the expressions they are used to define but serve instead to present effective criteria for the *use* of those expressions. It seems obvious that definitions of this sort present rhetorical rather than logical considerations as governing the "meaning" of words and that this should raise the question whether operational definitions provide the proper form for *all* explanations of meaning. But if the question has ever been raised in this form, it has not had any significant historical impact. For the most part operational definitions were conceived within a sort of semantic dualism, and it was assumed that the characteristic problems of dualism—in this case the logical aspects of words introduced only operationally—would sort themselves out without trouble. Certainly the question of the relation of operational meaning to conceptual meaning raises far deeper and more profound questions than have yet been effectively answered.

Philosophers who have given some impetus to the view that rhetoric rather than logic provides the foundation for linguistic meaning include Peirce and Royce in the nineteenth century and Wittgenstein and Austin in the postwar period. Peirce was undoubtedly one of the first to advocate operational definitions; but his more general philosophy of language is extremely difficult to interpret, largely because it is so difficult to know whether he would allow or encourage any priority among the various trichotomies that he sets down. Nonetheless, his emphasis on *interpretation* (as opposed to conception) suggests that meanings are to be explained ultimately in terms of the human context in which they are interpreted. If this is correct, Peirce would be the first philosopher who combined an emphasis upon operational definitions with the view that such operationally, or contextually, explained meaning is the primary source for all linguistic meaning. Certainly Royce interpreted Peirce this way and took his conception of meaning and interpretation as the crux for some important considerations in his social philosophy—especially in Lectures XI and XII of *The Problem of Christianity*.

Since 1940 in Britain, and moving from there to America, a considerable impetus to consider rhetoric rather than logic as the bedrock for language and for meaning has been given by the work of Wittgenstein and Austin. In the present context our attention must focus on Wittgenstein, since his own philosophical development, with respect to the foundations of language, is in many ways parallel to the movement in Continental philosophy from Husserl to Heidegger and Derrida. Lest this emphasis should seem to slight Austin, it should be said explicitly that in another context, where the concern was for revitalizing the discussion of rhetoric and incorporating it as a rigorous part of general linguistics, Austin's method would receive primary emphasis. Austin's rather conventional effort at classification, so as to provide a way to count what Wittgenstein referred to as the "countless different kinds of use of what we call 'symbols,' 'words,' 'sentences,'" and his patient attention to detail lend themselves much more readily to a scientific interest than does Wittgenstein's work; and something like Austin's theory of speech acts must be involved if rhetorical force is to be seen as the indispensable basis of linguistic meaning. But Wittgenstein provides a more useful framework for understanding the import, in Anglo-American terms, of Derrida's criticism of Husserl.

It is obvious that Wittgenstein's *Tractatus* bears close affinities to Husserl's *Logical Investigations*. Not only does Wittgenstein's notion of a *Begriffschrift* correspond closely with Husserl's conception of a *rein logisch-grammatische Formenlehre*, as Max Black points out,[2] but the whole idea of the *Tractatus* seems to be to provide what Husserl called a "pure logical grammar." Wittgenstein's aim, that is, is to show how it is possible for there to be language at all, by specifying the indispensable prerequisites for meaningful sentences, considered without reference to any of the accidental or empirical characteristics of those sentences. In this early work Wittgenstein—and here the hegemony of epistemology, of which Derrida complains, is apparent—allows only one sort of fully meaningful sentence, namely, those that describe the world. For there to be such sentences, there are

2. Max Black, *A Companion to Wittgenstein's 'Tractatus'* (Ithaca: Cornell University Press, 1964), p. 136.

(apart from the contingent and empirical prerequisites of human existence, vocal organs, and so on) two *a priori* requirements. The first is an elaboration of a Kantian image, namely, that there must be a single logical space, since each sentence or proposition determines a point in logical space. In its generalized form this requirement is the requirement that there must be a language if there are to be sentences, a view which persists in Wittgenstein's later work. The second requirement is that the sentences be composed of names that are correlated with noncontingent objects. Ultimately, logical space (the first requirement) is itself based upon this metaphysical foundation of simple and eternal objects. Here, then, is the crux of Wittgenstein's early theory of language: an invulnerable foundation, but one whose very invulnerability is its ultimate weakness. It is a metaphysical foundation which is determined and preserved by logical requirements and which in its turn preserves and determines logic.

Section 107 of the *Philosophical Investigations* presents as clearly and poignantly as one could wish the trend of his later thinking about the foundation for the pure logical grammar of his earlier work:

> The more narrowly we examine actual language, the sharper becomes the conflict between it and our requirement. (For the crystalline purity of logic was, of course, not a *result of investigation:* it was a requirement.) The conflict becomes intolerable; the requirement is now in danger of becoming empty.— We have got on to slippery ice, where there is no friction, and so in a certain sense the conditions are ideal; but also, just because of that, we are unable to walk. We want to walk: so we need *friction.* Back to the rough ground! [3]

When Wittgenstein turned from making demands to making observations—for his later philosophy is based firmly on the conviction that a philosopher has to look and see what happens and that he can only describe and in no way impose requirements —what he saw was that linguistic expressions are everywhere embedded in contexts of human activity. In order to conclude that they are in fact intrinsically and inextricably embedded in such activity, he had to present two sorts of consideration: one

3. Wittgenstein, *Philosophical Investigations,* trans. G. E. M. Anscombe (New York: Macmillan, 1963).

to break down the seeming necessity for metaphysical foundations, by showing that the metaphysical demands and hypotheses are ultimately incoherent; and the other to show how both the familiar and the problematic features of language and language use can be accounted for within a theory of language which takes rhetorical force rather than word meaning as the foundation for language.

It is very easy to overemphasize the importance of Wittgenstein's rejection of his earlier position, since such an overemphasis quickly leads us to overlook the remaining similarities. But there is nonetheless a strong negative component in Wittgenstein's presentation of his new position, a component consisting of at least four sorts of argument: against the primacy of names; against the possibility, or even the conceivability, of objects that are absolutely or metaphysically simple; against both the coherence and cogency of the demand for absolute exactness, which Frege had earlier persuaded him was essential if there is to be any conceptual meaning at all; and against the possibility of private language or private understandings or private meanings, such as seems to be presupposed by any theory which begins by associating words with ideas or by taking names to be signs for ideas in the mind of the person that uses them.

These negative arguments of Wittgenstein's against his former views (and against other philosophies which take logic as constituting the essence of language) are set firmly in an alternative constructive conception of language according to which the meaning of linguistic expressions is based ultimately on their rhetorical force, that is, on the role that they play in human activities. The central notions in terms of which Wittgenstein elaborates this new view of language are those of *language-games,* of *rules* and *practices,* and of *forms of life.* To understand a linguistic expression, one must know the "game" being played with it, which in turn often depends largely (never wholly) on knowing the "rules of the game" and always depends in part on being able (knowing how) to follow the rules. Being able to follow rules depends, in turn, on practice or training, on being initiated into a "form of life"—which is what is ultimately "given" as the basis of language. Thus language and logic (which are ideal) are founded on training (which is empirical)—a result which "seems to abolish logic, but does not do so." The reliance of this view on rhetorical force as the epitome of meaning, as well as its relevance to the dispute between Husserl and Derrida, comes out most forcefully in a slogan reported by Norman Malcolm: "Only in the stream of life does an expression have meaning."

DERRIDA'S POSITION is markedly similar. Derrida falls squarely within the movement which regards the role of utterances in actual discourse as the essence of language and meaning, and which therefore regards logic as derivative from rhetorical considerations. His penetrating consideration and ultimate rejection of the basic principles of Husserl's philosophy of language is the historical analogue of Wittgenstein's later consideration and rejection of his own earlier work, *The Tractatus Logicophilosophicus*. In both cases a work belonging to the first historical movement in the philosophy of language of the twentieth century is examined and found unintelligible, at least partly on its own terms; and the alternative to the rejected theory is one that belongs to the second movement, according to which rhetoric and the context of actual communication are an essential and ineradicable feature of all linguistic meaning. As we consider Derrida's criticism of Husserl, we should bear in mind that Derrida does not simply overthrow Husserl any more than Wittgenstein's later work simply overthrew his earlier work. In both cases the later work depends heavily upon the earlier; and with respect to other issues than those upon which we are focusing here, the common elements probably overshadow the differences.

In its negative component, the core of Derrida's analysis, or "deconstruction," is a sustained argument against the possibility of anything pure and simple which can serve as the foundation for the meaning of signs. It is an argument which strikes at the very idea of a transcendental phenomenology. The move is parallel with Wittgenstein's rejection of the idea of simples (which is also the core of the negative component in his later work); but whereas the simples that Wittgenstein came to reject were logical atoms, or objects free from any contingent or empirical properties, the simples that Derrida rejects are the simples of transcendental phenomenology rather than of logical atomism, viz., experience that is pure in the sense that it can be fully understood as it is found in our private mental life, without reference to transient circumstances or actual empirical objects. These pure experi-

ences must be some sort of direct and unmediated awareness of
the present moment and its content. Therefore, a central aspect
of Derrida's argument, in the next-to-the-last chapter, lies in his
examination of the claim that we can intelligibly think about
and talk about present moments that are pure and simple—even
though the present moments of Husserl's phenomenological account of meaning are not so pure and simple as, say, Hume's
"impressions," since their content includes "retentions" and "protentions" that have implications about the past and future. Here
we have an example of Husserl being followed out and used
against himself: just as Husserl criticized the British empiricists
for sneaking in metaphysical commitments with the assumption
that experience can be purely passive and free from implications
about the past and future, Derrida makes an analogous objection
to Husserl's own claim that there can be experience whose
Ausdruck is, in essence, independent of its *Anzeigen* and which
can therefore be fully comprehended in one's private mental life
without presupposing the actual world and transient circumstances.

In Chapter 7 he elaborates another aspect of the argument,
which culminates in the startling remark, "There never has been
any perception." This is, of course, not a rejection of any familiar
everyday experience, but a rejection of a concept, a concept that
is an idealized and, one might say, logicized abstraction from our
common everyday experience. It is the concept of perception,
not as the awareness of circumstances in which we live and move
and have our being, but rather as the pure immediate awareness
of a sensory content which, although complicated by retentions
and protentions, has no *intrinsic* reference to any such actual
circumstances. That such a concept of perception is not original
with Husserl but has been an integral part of the empiricist tradition since Locke, and in modern times can be found as well in
Russell, makes Derrida's point all the more important. It should
be noted, too, that this aspect of Derrida's central argument is an
echo of Wittgenstein's extended and fascinating discussion in
§ 11 of Part II of his *Philosophical Investigations*, of "seeing" and
"seeing as." In both Wittgenstein and Derrida the remarks about
perception are as difficult as they are important, and as puzzling
as they are intriguing; but it can at least be said that both impugn
the idea of pure perception and that what they have to say about
perception goes hand in glove with rejection of the idea that the

nature and essence of what is signified (*le signifié*) is wholly independent of the nature of the sign that signifies it (*le signifiant*).

Finally, there is an aspect of Derrida's attack upon the possibility of simples that seems to me to be original with him and to be highly interesting. It centers around his concept of *différance*. *Différance*, without which no language or meaningful sign can be conceived, is associated very closely in Derrida's work with what makes it possible to transcribe spoken language in writing. What makes writing possible is nothing having to do with the meaning of the spoken signs; what makes it possible is rather the pattern of vocalizations, the phonemics of the language. If I have understood Derrida right, one might say (though Derrida does not himself say it) that *voix* and *écriture* are ultimately in harmony rather than opposition because *différance* is essential to both. This may seem a perversely prosaic way to reduce the rich variety of remarks Derrida makes in his essay "Différance," so a word of explanation is in order. *Différance* is a complex essential characteristic of signs, being composed of (*a*) an actual difference which makes the sign possible, but which can be instituted and understood only in terms of (*b*) other times and circumstances in which the instituted difference *systematically* appears. Such a characteristic (which Derrida, it must be remembered, regards as somewhat puzzling and problematic) is no doubt essential at each level of language: it is what makes possible both meaning in the strict sense and also linguistic significance in general. Although it is a general characteristic of signs, its most fundamental application is at the phonological level, since spoken sound, *voix*, actual speech in actual circumstances, is the indispensable basis for all linguistic signification. In the sound system of a language, according to structuralist phonology, the sounds that are ultimately differentiated linguistically are phonemes. Derrida's remarks imply that phonemic difference is a matter of *différance* rather than either actual acoustic difference as such or ideal difference as such: both the above features are, essentially and indissolubly, involved in the differentiation of phonemes. Phonemes are, therefore, units or aspects of *différance* at the phonological level; as such they can be neither spoken nor written, but they are (and so is *différance*, if it is a viable concept) what makes it possible for sounds to be intelligible as *voix* and for marks to be intelligible as *écriture*. By following these notions back to their roots, Derrida shows that, although speech and writing *seem* to be opposed to each other, they cannot ultimately be so, since what is essential to the one necessarily makes the other possible.[4]

By taking *différance,* or the phonemic structure of the sound system of the language, as essential to any language or sign system, Derrida not only associates his central argument with a prominent element of contemporary linguistics but also strikes at the roots of the speculation about ideography that has often been associated with the logical conception of language—as, for example, in Descartes's letter to Mersenne of November 20, 1629, or Leibniz' project for a *characteristica universalis,* or the comments about a *Begriffschrift* that are to be found in the writings of Frege and Wittgenstein. Derrida's emphasis on *différance* being essential to any sign tells against any absolutely pure and simple signs, since the possibility of being transcribed in a writ-

---

4. While there can be no question of the originality of Derrida's formulation and his use of the concept of *différance,* there is an interesting historical precedent for some of the main points in Aristotle. Like Derrida, Aristotle bases his theory of meaning on *spoken* language; but what is spoken becomes *language* only if it can also be written down. Consider the following passage from the second chapter of the *De Interpretatione:*

"A name is a spoken sound significant by convention, without time, none of whose parts is significant in separation. . . . I say 'by convention' because no name is a name naturally but only when it has become a symbol. Even inarticulate [*agrammatoi*] noises (of beasts, for instance) do indeed reveal something, yet none of them is a name" (16a19–28; trans. J. L. Ackrill [Oxford: Clarendon Press, 1963]).

Here the key concept is that of being "articulated," that is, composed of segments or parts, for which Aristotle here uses the words *grammata* (elsewhere *stoicheia*) and *grammatoi.* Now *grammata* are normally thought of as letters; but since a *sound* cannot literally have letters, they must be thought of here as phonemes—that is, as the parts of a sound that can be represented by letters. The natural cries of animals do signify something, they are signs; but they are not symbols, and we know they are not conventional, *because* they are not composed of articulate parts and cannot faithfully be transcribed in writing. So Aristotle held that what characterizes human speech and distinguishes it from natural cries is the possibility of writing (*écriture*) and the internal segmentation or differentiation of even the simplest semantic elements (*différance*). For further discussion of this passage, see N. Kretzmann, "Aristotle on Sounds Significant by Convention," forthcoming from Reidel Publishing Company (Dordrecht) in J. Corcoran, ed., *Modernist Interpretations of Ancient Logic.*

ing system, which necessarily involves a reference both to other times *and* to a system, is not anything that is intrinsic to the physical presentation of the sign; and it tells against metaphysical simples when combined with his view that things cannot be conceived apart from the signs that represent them. If there is a parallel to this argument of Derrida's in the work of Wittgenstein, it would be found in Wittgenstein's insistence, in both his early and his later work, that a linguistic sign is always part of a system; but even if we were to regard these two points as significant analogues of each other, Derrida would deserve recognition for the power and force and originality of his formulation of the argument.

I HAVE ALREADY MENTIONED the attack on private language, and I would hope that philosophers in the analytic tradition would be able to find other familiar points presented in an exciting manner in Derrida's work. Nevertheless, I would not expect them to read the present work without frequent discomfort and occasional dismay. There are two aspects of the present work that contribute to such discomfort. One is Derrida's style. The work is full of metaphors, of plays upon words that often do not survive the translation, of florid language that sometimes leaves one mystified as to Derrida's intent, and of verbal contradictions or absurdities. Students of Wittgenstein are already familiar with the problem of having to read *through* someone's language in order to see the point lying behind it, presented obliquely but unstated—and perhaps even unstatable (in some sense which can be and needs to be stated), since both Wittgenstein and Derrida believe there is something ultimately incoherent about the notion of a "philosophical thesis." We cannot complain just because Derrida is often obscure, for the problems are exceedingly difficult, and a demand for pedestrian prose would be misplaced. But clarity is more than just pedestrian. Faced with Derrida's unrestrained literary extravagance, one cannot help wondering if the heavy reliance upon metaphor and paradox is not also misplaced.

It is often difficult to be sure that there is consistency or even intelligibility lying behind Derrida's manner of expression. I have in mind those passages where Derrida has been willing to risk equivocation for the sake of a pun or to pay the price of apparent absurdity in order to achieve a striking turn of phrase—as when he says that "there never has been any perception"; that speech (*voix*) without *différance* would be "at the same time absolutely dead and absolutely alive"; in regard to Husserl's essential distinctions, that "their possibility is their impossibility"; that the verb *différer* "seems to differ from itself"; that "la différance infinie est finie"; that the history of philosophy is "closed" (which, literally, is very like a child's claiming to be asleep); and so on. One cannot help wondering if the price is worth paying, and on at least one occasion in the last chapter Derrida himself is led into clearly fallacious reasoning that derives from his equivocation on "finite" and "infinite." But most of these locutions can be explained as intelligible comments, and the philosophical insight lying behind them is often profound. One might well bear in mind, through one's exasperation with Derrida's literary flourishes, that his obliqueness is caused at least in part by a virtue he shares with Socrates and Russell and other great philosophers, viz., the ability to retain a sense of how very perplexing the most familiar phenomena are and to expose the weaknesses in a proposed solution by articulating it in detail so that its presuppositions are laid bare.

The other worrisome aspect of the present work is the uncertainty about how Derrida views logic, knowledge, and philosophy. Just as the problem of reference is the one which presents the greatest challenge to the traditional logical conception of language, so the problem of logic is the greatest challenge to the conception of language that is found in Derrida and in the later work of Wittgenstein. Derrida gives us few hints, if any, as to how he will deal with this problem. In this respect there is a sharp contrast between Derrida and Wittgenstein, especially when we remember that in its wider implications the problem about logic includes the question whether we can ever really *know* anything; for in spite of his vigorous rejection of formalism, Wittgenstein never doubts the possibility of veridical knowledge and sound inference. One hopes that Derrida, having helped to shatter the reign of epistemology over our conception of language and metaphysics, will one day return to this problem.

Part of this problem is a much more specific question: a question about the tools of his trade, about what standpoint he takes from which to criticize Husserl. Derrida announces the end of metaphysics, the closure of the history of philosophy. But just as Derrida raises the question whether Husserl succeeded in eliminating all presuppositions from his phenomenological inquiry, so readers are bound to ask whether Derrida has succeeded

in eliminating all metaphysical presuppositions from his deconstruction. The question arises most forcefully when Derrida is
discussing what is real and what is unreal, a question which it
hardly seems possible to deal with without having a conception
of reality in one's mind. It arises again when he insists that language depends on a relation to "ma-mort," a claim which it is
difficult to conceive as other than metaphysical. No doubt the
answer to this question will depend in part on epistemological
views as well. Derrida *seems* at times to embrace a nominalism
combined with a sort of radical empiricism. What is "real" seems
to be the concrete reality immediately before me, and not aspects
of what I see and experience that refer to other times or possibilities. Thus, as Lionel Abel has pointed out,[5] Derrida's discussion of *différance* is reminiscent of Nelson Goodman's discussion
of likeness of meaning, in that the likeness or identity of meanings or phenomena is something ideal and hence unreal, standing
in sharp contrast to the reality of differences. This primacy of
difference over identity is an eerie departure from common
sense and is bound to be worrisome to Anglo-American readers.
No doubt it stems in part from the analytical methods of structural linguists such as Sapir and Bloomfield; but such a genesis
in structuralism can hardly be reassuring to those of us who
remember Bloomfield's close association with logical positivism
and who regard his linguistic methodological strictures as unduly
severe. The worry is that Derrida may not have left himself any
ground on which to stand and may be enticing us along a path to
nowhere—a worry, by the way, which some philosophers have
(mistakenly, I think) when they read Wittgenstein.

It may be that these worries about Derrida's standpoint are
unnecessary and that it is sufficient to note that his deconstruction, analysis, constantly harks back to the context of communication in which one person confronts another. Seen in this light,
the central point of the book may well be that memorable sentence in the last chapter: "Il reste alors à *parler*, à faire *resonner*
la voix dans les couloirs pour suppléer l'éclat de la présence" ("It
remains, then, for us to *speak*, to make our voices *resonate*
throughout the corridors in order to make up for the breakup of
presence"—though the last phrase is characteristically ambiguous and might also be rendered "in order to supplement the

5. Lionel Abel, *Important Nonsense* (New York: Basic Books,
1972).

impact of one's presence.") In the history of recent philosophy this remark can well be taken as an answer to Wittgenstein's equally memorable epigram at the end of the *Tractatus*, "Wovon man nicht sprechen kann, darüber muss man schweigen" ("What we cannot speak about we must consign to silence"). If these two slogans do not explicitly contradict each other, they at least present in dramatic form alternative conceptions of what is important; and readers will be well rewarded by taking the time to become acquainted with Derrida's view.

NEWTON GARVER

State University of New York
at Buffalo
June, 1972

Translator's Introduction

THE PRESENT WORK comprises a collection of three texts: *Speech and Phenomena*, which first appeared in 1967, together with two shorter pieces, "Form and Meaning" (1967), and "Differance" (1968). They were selected to appear together in translation with two reasons in mind; first, they present the English-speaking audience with a new generation of phenomenological criticism, indeed with one of the most thorough and reflective criticisms yet to appear on the work of Husserl. Second, they introduce the thought of Derrida himself to a new public, a thought that marks a considerable departure from the kind of exegesis and commentary that is all too present in current philosophical literature. It is not Derrida's intention, however, to remain confined within a particular framework of phenomenology. Rather, he sees it as his task to confront phenomenology with the tradition it has so often renounced up until now, the tradition of Western metaphysics itself.

In choosing to begin with a critique of the *Logical Investigations*, Derrida has selected perhaps the most important, if not the most influential, of Husserl's writings on language. Derrida's interpretation is instructive in that he demonstrates how the whole of phenomenology is implied in a reflection upon language, how a discussion of meaning, expression, grammar, and logic—the themes of the *Investigations*—will anticipate and later decide the forthcoming "transcendental" problems. The value of focusing the analysis here lies in the fact that Husserl begins the *Investigations* with a set of "essential distinctions," a group of operative concepts, that will rigorously and systematically guide his thought to the end.

[xxxi]

Derrida stresses the importance of these distinctions, not only because they dictate the course and structural unity of Husserl's own work, but because they repeat, in an explicit and cogent way, the very axioms of traditional metaphysics. This is only one stage of the argument, however, for he does not mean to portray Husserl and phenomenology as merely another example in the history of metaphysics. Derrida will argue even more emphatically that Husserl's thought is precisely the paradigm, the highest and final case of this tradition. And it is ultimately the claims and pretensions of this tradition—the parameters of which are admittedly vast—that Derrida wants to contest.

Derrida asserts that throughout his writings Husserl continually invokes the most traditional concepts of Western metaphysics to serve as the axiomatic foundation for phenomenology, and this is evident from the first "essential distinction." By this procedure a certain decision is taken to interpret the sense of being in a particular way. For Husserl and the tradition, the sense of being has always been interpreted as *presence,* and this interpretation assumes two forms: something *is* insofar as it presents itself or is capable of presenting itself to a subject—as the present object (*ob-jectum*) of a sensible intuition or as an objectivity presented to thought. Second, we say that a subject (*sub-jectum*) or self in general *is* only insofar as it is self-present, present to itself in the immediacy of a conscious act. The former marks the interpretation of being as objectivity (*ousia, physis,* etc.), the latter as subjectivity (*parousia, nous,* etc.). The interpretation of being as presence and self-presence entails a series of philosophical consequences and conceptual oppositions that persists to the present day, and nowhere are these consequences more strikingly evident than in the thought of Husserl. As part of his critical project of deconstruction,[1] Derrida discusses the

1. The term "deconstruction" (*déconstruction*), while perhaps unusual, should present no difficulties here. It signifies a project of critical thought whose task is to locate and "take apart" those concepts which serve as the axioms or rules for a period of thought, those concepts which command the unfolding of an entire epoch of metaphysics. "Deconstruction" is somewhat less negative than the Heideggerian or Nietzschean terms "destruction" or "reversal"; it suggests that certain foundational concepts of metaphysics will never be entirely eliminated, even if their importance may seem to be effectively diminished. There is no simple "overcoming" of metaphysics or the language of metaphysics. Derrida recognizes, nonetheless, that the system of Western thought is finite; it has a finite number of

genesis and derivation of this series as it functions in phenomenology. Among the many conceptual oppositions to be found here
are those of matter (*hylē*) and form (*eidos, idea*), corporeal and
incorporeal, body and soul, animate and inanimate, signifier and
signified.

Far from being "presuppositionless," therefore, the interpretation of being as presence will provide phenomenology with its
axial concepts. The highest principle of phenomenology, apodictic evidence, is precisely a call for the presentation or bringing-
forth (*e-videre*) of objects to an immediate and self-present intuition. The notion of transcendental consciousness, as well, is
nothing more than the immediate self-presence of this waking
life, the realm of what is primordially "my own." By contrast,
the concepts of empirical, worldly, corporeal, etc., are precisely
what stands opposed to this realm of self-present ownness; they
constitute the sphere of otherness, the mediated, what is different from self-present conscious life, etc. All these concepts
find their systematic unity in Husserl's account of language.

Language, for Husserl, serves scientific thought and finds
its model in the highest degree of scientific objectivity, the form
of logical predication. And, we should not forget, it is across and
through language that meaningful statements can be recorded
and transmitted, that a body of doctrine can be set down and
verified, that a community of scientists can communicate, that
science itself becomes possible. Meaningful language, consequently, has its own rules and purpose; it is a "pure logical grammar," and it expresses meanings in predicative form, i.e., in the
form of a possible reference to an object. This is where Husserl
makes the first "essential distinction" of the *Investigations*. In
language, there are two different sorts of signification: indication
and expression. For Husserl, however, only one of these—expres-

---

axioms and a finite number of permutations that will continue to
work themselves out in a given period of time as particular moments
within this tradition, e.g., as particular schools or movements of
philosophy. In this sense, Derrida also speaks of the "completion" of
metaphysics, the terminal point of "closure" (*clôture*) for the system.
But the work of deconstruction does not consist in simply pointing
out the structural limits of metaphysics. Rather, in breaking down
and disassembling the ground of this tradition, its task is both to
exhibit the source of paradox and contradiction within the system,
within the very axioms themselves, and to set forth the possibilities
for a new kind of meditation, one no longer founded on the metaphysics of presence.

sion—is meaningful. Expression alone, properly speaking, bears sense.

It is important to understand why Derrida seizes upon this distinction. Meaningful language is limited to expression. But how does expression differ from indication? Husserl understands indication to be a movement of *empirical* association. One sensible sign stands for something else; a mark, a note, an object makes us pass from something present to thought to something that is only anticipated or expected. There is no meaning-content present in indication; there is only an empty *signifier* and nothing that is *signified*. That is yet to come, it is yet to be presented. An expression, however, *carries* a meaning-content with it. Meaning is present as the *signified* content of expression. What is immediately at stake in this linguistic distinction, then, is Husserl's entire account of meaning. What is perhaps more remote, but what for Husserl will ensure the very possibility of meaningful language, is its foundation upon an interpretation of being as presence. Derrida argues not only that this account of language and meaning is impossible but that it is essentially contradictory, given the conceptual framework of the metaphysics of presence.

Rather than by pursuing this extremely complex argumentation in detail here, the purpose of such a general introduction would perhaps be better served by pointing out the directions it takes. For Husserl, the meaning-content of expression is ideal. An expression is composed of an explicit willed meaning-intention that "animates" a nonsensible signifier, for example, the "thought" or "imagined" word, the mere "form" of the actually uttered or written sign. In animating this purely formal signifier, the sign becomes invested with meaning, and meaning (*Bedeutung*) is ultimately the content of an interpretation (*Deutung*); the sign or signifier in general is always a sign *for* something. Now, for Husserl, all these elements of expression are nonreal because they all take place within the immediacy of a self-present consciousness—what in the *Investigations* he calls the sphere of "solitary mental life" and what he will later call "transcendental consciousness."

The difficulty in such a conception, and Husserl realizes this, is that actual communication always involves an abandonment of this privileged sphere. It involves the going-out into a world, into a realm of empirical fact. For this reason he maintains that expression is necessarily "interwoven" with indication in every case of effective communication. Husserl must preserve the dis-

tinction between the two kinds of sign, however, if he is to retain
the ideal status of meaning, the possibility of a purely present
and complete meaning. The original distinction is possible, in
turn, only if expression itself can effectively take place within
the purity of "solitary mental life." Communication, then, would
be a re-presentation of what primordially occurs in this inner
sphere. What is "meant" in communication is merely "indicated"
by means of sensible signs, by the actually spoken or written
signs. The problem here lies in the relation between expression
and indication. What is the nature of this "interweaving"? If
there is to be pure expression at all—and, consequently, pure
meaning—it must take place wholly within the internal sphere,
in the *absence* of indication; it would be a "silent" monologue.
There could be no meaningful communication per se in such a
case; and, following Husserl's account, communication would
come at the expense of meaning. But if indication were not
merely "interwoven" with expression, if it were shown to be absolutely necessary to the very concept of expression, then the possibility of their distinction becomes suspect. And it is just this
distinction that Derrida contests, together with the terms it rests
upon, i.e., the "solitary mental life" and the purely ideal, self-
present meaning.

Derrida first devotes a long critique to Husserl's account of
ideality. He insists that an ideal meaning is never a pure presentation to begin with; rather, it is itself a re-presentation (Husserl
uses the term *Vorstellung*) to consciousness, it is a product that
is constituted across a series of discrete acts. What constitutes
the ideality of meaning for Husserl is the possibility of its being
repeated an infinite number of times. Clearly, this is never com-
pleted; its completion would demand our disappearance as finite
beings. In any event, the ideal involves a relation of identity *between* acts, between a present act and an act that lies *outside*
present consciousness. Moreover, the very form of the signifier,
the sensory contour of a word or sign is itself a constituted historical product. The signifier is neither accidental nor idiomatic;
it always reflects a definite origin and heritage. In addition, each
occasion of its use represents (*Repräsentation*) only one instance
of its many possible uses; each use selectively repeats a pre-
existent convention. And what is it, finally, that really happens
in this "interior monologue," in this expression of "solitary mental
life"? The expression is not a communication, for there is nothing to communicate; meaning is immediately self-present to the

subject, so there is no need to communicate. What kind of expression is this, if there is no need to communicate anything to anyone? Husserl says this pure expression takes place entirely in the imagination. The interior monologue, then, is a phantasy representation (*Phantasievorstellung, Vergegenwärtigung*). But for Husserl, the imagination can never be purely "neutral"; it is always the modification of an antecedent experience, and its thetic character always testifies to an origin in empirical reality. No matter how it is modified, reality becomes represented in the imagination. The imagination, then, and consequently the expressive monologue, is fraught with all those elements Husserl sought to exclude from it, all those empirical references which enter in under the various headings of repetition and representation. From the very start, language must be just this; a structure of repetition and representation. There can be no refuge from empirical determination in such a structure.

Two consequences follow for Husserl: there can be no purely "ideal" meaning, no pure presence of ideality, for at every moment ideality would have to depend on precisely what is nonpresent, what is only repeated and represented in another presence. There can be no such sphere of pure self-presence either; for, in the simplest act of signifying, "solitary mental life" would be fractured by all that lies outside it, namely, the world. Once this occurs, the distinction between indication and expression can no longer be maintained. There is no presence or self-presence for signification; there is only an endless series of reverberations. What "presents" itself is the representation of nonpresence, what Derrida calls "otherness," "difference," or "alterity."

The distinction between indication and expression seems to be of questionable worth, therefore, once the important function of representation and repetition is made clear. But in carrying out the critical task of deconstruction, Derrida shows how Husserl's whole theory of language is undermined by a still more fundamental problem—one that leads back to the phenomenological form of experience itself—the problem of time. Husserl claimed there was no need for communication in the "interior monologue" because, among other reasons, it took place in an "instant," in the "blink of an eye." Following this account, meaning would be immediately present in the selfsame moment. There would be no need to mediate its presentation by means of signs. There would be no temporal distention in this process because signifier and signified are united in a punctual "now."

By Husserl's own premises, however, such an argument must fail. His theory of time dictates against any "punctually isolated" moment, for time is a "phasing," a continual movement of protentional and retentional traces. In *The Phenomenology of Internal Time-Consciousness,* Husserl argues that the present necessarily includes the phases of past and future under the heading of protention and retention. This conception of time denies the possibility of a temporally isolated "moment" or "instant." The very presence of the present is conditioned by what is absent or not yet realized. Far from being the point of origin for constitution, the "present" is itself constituted, produced, and *derived* from a more primordial source of nonpresence. Again, we find no *archē* of presence or self-presence. What we do find is a groundless play of differences that reflects an "outside and beyond" of past and future.

Derrida invokes the later account of temporality, not merely to play upon an inconsistency within Husserl's own thought, but rather to exhibit something far more important. In the *Logical Investigations* and elsewhere, the very concept of *life* had been understood as immediate self-presence, as the "living presence" of self-conscious thought. The historical importance of this concept cannot be overstated; it is what characterizes the modern thought of subjectivity since Descartes. Husserl, however, became increasingly skeptical of this view, as can be seen in his arguments against Brentano in *The Phenomenology of Internal Time-Consciousness,* against Hume in *Erste Philosophie,* and all throughout his later works, up to and including *The Origin of Geometry.* He came to see that, if the present "now" were conceived as a punctual instant, there could be no coherent account of experience as such; one would paradoxically end in denying the identity of one's own experience, one's own self, as did Hume. There could be no self-relation in such a case; in short, there could *be* no life, understood as absolute subjectivity.

Derrida concludes that the whole problem and history of language must be entirely rethought. Instead of trying to capture and retain a pure presence, we must conceive signification from the start as a movement *away* from self-presence, a movement away from the pure presence of a discrete origin and the ideal presence of an identical meaning-content. As a movement of difference, signification precedes and gives rise to the very concepts of self, presence, and meaning. The proper account of signification begins, not with the present and fulfilled meaning-content, but with the sense that remains to be assembled and built up across the itinerary of convention and practice. Following Saussure, Derrida maintains that linguistic meaning is not so much the product of an explicit meaning-intention as it is the arbitrary configuration of differences between signs. Meaning derives from the distance that extends between one particular sign and the system of other signs in linguistic use. It is this differential character of signs which must first be reckoned with, and this results from conventions existing within language; it is not a matter of meaning-intentions that supervene from without. There is no meaning, no signified content, that stands above and is free from this play of differences.[2] Nor could meaning withstand the continuous shifting of differences, the continuous sedimenting of traces, as some ideal *identity*. For Derrida, there is only a likeness or sameness to meaning, which is constituted across the history of ever-changing usage. Absolute objectivity, therefore, could never be claimed for meaning (yet for Husserl, the highest degree of objectivity is that of absolute ideality, the perfect identity of an omnitemporal meaning).

What is striking in Derrida's claim is the objection that linguistic meaning can never be completely present. There can never be an absolutely signified content, an absolutely identical or univocal meaning in language. All these values are denied to meaning once we admit its dependence upon nonpresent elements. Meaning can never be isolated or held in abstraction from its context, e.g., its linguistic, semiotic, or historical context. Each such context, for example, is a system of reference, a system of signifiers, whose function and reality point beyond the present. What is signified in the present, then, necessarily includes the differentiating and nonpresent system of signifiers in its very meaning. We can only assemble and recall the traces of what went before; we stand within language, not outside it.

Starting out with the metaphor of "presence," philosophy has generated a system of concepts whose import can be seen as essentially theological, what Heidegger has called the tradition of "onto-theology." [3] Ontology and theology are united in their

2. Derrida will discuss the concept of difference as it relates to the areas of semiotics, semantics, epistemology, and ontology, among others. Each of these uses finds its origin in the more primordial movement of "differance" (with an *a*). For an explanation of this term, see below, footnote 8, p. 82.

3. For an account of this, see, especially, Martin Heidegger, "Die

insistence upon a common ground and universal account of being, a first cause and final reason to things. For the tradition of
Western metaphysics, this unity has always been asserted under
the title of an absolute and nonempirical reality, a transcendent
being or principle that would subtend the empirical order by virtue of its role as cause and form, *archē* or *telos*. What invests
the world with order and substance is ultimately something
transcendent to that order: the Divine, the One, the principle of
intelligibility, the unconditioned.

Now it is precisely this kind of theological status that the
concept of meaning—interpreted as ideality or absolute identity
—has enjoyed in the history of Western thought, and particularly
when the account turns to problems of knowledge and signification. Despite the impurity of language and communication, the
possibility of an ideal and identical meaning has always been
held out, whether as pure "form," "*eidos*," "*idea*," "ideal," or as
absolute referent in the form of an ideal content of signification,
what Derrida elsewhere calls a "transcendental signified." [4]

Thus, for Husserl, what is "impure" in language is only the
adjunction of "the sensory or so to speak bodily" aspect, i.e., the
factually uttered phrase, the actually written word complex. The
"purity" of language, the very possibility of meaningful language,
lies outside this sphere in the nonempirical or ideal sphere of
meaning, in what can be purely "meant" or "intended" by language, in what can be "expressed" by language.[5] But Derrida's

Onto-Theo-Logische Verfassung der Metaphysik," in *Identität und
Differenz* (Pfullingen: Neske, 1957); English translation by Joan
Stambaugh, *Identity and Difference* (New York: Harper & Row,
1969), pp. 42–76.

4. Cf. Jacques Derrida, "Sémiologie et grammatologie," *Information sur les sciences sociales*, VII, No. 3 (June, 1968), esp. 136–40.
Also, Jacques Derrida, *De la grammatologie* (Paris: Editions de Minuit, 1967), esp. pp. 106–8.

5. In order to protect the pure presence of both solitary mental
life and the signified meaning, a "medium" of signification is required that would be free from all empirical resistance; a signifying
"element" is needed that would be absolutely nonempirical. For Husserl, this "medium" or "element" is the *voice* (and however silent it
may be, the internal monologue is still "spoken"). The voice is the
most "ideal" of signifiers in that it appears to be completely free of
any empirical substance. Only in speech does the signifier seem to be
completely "reduced" to its signified content; the spoken word is a
strangely diaphanous and transparent medium for meaning. Because
it animates a purely formal signifier (the "sensory contour" of the

reflection leads us to conclude that these distinctions can no longer be claimed for language for the precise reason that there can be no expression *without* indication, no *signified* without the *signifier*, no meaning or sense without the factually constituted complex of signifiers. To conclude that expression can never be "reduced" to an absolutely objective core of meaning, to conclude that meaning itself is no longer conceivable as a purely ideal presence, is also to conclude, for Derrida, that a certain period of metaphysical thought has come to a close.

THE MOST DIFFICULT task of any translator is to establish some effective compromise between transposition and transformation. However much one wishes to avoid altering the original style and vocabulary, they must inevitably succumb to modification and paraphrase, at least to some extent. In the present case this has been particularly true of such elements as sentence complexity and length. Yet, perhaps the greatest attention must be given to Derrida's terminology, which is sometimes at odds with English usage. I have tried to avoid his Latinate vocabulary, save for some few exceptions. One of these is the term "alterity," which arises in his discussion of difference. Like its French equivalent, *alterité*, the term is rich in connotations (to alter, to alternate, alternation, alternative, alteration, alter ego, etc.), and it has fewer ethical or personal overtones than other possible translations, such as "otherness." Similar ambiguities are also avoided by translating *auto-affection*, not as "self-affection" or "self-reference," but as the more extensive (for

---

phoneme—not the actually uttered sound complex itself), the silent speech stands as a pure phenomenon—what Derrida terms "the phenomenological voice."

The importance of the voice is not fortuitous with Husserl: implicitly or explicitly, the vocal medium has always functioned as the highest, the purest, form of signification. Its primacy is also that of reason and thought. How this complicity operates for Husserl and the tradition is one of the major themes of the present work. For Derrida, however, the primacy of speech—which is ultimately the primacy of presence—is illusory; it seems primary because it takes place "in an instant," in the apparent absence of the world. But in reality, speech is possible only because a certain kind of "writing" precedes it; the invisible and unconscious inscription of traces, the nonpresent and generative movement of differance that constitutes the system of language itself.

it applies to the processes or events of temporality, spacing, differance, etc., and not to an already constituted personality) "auto-affection" in general. Derrida takes the term in its Heideggerian sense.

There are cases, however, where ethical or axiological connotations are meant to be retained, as with the term "transgression." In attempting to break down the precepts and rules of Western—logocentric and phonocentric—thought, and by trying to bring its system to a close, one quite literally violates it. And when this order has been identified as the onto-theological ground of metaphysics, then the violation would surely constitute a "transgression" in the strictest sense.

Among other Heideggerian terms, Derrida occasionally uses the word *errance*. This is the accepted French translation of Heidegger's *die Irre*, a term which appears frequently throughout his work (especially in *Was ist Metaphysik?* and *Vom Wesen der Wahrheit*). Richardson first introduced the term into English as "errance," and he gives an admirable justification for it, noting that it incorporates not only the sense of "error" but also that of "aberrance," i.e., of being off course, wandering away from the truth.[6] Where Derrida introduces neologisms, such as "differance," I have added explanatory footnotes or have made reference to his own discussion of the term.

For Derrida's extensive quotations from Husserl, I have used existing English translations. Occasionally it has been necessary to modify these where the change was demanded by Derrida's own argument, e.g., in order to stress the etymology, or evocative import, of a particular term. In making these modifications, I have found Dorion Cairns's *Guide for Translating Husserl* extremely helpful and instructive.

In the course of preparing this translation, I have become deeply indebted to Professor Derrida himself, who, in the course of several long discussions, offered great encouragement as well as assistance with the text. My sincerest thanks must also be given to Professors Hubert Dreyfus and Newton Garver for their care and erudition in going over the manuscript and to Virginia Seidman for the patience and intelligence she devoted to the labor

6. See William J. Richardson, *Heidegger: Through Phenomenology to Thought*, 2d ed. (*Phaenomenologica XIII*) (The Hague: Nijhoff, 1967), p. 224.

of editing it. I would especially like to express my debt of gratitude and appreciation to Alphonso Lingis, whose suggestions and knowledgeable criticism were invaluable to me at every stage.

DAVID B. ALLISON

Stony Brook, New York
September, 1972

Speech and Phenomena: *Introduction to the Problem of Signs in Husserl's Phenomenology*

When we read this word "I" without knowing who wrote it, it is perhaps not meaningless, but is at least estranged from its normal meaning.

Logical Investigations

A name on being mentioned reminds us of the Dresden gallery and of our last visit there: we wander through the rooms and stop in front of a painting by Teniers which represents a gallery of paintings. Let us further suppose that the paintings of this gallery would represent in their turn paintings, which, on their part, exhibited readable inscriptions and so forth.

Ideas I

I have spoken both of "sound" and "voice." I mean to say that the sound was one of distinct, of even wonderfully, thrillingly distinct, syllabification. M. Valdemar *spoke*, obviously in reply to the question. . . . He now said:

"Yes;—no;—I have been sleeping—and now—now—*I am dead.*"

Poe, "The Facts in the Case of M. Valdemar"

Introduction

THE *Logical Investigations* (1900–1901) opened a path which, as we know, the whole of phenomenology has followed. Up to the fourth edition (1928) there was no fundamental change, no determined re-examination. Some touching up, certainly, and a powerful work of explication: *Ideas I* and *Formal and Transcendental Logic* develop without break the concepts of intentional or noematic sense, the difference between the two strata of analytics in the strong sense (the pure forms of judgments and consequence-logic), and suppress the deductivist or nomological form which had hitherto limited his concept of science in general.[1] In the *Crisis* and texts of the same period, particularly in *The Origin of Geometry*, the conceptual premises of the *Investigations* are still at work, notably when they concern all the problems of signification and language in general. In this area more than elsewhere, a patient reading of the *Investigations* would show the germinal structure of the whole of Husserl's thought. On each page the necessity—or the implicit practice—of eidetic and phenomenological reductions is visible, and the presence of everything to which they will give access is already discernible.

But the first of the *Investigations* ("Expression and Mean-

---

1. Edmund Husserl, *Formale und transzendentale Logik* (Halle: Max Niemeyer, 1929), § 35b. English translation by Dorion Cairns, *Formal and Transcendental Logic* (The Hague: Martinus Nijhoff, 1969), p. 102. [English translations will be referred to throughout as "ET." For general information about my use of English translations of Husserl, see my Translator's Introduction.—Translator.]

[3]

ing") [2] opens with a chapter devoted to some "essential distinctions" which rigorously command all the subsequent analyses. And the coherence of this chapter is entirely due to a distinction proposed in the first paragraph; the word "sign" (*Zeichen*) will have a "twofold sense" (*ein Doppelsinn*); "sign" may signify "expression" (*Ausdruck*) or "indication" (*Anzeichen*).

In terms of what question are we to accept and read this apparently so portentous distinction?

Before proposing this purely "phenomenological" distinction between the two senses of the word "sign," or rather, even before recognizing it, before setting it off in what purports to be a simple description, Husserl proceeds to what is in effect a phenomenological reduction: he puts out of play all constituted knowledge, he insists on the necessary absence of presuppositions (*Voraussetzungslosigkeit*), whether they come from metaphysics, psychology, or the natural sciences. The point of departure in the *"Faktum"* of language is not a presupposition, provided that one is attentive to the contingency of the example. Analyses thus directed keep their "sense" and their "epistemological value"—their import for the theory of knowledge (*erkenntnistheoretischen Wert*)—whether or not there exist any languages; whether beings such as men use them effectively or not; whether men or nature really exist, or exist only "in the imagination and according to the mode of possibility."

We have thus a prescription for the most general form of our question: do not phenomenological necessity, the rigor and subtlety of Husserl's analysis, the exigencies to which it responds and which we must first recognize, nonetheless conceal a metaphysical presupposition? Do they not harbor a dogmatic or speculative commitment which, to be sure, would not keep the phenomenological critique from being realized, would not

---

2. With the exception of several overtures or indispensable anticipations, the present essay analyzes the doctrine of signification as it is formed in the first of the *Logical Investigations*. In order to better follow the difficult and tortuous itinerary, we have generally abstained from comparisons, reconciliations, or oppositions which seem to impose themselves, here or there, between Husserl's phenomenology and other theories, classical or modern, of signification. Each time that we go beyond the text of the First Logical Investigation, it is to indicate the principle of a general interpretation of Husserl's thought and to sketch that systematic reading which we hope to try one day.

be a residue of unperceived naïveté, but would *constitute* phenomenology from within, in its project of criticism and in the instructive value of its own premises? This would be done precisely in what soon comes to be recognized as the source and guarantee of all value, the "principle of principles": i.e., the original self-giving evidence, the *present* or *presence* of sense to a full and primordial intuition. In other words, we shall not be asking whether such and such metaphysical heritage has been able, here or there, to restrict the vigilance of the phenomenologist, but whether the phenomenological form of this vigilance is not already controlled by metaphysics itself.

In the few lines just touched upon, distrust of metaphysical presuppositions is already presented as the condition for an authentic "theory of knowledge," as if the project of a theory of knowledge, even when it has freed itself by the "critique" of such and such speculative system, did not belong at the outset to the history of metaphysics. Is not the idea of knowledge and of the theory of knowledge in itself metaphysical?

What is at issue, then, in the privileged example of the concept of sign, is to see the phenomenological critique of metaphysics betray itself as a moment within the history of metaphysical assurance. Better still, our intention is to begin to confirm that the recourse to phenomenological critique is metaphysics itself, restored to its original purity in its historical achievement.

We have tried elsewhere [3] to follow the movement by which Husserl, while ceaselessly criticizing metaphysical speculation, in fact had his eye on only the perversion or the degeneracy of what he continued to believe in and wished to restore as authentic metaphysics or *philosophia prōtē*. Concluding his *Cartesian Meditations*, Husserl again opposes authentic metaphysics (which will owe its accomplishment to phenomenology) to metaphysics in the customary sense. The results which he presents there are, he says,

> metaphysical, if it be true that ultimate cognitions of being should be called metaphysical. On the other hand, what we have here is *anything but metaphysics in the customary sense:* a historically degenerate metaphysics, which by no means conforms to the sense with which metaphysics, as "first philosophy," was instituted origi-

3. "La Phénoménologie et la clôture de la métaphysique," ΕΠΟΧΕΣ (Athens), February, 1966.

nally. Phenomenology's purely intuitive, concrete, and also apodictic mode of demonstration excludes all "metaphysical adventure," all speculative excesses (*Cartesian Meditations*, § 60; ET, p. 139).[4]

The unique and permanent motif of all the mistakes and distortions which Husserl exposes in "degenerated" metaphysics, across a multiplicity of domains, themes, and arguments, is always a blindness to the authentic mode of *ideality*, to that which *is*, to what may be indefinitely *repeated* in the *identity* of its *presence*, because of the very fact that it *does not exist*, is *not real* or is *irreal*—not in the sense of being a fiction, but in another sense which may have several names, whose possibility will permit us to speak of nonreality and essential necessity, the noema, the intelligible object, and in general the nonworldly. This nonworldliness is not another worldliness, this ideality is not an existent that has fallen from the sky; its origin will always be the possible repetition of a productive act. In order that the possibility of this repetition may be open, *ideally to infinity*, one ideal form must assure this unity of the *indefinite* and the *ideal:* this is the present, or rather the presence of the *living present*. The ultimate form of ideality, the ideality of ideality, that in which in the last instance one may anticipate or recall all repetition, is the *living present*, the self-presence of transcendental life. Presence has always been and will always, forever, be the form in which, we can say apodictically, the infinite diversity of contents is produced. The opposition between form and matter—which inaugurates metaphysics—finds in the concrete ideality of the living present its ultimate and radical justification. We will come back to the enigma of the concept of *life* in such expressions as "living present" and "transcendental life." Let us note only, in order to here specify our intention, that phenomenology seems to us tormented, if not contested from within, by its own descriptions of the movement of temporalization and of the constitution of intersubjectivity. At the heart of what ties together these two decisive moments of description we recognize an irreducible nonpresence as having a constituting value,

4. Edmund Husserl, *Cartesianische Meditationen und Pariser Vorträge, Husserliana I* (The Hague: Martinus Nijhoff, 1950). English translation by Dorion Cairns, *Cartesian Meditations* (The Hague: Martinus Nijhoff, 1960).

and with it a nonlife, a nonpresence or nonself-belonging of the living present, an ineradicable nonprimordiality. The names which it assumes only render more palpable the resistance to the form of presence. Briefly, it is a question of (1) the necessary transition from retention to re-presentation (*Vergegenwärtigung*) in the constitution of the presence of a temporal object (*Gegenstand*) whose identity may be repeated; and (2) the necessary transition by way of *appresentation* in relation to the *alter ego*, that is, in relation to what also makes possible an ideal objectivity in general; for intersubjectivity is the condition for objectivity, which is absolute only in the case of ideal objects. What in the two cases is called a modification of presentation (*re*-presentation, *ap*-presentation) (*Vergegenwärtigung* or *Appräsentation*) is not something that happens to presentation but rather conditions it by bifurcating it *a priori*. This does not impugn the apodicticity of the phenomenological-transcendental description, nor does it diminish the founding value of presence. Besides, "founding value of presence" is a pleonastic expression. It is only a question of bringing out that the lack of foundation is basic and nonempirical and that the security of presence in the metaphorical form of ideality arises and is set forth again upon this irreducible void. It is within this compass that we will now question the phenomenological concept of the sign.

The concept of metaphysics with which we shall be operating will have to be made precise and the excessive generality of this question narrowed. First, how can we justify the *decision* which subordinates a reflection on the sign to a logic? And if the concept of sign precedes logical reflection, is given to it, and is freed from its critique, from whence does it come? Where does the essence of the sign, according to which the concept is regulated, come from? What gives a theory of knowledge the authority to determine the essence and origin of language? We do not impute such a *decision* to Husserl; he explicitly assumes it—or rather he explicitly assumes its tradition and its validity. The consequences of this are limitless. On the one hand, Husserl had to postpone, from one end of his itinerary to the other, all explicit meditation on the essence of language *in general*. He still puts it "out of play" in the *Formal and Transcendental Logic* ("Preliminary Considerations," § 2). And, as Fink has well shown, Husserl never raised the question of the transcendental logos, the inherited language in which phenomenology produces and exhibits the results of its reductive operations. The unity of ordinary language (or the language of traditional metaphysics) and the language of phenomenology is never broken in spite of the precautions, the "brackets," the renovations or innovations. Transforming a traditional concept into an indicative or metaphorical concept does not eliminate its heritage; it imposes questions, rather, to which Husserl never ventured a response. This is due to the fact that, on the other hand, being interested in language only within the compass of rationality, determining the logos from logic, Husserl had, in a most traditional manner, determined the essence of language by taking the logical as its telos or norm. That this telos is that of being as presence is what we here wish to suggest.

Thus, for example, when Husserl redefines the relation between the purely grammatical and the purely logical (a relation which traditional logic would have lacked, distorted as it was by metaphysical presuppositions), when he institutes a pure morphology of *Bedeutungen* (we do not translate this word for reasons which will appear in a moment) to explain the purely grammatical, what results is that the generality of this meta-empirical grammar is not sufficient to cover the whole field of possibility for language in general; it does not exhaust the whole extension of language's *a priori*. When we speak of the purely grammatical, we mean that system of rules which enables us to recognize whether or not a discourse is, properly speaking, a discourse. Speech, to be sure, must make *sense;* but do falsity and the absurdity of contradiction (*Widersinnigkeit*) necessarily make it unintelligible? Do they necessarily deprive discourse of its experienced and intelligible character, thereby rendering it *sinnlos?* This grammar concerns only the *logical a priori* of language; it is *pure logical grammar.*

This restriction is operative from the beginning, although Husserl does not insist on it in the first edition of the *Investigations:*

> In the first edition I spoke of "pure grammar," a name conceived and expressly devised to be analogous to Kant's "pure science of nature." Since it cannot, however, be said that pure formal semantic (*Bedeutungen*) theory comprehends the entire *a priori* of general grammar—there is, e.g., a peculiar *a priori* governing relations of mutual understanding among minded persons, relations

very important for grammar—talk of pure *logical* grammar is to be preferred.[5]

The delineation of the logical *a priori* within the general *a priori* of language does not set apart a region; rather it designates, as we shall see, the dignity of a telos, the purity of a norm, and the essence of a destination.

That this gesture, whereby the whole of phenomenology is already involved, repeats the original intention of metaphysics itself is what we wish to show here by pointing out in the first of the *Investigations* those roots which will remain undisturbed by Husserl's subsequent discourse. The factor of *presence*, the ultimate court of appeal for the whole of this discourse, is itself modified, without being lost, each time there is a question of the presence (in the two related senses, of the proximity of what is set forth as an object of an intuition, and the proximity of the temporal present which gives the clear and present intuition of the object its form) of any object whatever to consciousness, in the clear evidence of a fulfilled intuition. Indeed, the element of presence is modified whenever it is a question of self-presence in consciousness—where "consciousness" means nothing other than the possibility of the self-presence of the present in the living present. Every time this element of presence becomes threatened, Husserl will awaken it, recall it, and bring it back to itself in the form of a telos—that is, an Idea in the Kantian sense. There is no *ideality* without there being an Idea in the Kantian sense at work, opening up the possibility of something indefinite, the infinity of a stipulated progression or the infinity of permissible repetitions. This ideality is the very form in which the presence of an object in general may be indefinitely repeated as the *same*. The nonreality of the *Bedeutung*, the nonreality of the ideal object, the nonreality of the inclusion of sense or noema in consciousness (Husserl will say that the noema does not really—*reell*—belong to consciousness) will thus give the assurance that presence to consciousness can be indefinitely repeated—ideal presence to an ideal or transcendental consciousness. Ideality is the preservation or mastery of presence

5. Edmund Husserl, *Logische Untersuchungen*, 1st ed., 2 vols. (Halle: Max Niemeyer, 1900; 2d ed., 1913). English translation by J. N. Findlay, *Logical Investigations*, 2 vols. (New York: Humanities Press, 1970), II, 527.

in repetition. In its pure form, this presence is the presence of nothing *existing* in the world; it is a correlation with the acts of repetition, themselves ideal.

Is this to say that what opens the repetition to the infinite, or what is opened up when the movement of idealization is assured, is a certain relation of an "existent" to his death? And that the "transcendental life" is the scene of this relationship? It is too soon to tell. First we must deal with the problem of language. No one will be surprised if we say that language is properly the medium for this play of presence and absence. Is there not within language—is it not language itself that might seem to unify *life and ideality*? But we ought to consider, on the one hand, that the element of signification—or the substance of expression—which best seems to preserve ideality and living presence in all its forms is living speech, the spirituality of the breath as *phōnē;* and, on the other hand, that phenomenology, the metaphysics of presence in the form of ideality, is also a philosophy of *life.*

It is a philosophy of life, not only because at its center death is recognized as but an empirical and extrinsic signification, a worldly accident, but because the source of sense in general is always determined as the act of *living,* as the act of a living being, as *Lebendigkeit.* But the unity of living, the focus of *Lebendigkeit* which diffracts its light in all the fundamental concepts of phenomenology (*Leben, Erlebnis, lebendige Gegenwart, Geistigkeit,* etc.), escapes the transcendental reduction and, as unity of worldly life, even opens up the way for it. When the empirical life, or even the region of the purely psychic, is bracketed, it is still a transcendental life or, in the final instance, the transcendentality of a *living* present that Husserl uncovers. And yet he thematizes the concept of *life* without as much as raising the question of its unity. The "soulless (*seelenloses*) consciousness," whose essential possibility is redeemed in *Ideas I* (§ 54) is still a *living* transcendental consciousness. If we concluded, with a very Husserlian gesture, that the concepts of empirical (or in general, worldly) life and transcendental life are radically heterogeneous and that the two names sustain a simply indicative or metaphorical relation between themselves, then it is upon the possibility of this relation that the whole weight of the question falls. The common root that makes all these metaphors possible still seems to us to be the concept of *life*. There is, in the final instance, says Husserl, a relation of *parallelism* between the purely mental—the region of the world opposed to transcendental consciousness and discovered by the reduction of the totality of the natural and transcendent world—and pure transcendental life.

Phenomenological psychology will have to continue to call upon psychology to work over its fund of eidetic presuppositions and the conditions for its own language. It has the task of fixing the sense of concepts derived from psychology, and first of all the sense of what is called the *psychē*. But what will distinguish this phenomenological psychology, this descriptive science, eidetic and *a priori*, from transcendental phenomenology itself? What will distinguish the epochē which discloses the immanent domain of the purely psychic from the transcendental epochē itself? For the field opened up by this pure psychology has a privilege with respect to all other regions, and its generality dominates all others. Its domain necessarily includes all lived experiences, and the sense of every determinate region or object is betokened through it. Also, the dependence of the purely psychic upon the transcendental consciousness, as protoregion, is quite singular. For the domain of pure psychological experience incorporates the total domain of what Husserl calls transcendental experience. Yet despite this perfect *incorporation*, a radical difference remains, one having nothing in common with any other difference, a difference in fact distinguishing nothing, a difference separating no state, no experience, no determined signification—but a difference which, without altering anything, changes all the signs, and in which alone the possibility of a transcendental question is contained. That is to say, freedom itself. A fundamental difference, thus, without which no other difference in the world would either make any sense or have the chance to appear *as such*. Without the possibility and the recognition of such a *duplication* (*Verdoppelung*), whose rigor tolerates no duplicity, without this invisible distance held out between the two acts of the epochē, transcendental phenomenology would be destroyed in its root.

The difficulty lies in that this duplication of sense must correspond to no ontological double. Husserl specifies, for example, that my transcendental ego is radically different from my natural and human ego;[6] and yet it is distinguished by nothing, nothing that can be determined in the natural sense of distinction. The (transcendental) ego is not an other. It is certainly not the formal or metaphysical phantom of the empirical ego. Indeed this leads us to take the ego—as absolute spectator of its own psychic self—to be but a theoretical image and metaphor. We would also expose the analogical character of language which must sometimes be used to announce the transcendental reduction as well as to describe that unusual "object," the psychic self as it confronts the absolute transcendental self. In fact no language can cope with the operation by which the transcendental ego constitutes and opposes itself to its worldly self, its soul, reflecting itself in a *verweltlichende Selbstapperzeption*.[7] The pure soul is this strange self-objectification (*Selbstobjektivierung*) of the monad in and by itself.[8] Here, too, the Soul originates in the One (monadic ego) and may be freely turned toward it in a reduction.

All these difficulties are concentrated in the enigmatic concept of "parallelism." Husserl evokes [9] the surprising "parallelism" and even, "if one may say, incorporation" of phenomenological psychology and transcendental phenomenology, "both of them understood as eidetic disciplines." "The one inhabits the other, as it were, implicitly."

This *nothing* that distinguishes the parallels, this nothing without which precisely no explication, that is, no language, could be freely developed in the service of truth without being deformed by some real contact, this nothing without which no transcendental (that is, philosophical) question could be opened, this nothing arises, so to speak, when the *totality* of the world is neutralized in its existence and is reduced to its phenomenal being. *This operation is that of the transcendental reduction; it may in no case be that of the psychophenomenological reduction.* The pure eidetic of psychic experience doubtless concerns no determined existence, no matter of empirical fact; it makes no appeal to any signification transcendent to consciousness. But the essences it fixes intrinsically

6. Edmund Husserl, *Phänomenologische Psychologie* (lectures delivered in the summer semester, 1925), ed. Walter Biemel, *Husserliana IX* (The Hague: Martinus Nijhoff, 1962), p. 342.

7. *Cartesian Meditations*, § 45.

8. *Ibid.*, § 57.

9. *Phänomenologische Psychologie*, p. 343.

presuppose the existence of the world in the form of that worldly region called *psychē*. Moreover, we must notice that this parallelism does more than release transcendental ether; it renders more mysterious still (as it alone is capable of doing) the meaning of the *mental* and of mental *life*, that is, of a *worldliness* capable of sustaining, or in some way nourishing, *transcendentality*, and of equaling the full scope of its domain, yet without being merged with it in some total adequation. To conclude that this parallelism is an adequation is the most tempting, the most subtle, but also the most obscuring of confusions: *transcendental psychologism*. Against it we must maintain the precarious and fragile distance between the parallels; against it we must ceaselessly direct our questions. But since the meaning of the transcendental consciousness is not affected by the hypothesis of the destruction of the world (*Ideas I*, § 49), "Certainly an incorporeal and, paradoxical as it may sound, even an inanimate (*seelenloses*) and nonpersonal consciousness is conceivable" (*ibid.*, § 54; ET, p. 167).[10] Moreover, the transcendental consciousness is *nothing more and nothing other* than the psychological consciousness. Transcendental psychologism misunderstands this: if the world needs the *supplement of a soul*, the soul, which is in the world, needs this *supplementary nothing* which is the transcendental and without which no world would appear. But, on the other hand, we must, if we are to be attentive to Husserl's renewal of the notion of "transcendental," refrain from attributing any reality to this distance, substantializing this nonconsistency or making it be, even merely analogically, some thing or some moment of the world. This would be to extinguish the light at its source. If language never escapes analogy, if it is indeed analogy through and through, it ought, having arrived at this point, at this stage, freely to assume its own destruction and cast metaphor against metaphor: all of which amounts to complying with the most traditional of imperatives, something which has received its most explicit but not most original form in the *Enneads* and has ceaselessly

10. Edmund Husserl, *Ideen zu einer reinen Phänomenologie und phänomenologische Philosophie, Husserliana III* (The Hague: Martinus Nijhoff, 1913). English translation by W. R. Boyce Gibson, *Ideas: General Introduction to Pure Phenomenology* (New York: Humanities Press, 1931), p. 167.

and faithfully been transmitted right up to the *Introduction to Metaphysics* (especially by Bergson). It is at the price of this war of language against itself that the sense and question of its origin will be thinkable. This war is obviously not one war among others. A polemic for the possibility of sense and world, it takes place in this *difference*, which, we have seen, cannot reside in the world but only in language, in the transcendental disquietude of language. Indeed, far from only living in language, this war is also the origin and residence of language. Language preserves the difference that preserves language.

Later, in his "Nachwort zu meinen 'Ideen,' " [11] and in the *Cartesian Meditations* (§§ 14 and 57), Husserl will again briefly invoke this "precise parallel" between the "pure psychology of consciousness" and the "transcendental phenomenology of consciousness." And in order to deny that transcendental psychologism which "makes a genuine philosophy impossible" (*Cartesian Meditations*, § 14), he will then say that at all costs we shall have to practice the *Nuancierung* ("Nachwort," p. 557) which distinguishes the parallels, one of which is in the world and the other outside the world without being in another world, that is, without ceasing to be, like *every parallel, alongside, right next to the other*. We must stringently assemble and protect in our discourse these frivolous, subtle (*geringfügigen*), "seemingly trivial nuances" which "make a decisive difference between right and wrong paths (*Wege und Abwege*) of philosophy" (*Cartesian Meditations*, § 14). Our discussion ought to incorporate these protected nuances and thereby at the same time *consolidate in them its own possibility and rigor*. But the strange unity of these two parallels, that which refers the one to the other, does not allow itself to be sundered by them and, by dividing itself, finally joins the transcendental to its other; this unity is *life*. One finds out quickly enough that the sole nucleus of the concept of *psyche* is life as self-relationship, whether or not it takes place in the form of consciousness. "Living" is thus the name of that which precedes the reduction and finally

11. "Nachwort zu meinen 'Ideen zu einer reinen Phänomenologie und phänomenologische Philosophie,' " *Jahrbuch für Philosophie und phänomenologische Forschung*, XI (Halle, 1930), 549–70. The "Nachwort," translated by Boyce Gibson, appears as the Preface to the English edition of *Ideas*.

escapes all the divisions which the latter gives rise to. But
this is precisely because it is its own division and its own opposition to its other. In determining "living" in this way, we
come to designate the origin of the insecurity of discourse,
precisely the point where it can no longer *assure its possibility
and rigor within the nuance.* This concept of *life* is then
grasped in an instance which is no longer that of pretranscen-
dental naïveté, the language of day-to-day life or biological
science. But if this ultratranscendental concept of life enables
us to conceive life (in the ordinary or the biological sense),
and if it has never been inscribed in language, it requires
another name.

We will be less astonished before this oblique and laborious,
tenacious endeavor of phenomenology to protect the spoken
word, to affirm an essential tie between *logos* and *phōnē*, when
we remember that consciousness owes its privileged status
(about which Husserl in the end never asked *what it was,* in
spite of the admirable, interminable, and in so many respects
revolutionary, meditation he devoted to it) to the possibility
of a living vocal medium [*la vive voix*]. Since self-consciousness appears only in its relation to an object, whose presence it
can keep and repeat, it is never perfectly foreign or anterior
to the possibility of language. Husserl no doubt did want to
maintain, as we shall see, an originally silent, "pre-expressive"
stratum of experience. But since the possibility of constituting
ideal objects belongs to the essence of consciousness, and
since these ideal objects are historical products, only appearing thanks to acts of creation or intending, the element of
consciousness and the element of language will be more and
more difficult to discern. Will not their indiscernibility introduce nonpresence and difference (mediation, signs, referral
back, etc.) in the heart of self-presence? This difficulty *calls
for* a response. This response is the voice [*la voix*]. The voice
is richly and profoundly enigmatic in all that it here seems to
answer. That the voice simulates the conservation of presence,
and that the history of spoken language is the archives of
this simulation, this at once prevents us from considering the
"difficulty" to which, in Husserl's phenomenology, the voice
answers as a difficulty of the system or a contradiction proper
to it. This prevents us also from describing this simulation,
whose structure is of an infinite complexity, as an illustration,
phantasm, or hallucination. These last concepts, on the con-

trary, refer to the simulation of language as well as to their common root.

It remains that this "difficulty" structures the whole of Husserl's discourse and that we ought to recognize the work involved therein. Husserl will radicalize the necessary privilege of the *phonē*, which is implied by the whole history of metaphysics, and exploit all its resources with the greatest critical refinement. For it is not in the sonorous substance or in the physical voice, in the body of speech in the world, that he will recognize an original affinity with the logos in general, but in the voice phenomenologically taken, speech in its transcendental flesh, in the breath, the intentional animation that transforms the body of the word into flesh, makes of the *Körper* a *Leib*, a *geistige Leiblichkeit*. The phenomenological voice would be this spiritual flesh that continues to speak and be present to itself—*to hear itself*—in the absence of the world. Of course, what one accords to the voice is accorded to the language of *words*, a language constituted of unities—which one might have believed irreducible, which cannot be broken down—joining the signified concept to the signifying "phonic complex." Despite the vigilance of the description, a perhaps naïve treatment of the concept of "word" has doubtless left unresolved the tension of the two major motifs in phenomenology: the purity of formalism and the radicality of intuitionism.

That the privilege of presence as consciousness can be established—that is, historically constituted and demonstrated—only by virtue of the excellence of the voice is a truism which has never occupied the forefront of the phenomenological stage. In a mode neither simply operative nor directly thematic, in a place neither central nor peripheral, the necessity of this truism seems to have assured itself a sort of "hold" throughout phenomenology. The nature of this "hold" is poorly conceived in the concepts habitually sanctioned in the philosophy of the history of philosophy. But our purpose here is not directly to meditate upon the form of this "hold" but only to show it already—and powerfully—at work from the start, in the first of the *Logical Investigations*.

1 / Sign and Signs

HUSSERL BEGINS by pointing out a confusion: The word "sign" (*Zeichen*) covers, always in ordinary language and occasionally in philosophical language, two heterogeneous concepts: that of *expression* (*Ausdruck*), which is often wrongly taken as a synonym for sign in general, and that of *indication* (*Anzeichen*). But, according to Husserl, there are signs that express nothing because they convey nothing one could call (we still have to put it in German) *Bedeutung* or *Sinn*. Such is the indicative sign [*indice*].[1] Certainly an indicative sign is a sign, as is an expression. But, unlike an expression, an indicative sign is deprived of *Bedeutung* or *Sinn;* it is *bedeutungslos, sinnlos*. But, nonetheless, it is not without signification. By definition there can be no sign without signification, no signifying without the signified. This is why the traditional translation of *Bedeutung* by "signification," although time-honored and practically inevitable, risks confusing the whole text of Husserl. Rendering it unintelligible in its axial intention, it would subsequently make unintelligible all that depends on these first "essential distinctions." In German one may, with Husserl, say without absurdity that a sign (*Zeichen*) is without *Bedeutung* (is *bedeutungslos*, is not *bedeutsam*), as in English one may say that a sign has no meaning; but in French one cannot say without contradiction that *un*

1. [Derrida's use of the French *indice* as a translation of the German *Anzeichen* is perhaps best rendered in English by the term "indicative sign." The indicative sign serves as a pointer or indicator, that substantive found in the act of indication—Translator.]

[17]

signe lacks *signification.* In German one can speak of expression (*Ausdruck*) as *bedeutsame Zeichen,* as Husserl does, and as one speaks in English of "meaningful signs"; but one cannot without redundance translate *bedeutsame Zeichen* into French by *signe signifiant.* That would lead one to imagine, contrary to all evidence and contrary to Husserl's intention, that there could be nonsignifying signs. While we thus hold suspect the hallowed French translations, we ought to acknowledge the difficulty in replacing them. This is why our remarks are in no way to be construed as criticisms of existent and valuable translations. We will nonetheless try to propose solutions halfway between commentary and translation, which are meant to be restricted to Husserl's texts themselves. Being faced with such difficulties, we shall more often than not retain the German word while attempting to clarify it by analysis (a procedure whose worth is sometimes questionable).

It will then be quickly seen that, for Husserl, the expressiveness of expression—which always supposes the ideality of a *Bedeutung*—has an irreducible tie to the possibility of spoken language (*Rede*). An expression is a purely linguistic sign, and it is precisely this that in the first analysis distinguishes it from an indicative sign. Although spoken language is a highly complex structure, always containing *in fact* an indicative stratum, which, as we shall see, is difficult to confine within its limits, Husserl has nonetheless reserved for it the power of expression exclusively—and thereby pure logicality. Without forcing Husserl's intention we could perhaps define, if not translate, *bedeuten* by "mean" [or "want to say"; in French, *vouloir-dire*], in the sense that a speaking subject, "expressing himself," as Husserl says, "about something," *means* or *wants to say* [*veut dire*] something and that an expression likewise means or "wants to say" something.[2] One would thus be assured that the meaning (*Bedeutung*) is always *what* a discourse or somebody *wants to say:* what is conveyed, then, is always a linguistic sense, a discursive content.

Everyone knows that, contrary to Frege, Husserl in the *Investigations* makes no distinction between *Sinn* and *Bedeutung:*

2. "To mean" and "meaning" are, for *bedeuten* and *Bedeutung,* those happy equivalents which we cannot avail ourselves of in French.

"Meaning" (*Bedeutung*) is further used by us as synonymous with "sense" (*gilt als gleichbedeutend mit Sinn*). It is agreeable to have parallel, interchangeable terms in the case of this concept, particularly since the sense of the term "meaning" is itself to be investigated. A further consideration is our ingrained tendency to use the two words as synonymous, a circumstance which makes it seem rather a dubious step if their "meanings" are differentiated, and if (as G. Frege has proposed) we use one for meaning in our sense, and the other for the objects expressed (First Investigation, § 15; ET, p. 292).

In *Ideas I*, the dissociation which occurs between the two notions does not at all have the same function as for Frege, and this confirms our reading: *meaning* is reserved for the content in the ideal sense of *verbal* expression, spoken language, while sense (*Sinn*) covers the whole noematic sphere right down to its nonexpressive stratum:

> Let us start from the familiar distinction between the sensory, the so to speak bodily aspect of expression, and its non-sensory "mental" aspect. There is no need for us to enter more closely into the discussion of the first aspect, nor upon the way of uniting the two aspects, though we clearly have title-headings here indicated for phenomenological problems that are not unimportant.
>
> We, however, are exclusively concerned with the "to mean" or "*bedeuten*" and the "meaning" (*Bedeutung*). Originally, these words relate only to the sphere of speech (*sprachliche Sphäre*), that of "expressing" (*des Ausdrückens*). But it is almost inevitable, and at the same time an important step for knowledge, to extend the meaning of these words, and to modify them suitably so that they may be applied in a certain way to the whole noetico-noematic sphere, to all acts, therefore, whether these are interwoven (*verflochten*) with expressive acts or not. With this in view we ourselves, when referring to any intentional experiences, have spoken all along of "sense" (*Sinn*), a word which is generally used as an equivalent for "meaning" (*Bedeutung*). We propose in the interests of distinctness to favour the word "meaning" when referring to the old concept, and more particularly in the complex speech-form "*logical*" or "*expressive*" meaning. We use the word "sense" in future, as before, in its more embracing breadth of application (*Ideas, I,* § 124; ET [modified], p. 346).

And after having (in a passage to which we will have to return) affirmed that there was, notably in perception, a pre-expressive stratum of lived experience or sense, since this stratum of sense was always able to receive expression and meaning, Husserl stipulates that "logical meaning (*Bedeutung*) is an expression" (*ibid.*).

The difference between indication and expression very quickly appears in the course of the description to be a difference more *functional* than *substantial*. Indication and expression are functions or signifying relations, not terms. One and the same phenomenon may be apprehended as an expression or as an indication, a discursive or nondiscursive sign depending on the intentional experience [*vécu intentionnel*] which animates it. This functional character of the description immediately presents us with the full extent of the difficulty and brings us to the center of the problem. Two functions may be interwoven or entangled in the same concatenation of signs, the same signification. Husserl speaks first of an addition or juxtaposition of function: "signs in the sense of indications (*Anzeichen*) (notes, marks, etc.) *do not express anything,* unless they happen to fulfill a meaning *as well as* [*neben,* alongside; the italics are Husserl's] an indicative function." But several lines further he speaks of an intimate involvement, an entanglement (*Verflechtung*). This word will often reappear at decisive moments, and this is not fortuitous. In the very first paragraph he says: "Meaning (*bedeuten*)— in communicative speech (*in mitteilender Rede*)—is always interwoven (*verflochten*) with such an indicative relation."

We know already *in fact* that the discursive sign, and consequently the meaning, is *always* involved, always *caught up* in an indicative system. Caught up is the same as contaminated: Husserl wants to grasp the expressive and logical purity of meaning as the possibility of logos. *In fact and always* (*allzeit verflochten ist*) to the extent to which the meaning is taken up in communicative speech. To be sure, as we shall see, communication itself is for Husserl a stratum extrinsic to expression. But each time an expression is in fact produced, it communicates, even if it is not exhausted in that communicative role, or even if this role is simply associated with it.

We will have to clarify the modalities of this interweaving. But it is already evident that this *de facto* necessity of entanglement, intimately associating expression and indication, must not, according to Husserl, cut off the possibility of a rigorous distinction of essence. This possibility is purely *de jure* and phenomenological. The whole analysis will thus advance in this separation between *de facto* and *de jure*, existence and essence, reality and intentional function. Skipping over many mediations and inverting the apparent order, we would be tempted to say that this separation, which defines the very space of phenomenology, does not exist prior to the question of language, nor does it enter into it, so to speak, as into an already bounded domain or as one problem among others; it is discovered only in and through the possibility of language. And its *de jure* import, the right to a distinction between fact and intention, depends entirely on language and, in language, on the validity of a radical distinction between indication and expression.

We return to the text. Every expression would thus be caught up, despite itself, in an indicative process. But the reverse, Husserl recognizes, is not true. One might well be tempted, then, to make the expressive sign a species of the genus "indication." In this case, we would have to say in the end that the spoken word, whatever dignity or originality we still accorded it, is but a form of gesture. In its essential core, then, and not only by what Husserl considers its accidents (its physical side, its communicative function), it would belong to the general system of signification and would not surpass it. The general system of signification then would be coextensive with the system of indication.

This is just what Husserl contests. To do so, he must demonstrate that expression is not a species of indication. While all expressions are mixed with indication, the converse is not true.

> If, as one unwillingly does, one limits oneself to expressions employed in living discourse, the notion of an indication seems to apply more widely than that of an expression, but this does not mean that its content is the genus of which an expression is the species. To mean (*bedeuten*) is *not a particular way of being a sign* (*Zeichenseins*) *in the sense of indicating* (*Anzeige*) *something*. It has a narrower application only because meaning—in communicative speech—is always bound up (*verflochten*) with such an indicative relation (*Anzeichensein*), and this in its turn leads to a wider concept, since meaning is also capable of occurring without such a connection (First Investigation, § 1; ET, p. 269).

In order to show the breakup of the genus-species relation we would have to find a phenomenological situation in which expression is no longer caught up in this entanglement, no longer intertwined with the indication. As this contamination is always produced in real colloquy (this for two reasons: because expression indicates a content forever hidden from intuition, that is, from the lived experience of another, and also because the ideal content of the meaning and spirituality of expression are here united to sensibility), we have to ferret out the unshaken purity of expression in a language without communication, in speech as monologue, in the completely muted voice of the "solitary mental life" (*im einsamen Seelenleben*). By a strange paradox, meaning would isolate the concentrated purity of its *ex-pressiveness* just at that moment when the relation to a certain *outside* is suspended. Only to a certain outside, because this reduction does not eliminate, but rather reveals, within pure expression, a relation to an object, namely, the intending [*visée*] of an objective ideality, which stands face to face with the meaning-intention, the *Bedeutungsintention*. What we just called a paradox is in fact only the phenomenological project in its essence. Beyond the opposition of "idealism" and "realism," "subjectivism" and "objectivism," etc., transcendental phenomenological idealism answers to the necessity of describing the *ob*jectivity of the *ob*ject (*Gegenstand*) and the *pre*sence of the present (*Gegenwart*)—and objectivity in presence—from the standpoint of "interiority," or rather from a self-proximity, an *ownness* (*Eigenheit*), which is not a simple *inside* but rather the intimate possibility of a relation to a beyond and to an outside in general. This is why the essence of intentional consciousness will only be revealed (for example, in *Ideas I,* § 49) in the reduction of the totality of the existing world in general.

This movement is already adumbrated in the First Investigation with regard to expression and meaning as a relation to objects. "*Expressions* function meaningfully (*Bedeutungsintention*) even in *solitary mental life, where they no longer serve to indicate anything.* The two notions of sign do not therefore really stand in the relation of more extensive genus to narrower species" (§ 1; ET, [modified], p. 269).

Before opening the field of this solitary mental life in order to apprehend the nature of expression in it, we must first determine and reduce the domain of indication. Husserl begins with this. But before following him in this analysis, let us pause for a moment.

The moves we have just been commenting upon are subject to two possible readings.

On the one hand, Husserl seems to repress, with dogmatic haste, a question concerning the *structure of the sign in general.* By proposing from the start a radical dissociation between the two *heterogeneous* kinds of sign, between indication and expression, he has not asked what is meant by a sign *in general.* The concept of a sign in general, which he has to use to start with, and in which he must recognize a core of sense, can receive its unity only from an essence; it can only be ordered according to such. The latter must be recognized in an essential structure of experience and within a familiar horizon. In order to understand the word "sign" at the opening of the problem, we must already have a precomprehension of the essence, the function, or essential structure of the sign in general. Only later on will we be able eventually to distinguish between sign as indication and sign as expression, even if these two kinds of sign are not ordered according to relations of genus and species. According to a distinction of Husserl's (cf. § 13) we can say that the category of sign in general if not a genus but a form.

What then is a sign in general? We do not propose to answer this question here for various reasons. We only wish to suggest in what sense Husserl may seem to evade it. "Every sign is a sign for something," about something (*für etwas*). These are the words Husserl first uses to *immediately* introduce the following dissociation: "but not every sign has a 'meaning,' a 'sense' that the sign 'expresses.' " This would suppose we implicitly knew what "being-for" means—in the sense of "being-in-the-place-of." We have to understand and acquaint ourselves with this structure of substitution or reference so that the heterogeneity between the indicative reference and the expressive reference could then become intelligible, indeed demonstrable—if for no other reason than that their relationship, as Husserl understands it, might become clear to us. Husserl will demonstrate a little further on (§ 8) that the expressive reference (*Hinzulenken, Hinzeigen*) is not the indicative reference (*Anzeigen*). But no basic question is raised as to the sense of the *Zeigen in general,* which points to the invisible and may then be modified into *Hinzeigen* or *Anzeigen.* However, one can already guess—perhaps we shall verify it further on—that this *"Zeigen"* is the place where the root and necessity of all "interweaving" of indication and expression is manifested. This is the place where all those oppositions and differences which will henceforth structure Husserl's analysis (and which will all be framed in concepts derived from traditional metaphysics) have not yet taken shape. But by choosing the logical character of signification as his theme, and by believing he can isolate the *logical a priori* of pure grammar in the general *a priori* of grammar, Husserl is already resolutely engaged in one of the modifications of the general structure of the *Zeigen: Hinzeigen* and not *Anzeigen*.

Does this absence of questioning about the starting point and about the precomprehension of an operative concept (that of signs in general) necessarily denote dogmatism? May we not interpret this *on the other hand* as critical vigilance? Is this not precisely to refuse or deny precomprehension as the apparent starting point because it would be a prejudice or presumption? By what right may we assume the essential unity of something like the sign? What if Husserl wanted to break down the unity of the sign by dismantling its appearance and thus reduce it to a conceptually unfounded verbality? What if there were not *a* concept of sign and *different* kinds of sign but two irreducible concepts which were improperly attached to a single word? At the beginning of the second section Husserl speaks precisely of the "two concepts attached to the word 'sign.'" In reproaching him for not beginning by asking himself about the being of the sign in general, do we not extend a precipitate confidence to the unity of a word?

More seriously still: by asking *"What is* the sign in general?,"* we raise the question of the sign to an ontological plane, we pretend to assign a fundamental or regional place to signification in an ontology. This would be a classical procedure. One would subject sign to truth, language to being, speech to thought, and writing to speech. To say that there could be a truth for the sign in general, does this not suppose that the sign is not the possibility of truth, does not constitute it, but is satisfied to signify it—to reproduce, incarnate, secondarily inscribe, or refer to it? For if the sign in some way preceded what we call truth or essence, there would be no sense in speaking about the truth or essence of the sign. May we not think—as Husserl no doubt did—that if one considers the sign as the structure of an intentional movement, it does not fall under the category of a thing in general (*Sache*), it is not a "being" whose own being would be questioned? Is not the sign something other than a being—the sole "thing" which, not being a thing, does not fall under the question "what is . . . ?" but on the contrary, should the occasion arise, produces "philosophy" in this way as the empire of the *ti esti*?

In affirming that "logical meaning (*Bedeutung*) is an expression," that there is theoretical truth only in a statement,[3] in resolutely concerning himself with linguistic expression as the possibility of truth and in not presupposing the essential unity of the sign, Husserl might seem to reverse the traditional procedure and, in the activity of signification, attend to what —although it has no truth in itself—conditions the movement and concept of truth. Along a whole itinerary which ends in *The Origin of Geometry*,[4] Husserl will accord a growing attention to that which, in signification, in language, and in inscription, deposits [*consigne*] ideal objectivity, *produces* truth or ideality, rather than simply *records* it.

But this last move is not simple. This is our problem, and we shall have to return to it. The historic destiny of phenomenology seems in any case to be contained in these two motifs: on the one hand, phenomenology is the reduction of naïve ontology, the return to an active constitution of sense and value, to the activity of a *life* which produces truth and value in general through its signs. But at the same time, without being simply juxtaposed to this move,[5] another factor

3. A very frequent affirmation, from the *Logical Investigations* (cf., e.g., Introduction, § 2) right up until *The Origin of Geometry*.

4. "Der Ursprung der Geometrie als intentional-historisches Problem," ed. Eugen Fink, *Revue internationale de philosophie*, I, No. 2 (1939). English translation by David Carr, "The Origin of Geometry," Appendix VI of *The Crisis of European Sciences* (Evanston: Northwestern University Press, 1970). [The French translation by Derrida, *L'Origine de la géométrie* (Paris: Presses Universitaires de France, 1962), also contains an introduction by Derrida.—Translator.]

5. A move whose relation to classical metaphysics or ontology can be interpreted in different ways. It is a critique which would have limited but certain affinities with that of Nietzsche or Bergson. In any case it belongs to the unity of a historical configuration. That this critique, in the historical configuration of these reversals, continues metaphysics is one of the most enduring themes of Heidegger's meditation. Concerning these problems (the starting point to be found in the precomprehension of the sense of a word, the privilege of the

will necessarily confirm the classical metaphysics of presence and indicate the adherence of phenomenology to classical ontology.

It is with this adherence that we have chosen to interest ourselves.

---

question, "what is . . . ?," the relations between language and being or truth, the belonging to a classical ontology, etc.), it is only by a superficial reading of Heidegger's texts that one could conclude that these texts themselves fall under these, Heidegger's own objections. We think, on the contrary, without being able to go into it here, that no one before has better escaped them. This does not mean, of course, that one often escapes them afterwards.

2 / The Reduction of Indication

THIS METAPHYSICAL ATTACHMENT is evidenced in the theme to which we now return, the extrinsic relation of the indicative sign to expression. Husserl devotes only three paragraphs to *"the essence of indication"* and, in the same chapter, eleven paragraphs to *expression*. His logical and epistemological concern here is to secure the originality of expression as "meaning" and as relation to an ideal object. The treatment of indication therefore must be brief, preliminary, and "reductive." Indication must be set aside, abstracted, and "reduced" as an extrinsic and empirical phenomenon, even if it is in fact closely related to expression, empirically interwoven with expression. But such a reduction is difficult. It is only apparently accomplished at the end of the third paragraph. Indicative functions, sometimes of another kind, continually reappear further on, and getting rid of them will be an infinite task. Husserl's whole enterprise—and far beyond the *Investigations*—would be threatened if the *Verflechtung* which couples the indicative sign to expression were absolutely irreducible, if it were in principle inextricable and if indication were essentially internal to the movement of expression rather than being only conjoined to it, however tenaciously.

What is an indicative sign? First, it may be *natural* (the canals of Mars *indicate* the possible presence of intelligent beings) as well as *artificial* (the chalk mark, the stigmata, all the instruments of conventional designation).[1] Here the op-

1. By the logic of his example and analysis, Husserl would have been able to cite writing in general. While it cannot be doubted that, for Husserl, writing is *indicative* in its own sphere, it poses a formi-

position between nature and convention has no pertinence whatsoever and in no way divides the unity of the indicative function. What is this unity? Husserl describes it as being a certain "motivation" (*Motivierung*): it is what moves something such as a "thinking being" *to pass* by thought from something to something else. For the moment, this definition must remain quite general. This passage may be effected in conviction (*Überzeugung*) or presumption (*Vermutung*), and it always links an *actual* consciousness to a *nonactual* consciousness. For motivation considered in this degree of generality, this cognition may concern any object (*Gegenstand*) or state of affairs (*Sachverhalt*), and not necessarily empirical existents, that is, individuals. In order to designate the category of the known (actual or nonactual), Husserl intentionally uses very general concepts (*Sein, Bestand*), which may cover being or subsistence and the structure of both ideal objects and empirical existents. *Sein, bestehen,* and *Bestand*—frequent and fundamental words in the beginning of the section—are not reducible to *Dasein, existieren,* and *Realität,* and this difference matters a great deal for Husserl, as we shall see in a moment.

Husserl thus defines the essential character which most generally incorporates all of the indicative functions:

> In these we discover as a common circumstance the fact that certain objects or states of affairs *of whose reality (Bestand) someone has actual knowledge* indicate (*anzeigen*) to him *the reality of certain other objects or states of affairs,* in the sense that *his belief in the being (Sein) of the one is experienced* (though not at all evidently) *as motivating a belief or surmise in the being of the other* (First Investigation, § 2; ET [modified], p. 270).

But this essential character is still so general that it covers the whole field of indication and even more. Or, rather, since

---

dable problem, which probably here explains his prudent silence. For in supposing that writing is indicative in the sense that he gives to the term, it has a strange privilege which endangers all the essential distinctions: in phonetic writing (or rather that purely phonetic part of writing, which is universally and perhaps abusively called phonetics) what it would "indicate" would be an "expression," whereas in nonphonetic writing it would take the place of expressive discourse and immediately connect with the "meaning" (*bedeuten*). We are not here insisting upon this problem, but it does belong to the wider horizon of this essay.

it is certainly an *Anzeigen* that is described here, let us say that this common character goes beyond indication *in the strict sense*, something with which he will now have to deal. Thus we see why it was so important to distinguish between *Sein* and *Bestand*, on the one hand, and *Existenz, Dasein,* or *Realität*, on the other. General motivation thus defined is a simple "because" which may just as well have the sense of indicative allusion (*Hinweis*) as that of deductive, evident, and apodictic demonstration (*Beweis*).

In this latter case, the "because" links together the evident and ideal necessities which are permanent and which persist beyond every empirical *hic et nunc.* "An ideal rule is here revealed which extends its sway beyond the judgements here and now united by 'motivation'; in a supraempirical generality .it comprehends as such all judgements having a like content, all judgements, even, having a like form" (§ 3; ET, p. 271). Motivations linking together lived experiences, as well as *acts* which grasp necessary and evident idealities and ideal objectivities, may belong to the contingent and empirical order of "nonevident" indication. However, the relations which unite the *contents* of ideal objects in evident demonstration are not cases of indication. The whole analysis of section 3 demonstrates the following: (1) Even if *A* indicates *B* with complete *empirical* certitude (with the highest probability), this indication will never be a demonstration of apodictic necessities or (to employ classical terms) "truths of reason" in contrast to "truths of fact." (2) Even if, on the contrary, indication does seem to intervene in a demonstration, it will always be on the side of psychic motivations, acts, beliefs, etc., and never on the side of the content of the truths involved.

This indispensable distinction between *Hinweis* and *Beweis*, indication and demonstration, does not merely pose a problem whose form is analogous to the one which we raised earlier apropos of the *Zeigen.* What can be meant by "showing (*Weisen*) in general" before it is divided up into the indicative pointing-out (*Hinweis*) of the nonseen and the demonstration (*Beweis*) which exhibits in the evidence of proof? This distinction also sharpens the difficulty which we already noted in the problem of "interweaving."

We now know in fact that, for the order of signification in general, the whole of psychic experience (under the surface character of its *acts*—even when they intend idealities and objective necessities) contains only indicative concatenations. The indicative sign falls outside the content of absolutely ideal objectivity, that is, outside truth. Here again, the very possibility of this exteriority, or rather this extrinsic character of the indicative sign, is inseparable from the possibility of all the forthcoming reductions, be they eidetic or transcendental. Having its "origin" in the phenomena of association,[2] and always connecting empirical existents in the world, indicative signification in language will cover everything that falls subject to the "reductions": factuality, worldly existence, essential nonnecessity, nonevidence, etc. Would we not be already justified in saying that the whole future problem of the reduction and all the conceptual differences in which it is articulated (fact/essence, worldliness/transcendentality, and all the oppositions systematically involved with it) are opened up in a *divergence* between two kinds of signs? And would we not be right again in saying that this system is set up at the same time as this divergence, if not in it and as a result of it? Does not the concept of *parallelism*, which defines the relations between the purely psychic—which is in the world—and the purely transcendental—which is not—and which thus sums up the whole enigma of Husserl's phenomenology, already present itself here in the form of a relation between two modes of signification?

2. Cf. § 4: "The mental facts in which the notion of indication has its 'origin,' i.e., in which it can be abstractively apprehended, belong to the wider group of facts which fall under the historical rubric of the 'association of ideas'" (ET, p. 273). We know that Husserl never stopped using the concept of "association," although he continually renewed and utilized it in the field of transcendental experience. Here, what is excluded from pure expression as such is indication, and thus association in the sense of empirical psychology. It is the empirical mental experiences which must be bracketed in order to recognize the ideality of meaning at work governing expression. The distinction between indication and expression appears first of all in the necessary and provisionally "objectivist" phase of phenomenology, when empirical subjectivity has to be neutralized. Will it retain all its value when transcendental themes deepen the analysis? Will it do so when we come back to the constituting subjectivity? Such is the question. Husserl never again broached it. He continued to use the "essential distinctions" from the beginning of the *Investigations*. Yet he never recommenced, never repeated, on them that work of thematization by which all his other concepts were untiringly reworked, verified, and confirmed, reappearing continually in the midst of a description.

And yet Husserl, who never wanted to assimilate experience in general (empirical or transcendental) with language, will ceaselessly strive to keep signification outside the self-presence of transcendental life.

The question we have just raised brings us from commentary to interpretation. If we could reply in the affirmative, we would have to conclude, against the express intention of Husserl, that even before becoming a method the "reduction" would already be at work in the most spontaneous act of spoken discourse, the simple practice of the spoken word, the power of expression.

Although this conclusion would constitute for us in a certain sense the "truth" of phenomenology, it would at a certain level contradict the express intention of Husserl for two sorts of reasons. For on the one hand, as we mentioned above, Husserl believes in the existence of a pre-expressive and prelinguistic stratum of sense, which the reduction must sometimes disclose by excluding the stratum of language. On the other hand, although there is no expression and meaning without speech, not everything in speech is "expressive." Although discourse would not be possible without an expressive core, one could almost say that the totality of speech is caught up in an indicative web.

3 / Meaning as Soliloquy

LET US SUPPOSE that indication is excluded; expression remains. What is expression? It is a sign charged with meaning. Husserl undertakes to define meaning (*Bedeutung*) in section 5 of the First Investigation: "Expressions as Meaningful Signs" (*Ausdrücke als bedeutsame Zeichen*). Expressions are signs which "want to say," which "mean."

A) Meaning doubtless comes to the sign and transforms it into expression only by means of speech, oral discourse. "From indicative signs we distinguish *meaningful* signs, i.e., *expressions*" (§ 5; ET, p. 275).[1] But why "expressions" and why "meaningful" signs? This can only be explained by bringing together a whole sheaf of reasons, unified by a single underlying intention.

1. Ex-pression is exteriorization. It imparts to a certain outside a sense which is first found in a certain inside. We suggested above that this outside and this inside were absolutely primordial: the outside is neither nature, nor the world, nor a real exterior relative to consciousness. We can now be more precise. The meaning (*bedeuten*) intends an outside which is that of an ideal ob-ject. This outside is then ex-pressed and goes forth beyond itself into another outside, which is always "in" consciousness. For, as we shall see, the expressive discourse, as such and in essence, has no need of being effectively uttered in the world. Expressions as meaningful signs are a twofold

---

1. [Unless otherwise indicated, all quotations from Husserl are from the First Investigation.—Translator.]

going-forth beyond itself of the sense (*Sinn*) in itself, existing in consciousness, in the with-oneself or before-oneself which Husserl first determined as "solitary mental life." Later, after the discovery of the transcendental reduction, he will describe this solitary life of the soul as the noetic-noematic sphere of consciousness. If, by anticipation and for greater clarity, we refer to the corresponding sections in *Ideas I*, we see how the "unproductive" stratum of expression comes to reflect, "to mirror" (*widerzuspiegeln*) every other intentionality in both its form and its content. The relation to objectivity thus denotes a "preexpressive" (*vorausdrücklich*) intentionality aiming at a sense which is to be transformed into meaning and expression. It is not self-evident, however, that this repeated and reflected "going-forth" toward the noematic sense and then toward expression is an unproductive reduplication, especially if we consider that by being "unproductive" Husserl understands the "*productivity* that *exhausts itself in expressing,* and in the *form of the conceptual* introduced with this function." [2]

We shall have to return to this. We only wanted to note here what "expression" means for Husserl: the going-forth-beyond-itself of an act, then of a sense, which can remain in itself, however, only in speech, in the "phenomenological" voice.

2. The word "expression" is already required in the *Investigations* for another reason. Expression is a voluntary exteriorization; it is meant, conscious through and through, and intentional. There is no expression without the intention of a subject animating the sign, giving it a *Geistigkeit*. In indication the animation has two limits: the body of the sign, which is not merely a breath, and that which is indicated, an existence in the world. In expression the intention is absolutely explicit because it animates a voice which may remain entirely internal and because the expressed is a meaning (*Bedeutung*), that is, an ideality "existing" nowhere in the world.

3. That there can be no expression without voluntary intention can be confirmed from another point of view. If expression is always inhabited and animated by a meaning (*bedeuten*), as *wanting* to say, this is because, for Husserl, the

2. *Ideas I*, § 124; ET, p. 321. Elsewhere we examine more closely the problem of meaning and expression in *Ideas I*; cf. "La Forme et le vouloir-dire: Note sur la phénoménologie du langage," *Revue internationale de philosophie*, LXXXI (September 1967), 277–99. [This essay is translated below, pp. 107–28, as "Form and Meaning."]

Deutung (the interpretation or the understanding of the *Bedeutung*) can never take place outside oral discourse (*Rede*). Only such discourse is subject to a *Deutung*, which is never primarily reading, but rather listening. What "means," i.e., *that which* the meaning means to say—the meaning, *Bedeutung*—is left up to whoever is speaking, insofar as he says what he *wants* to say, what he *means* to say—expressly, explicitly, and consciously. Let us examine this.

Husserl recognizes that his use of the word "expression" is somewhat "forced." But the constraint thus exercised over language clears up his own intentions and at the same time reveals a common fund of metaphysical implications.

> We shall lay down, for provisional intelligibility, that all speech (*Rede*) and every part of speech (*Redeteil*), as also each sign that is essentially of the same sort, shall count as an expression, whether or not such speech is actually uttered (*wirklich geredet*), or addressed with communicative intent to any persons or not (§ 5; ET, p. 275).

Thus everything that constitutes the effectiveness of what is uttered, the physical incarnation of the meaning, the body of speech, which in its ideality belongs to an empirically determined language, is, if not outside discourse, at least foreign to the nature of expression as such, foreign to that pure intention without which there could be no speech. The whole stratum of empirical effectiveness, that is, the factual totality of speech, thus belongs to indication, which is still more extensive than we had realized. The effectiveness, the totality of the events of discourse, is indicative, not only because it is in the world, but also because it retains in itself something of the nature of an *involuntary* association.

For if intentionality never simply meant will, it certainly does seem that in the order of expressive experiences (supposing it to be limited) Husserl regards intentional consciousness and voluntary consciousness as synonymous. And if we should come to think—as Husserl will authorize us to do in *Ideas I*—that every intentional lived experience may in principle be taken up again in an expressive experience, we would perhaps have to conclude that, in spite of all the themes of receptive or intuitive intentionality and passive genesis, the concept of intentionality remains caught up in the tradition of a voluntaristic metaphysics—that is, perhaps, in metaphysics *as such*. The explicit teleology that commands the whole of transcendental phenomenology would be at bottom nothing but a transcendental voluntarism. Sense wants to be signified; it is expressed only in a meaning [*vouloir-dire*] which is none other than a wanting-to-tell-itself proper to the presence of sense.

This explains why everything that escapes the pure spiritual intention, the pure animation by *Geist*, that is, the will, is excluded from meaning (*bedeuten*) and thus from expression. What is excluded is, for example, facial expressions, gestures, the whole of the body and the mundane register, in a word, the whole of the visible and spatial as such. As such: that is, insofar as they are not worked over by *Geist*, by the will, by the *Geistigkeit* which, in the word just as in the human body, transforms the *Körper* into *Leib* (into flesh). The opposition between body and soul is not only at the center of this doctrine of signification, it is confirmed by it; and, as has always been at bottom the case in philosophy, it depends upon an interpretation of language. Visibility and spatiality as such could only destroy the self-presence of will and spiritual animation which opens up discourse. *They are literally the death of that self-presence*. Thus:

> Such a definition excludes (from expression) facial expression and the various gestures which involuntarily (*unwillkürlich*) accompany speech without communicative intent, or those in which a man's mental states achieve understandable "expression" for his environment, without the added help of speech. Such "utterances" (*Äusserungen*) are not expressions in the sense in which a case of speech (*Rede*) is an expression, they are not phenomenally one with the experiences made manifest in them in the consciousness of the man who manifests them, as is the case with speech. In such manifestations one man communicates nothing to another: their utterance involves no intent to put certain "thoughts" on record expressively (*in ausdrücklicher Weise*), whether for the man himself, in his solitary state, or for others. Such "expressions," in short, have properly speaking, *no meaning (Bedeutung)* (§ 5; ET, p. 275).

They do not have anything to *say*, for they do not *want* to say anything. In the order of signification, explicit intention is an intention to express. What is implicit does not belong to the essence of speech. What Husserl here affirms concerning gestures and facial expressions would certainly hold *a fortiori* for preconscious or unconscious language.

That one may eventually "interpret" gesture, facial expression, the nonconscious, the involuntary, and indication in general, that one may sometime take them up again and make them explicit in a direct and discursive commentary—for Husserl this only confirms the preceding distinctions. This interpretation (*Deutung*) makes a latent expression *heard*, brings a meaning (*bedeuten*) out from what was still held back. Nonexpressive signs mean (*bedeuten*) only in the degree to which they can be made to say what was murmuring in them, in a stammering attempt. Gestures mean something only insofar as we can hear them, interpret (*deuten*) them. As long as we identify *Sinn* and *Bedeutung*, nothing that resists the *Deutung* can have sense or be language in the strict sense. The essence of language is in its telos; and its telos is voluntary consciousness as meaning [*comme vouloir-dire*]. The indicative sphere which remains outside expression so defined circumscribes the failure of this telos. However interwoven with expression, the indicative sphere represents everything that cannot itself be brought into deliberate and meaningful speech.

For all these reasons, the distinction between indication and expression cannot rightfully be made as one between a non-linguistic and linguistic sign. Husserl draws a boundary which passes, not between language and the nonlinguistic, but, within language in general, between the explicit and nonexplicit (with all their connotations). For it would be difficult—and *in fact* impossible—to exclude all the indicative forms from language.

At most, then, we can distinguish with Husserl between linguistic signs "in the strict sense" and linguistic signs in the broader sense. For, justifying his exclusion of gestures and facial expressions, Husserl concludes:

> It is not to the point that another person may interpret (*deuten*) our involuntary manifestations (*unwillkürlichen Äusserungen*), e.g., our "expressive movements," and that he may thereby become deeply acquainted with our inner thoughts and emotions. They [these manifestations or "utterances"] "mean" (*bedeuten*) something to him in so far as he interprets (*deutet*) them, but even for him they are without meaning (*Bedeutungen*) in the special sense in which verbal signs have meaning (*im prägnanten Sinne sprachlicher Zeichen*): they only mean in the sense of indicating (§ 5; ET, p. 275).

This leads us to seek the limit of the indicative field still further. Even for him who finds something discursive in another person's gestures, the indicative manifestations of the other are not thereby transformed into expressions. It is he, the interpreter, who expresses himself about them. In the relation to the other perhaps there is something that makes indication irreducible.

B) It does not suffice, in short, to recognize oral discourse as the medium of expressivity. Once we have excluded all the nondiscursive signs immediately given as extrinsic to speech (gestures, facial expressions, etc.), there still remains a considerable sphere of the nonexpressive within speech itself. This nonexpressiveness is not only restricted to the physical aspect of expression ("the sensible sign, the articulate sound-complex, the written sign on paper"). "A mere distinction between physical signs and sense-giving experiences is by no means enough, and not at all enough for logical purposes" (§6; ET, p. 276).

Considering now the nonphysical side of speech, Husserl excludes from it, as belonging to indication, everything that belongs to the *communication* or *manifestation* of mental experiences. The move which justifies this exclusion should teach us a great deal about the metaphysical tenor of this phenomenology. The themes which will arise therein will never again be re-examined by Husserl; on the contrary, they will repeatedly be confirmed. They will lead us to think that in the final analysis what separates expression from indication could be called the immediate nonself-presence of the living present. The elements of worldly existence, of what is natural or empirical, of sensibility, of association, etc., which determined the concept of indication, will perhaps (certainly across a number of mediations we can anticipate) find their ultimate unity in this nonpresence. And this nonpresence to itself of the living present will simultaneously qualify the relation to others in general as well as the relation to the self involved in temporalization.

This takes form slowly, prudently, but rigorously in the *Investigations*. We have seen that the difference between indication and expression was functional or intentional, and not substantial. Husserl can thus think that some elements of a substantially discursive order (words, parts of speech in general) function in certain cases as indicative signs. And this indicative function of speech is everywhere at work. *All speech inasmuch as it is engaged in communication and manifests lived experience operates as indication.* In this way words act like gestures. Or rather, the very concept of gesture would have to be determined on the basis of indication as what is not expressive.

Husserl indeed admits that expression is "originally framed" to serve the function of communication (First Investigation, § 7). And yet expression itself is never purely expression as long as it fulfills this original function; only when communication is suspended can pure expression appear.

What in effect happens in communication? Sensible phenomena (audible or visible, etc.) are animated through the sense-giving acts of a subject, whose intention is to be simultaneously understood by another subject. But the "animation" cannot be pure and complete, for it must traverse, and to some degree lose itself in, the opaqueness of a body:

> Such sharing [of communication] becomes a possibility if the auditor also understands the speaker's intention. He does this inasmuch as he takes the speaker to be a person, who is not merely uttering sounds but *speaking to him,* who is accompanying those sounds with certain sense-giving acts, which the sounds reveal to the hearer, or whose sense they seek to communicate to him. What first makes mental commerce possible, and turns connected speech into discourse, lies in the correlation among the corresponding physical and mental experiences of communicating persons which is effected by the physical side of speech (§ 7; ET, p. 277).

Everything in my speech which is destined to manifest an experience to another must pass by the mediation of its physical side; this irreducible mediation involves every expression in an indicative operation. The manifesting function (*kundgebende Funktion*) is an indicative function. Here we find the core of indication: indication takes place whenever the sense-giving act, the animating intention, the living spirituality of the meaning-intention, is not fully present.

When I listen to another, his lived experience is not present to me "in person," in the original. Husserl thinks I may have a primordial intuition, that is, an immediate perception of what is exposed of the other in the world: the visibility of his body, his gestures, what may be understood of the sounds he utters. But the subjective side of his experience, his consciousness, in particular the acts by which he gives sense to his signs, are not immediately and primordially present to me as they are for him

and mine are for me. Here there is an irreducible and defini-
tive limit. The lived experience of another is made known to
me only insofar as it is mediately indicated by signs involving
a physical side. The very idea of "physical," "physical side," is
conceivable in its specific difference only on the basis of this
movement of indication.

To explain the irreducibly indicative character of manifestation, even in speech, Husserl already proposes certain
themes which will be meticulously and systematically elaborated in the fifth *Cartesian Meditation:* outside the transcendental monadic sphere of what is my own (*mir eigenes*), the
ownness of my own (*Eigenheit*), my own self-presence, I only
have relations of *analogical appresentation, of mediate and
potential intentionality,* with the other's ownness, with the self-
presence of the other; its primordial presentation is closed to
me. What will there be described under the surveillance of a
differentiated, bold, and rigorous transcendental reduction is
here, in the *Investigations,* sketched out in the "parallel" dimension of the mental.

> The hearer perceives the intimation in the same sense in which he
> perceives the intimating person—even though the mental phe-
> nomena which make him a person cannot fall, for what they are,
> in the intuitive grasp of another. Common speech credits us with
> percepts even of other people's inner experiences; we "see" their
> anger, their pain, etc. Such talk is quite correct, as long as, e.g.,
> we allow outward bodily things likewise to count as perceived, and
> as long as, in general, the notion of perception is not restricted to
> the adequate, the strictly intuitive percept. If the essential mark
> of perception lies in the intuitive persuasion (*Vermeinen*) that a
> thing or event is itself before us (*gegenwärtigen*) for our grasping
> —such a persuasion is possible, and in the main mass of cases
> actual, without verbalized, conceptual apprehension—then the
> receipt of such an intimation (*Kundnahme*) is the mere perceiving
> of it. . . . The hearer perceives the speaker as manifesting cer-
> tain inner experiences, and to that extent he also perceives these
> experiences themselves: he does not, however, himself experience
> them, he has not an "inner" but an "outer" percept of them. Here
> we have the big difference between the real grasp of what is in
> adequate intuition, and the putative (*vermeintlichen*) grasp of
> what is on a basis of inadequate, though intuitive, presentation.
> In the former case we have to do with an experienced, in the latter
> case with a presumed (*supponiertes*) being, to which no truth
> corresponds at all. Mutual understanding demands a certain corre-

lation among the mental acts mutually unfolded in intimation and in the receipt of such intimation, but not at all their exact resemblance (§ 7; ET, p. 278).

The notion of *presence* is the core of this demonstration. If communication or intimation (*Kundgabe*) is essentially indicative, this is because we have no primordial intuition of the presence of the other's lived experience. Whenever the immediate and full presence of the signified is concealed, the signifier will be of an indicative nature. (This is why *Kundgabe*, which has been translated a bit loosely by "manifestation" ["intimation" in Findlay's English translation], does not manifest, indeed, renders nothing manifest, if by manifest we mean evident, open, and presented "in person." The *Kundgabe* announces and at the same time conceals what it informs us about.)

All speech, or rather everything in speech which does not restore the immediate presence of the signified content, is inexpressive. Pure expression will be the pure active intention (spirit, *psychē*, life, will) of an act of meaning (*bedeuten*) that animates a speech whose content (*Bedeutung*) is present. It is present not in nature, since only indication takes place in nature and across space, but in consciousness. Thus it is present to an "inner" intuition or perception. We have just understood why the intuition to which it is present cannot be that of the other person in communication. The meaning is therefore *present to the self* in the life of a present that has not yet gone forth from itself into the world, space, or nature. All these "goings-forth" effectively exile this life of self-presence in indications. We know now that indication, which thus far includes practically the whole surface of language, is the process of death at work in signs. As soon as the other appears, indicative language—another name for the relation with death —can no longer be effaced.

The relation with the other as nonpresence is thus impure expression. To reduce indication in language and reach pure expression at last, the relation with the other must perforce be suspended. I will no longer then have to pass through the mediation of the physical side, or any appresentation whatever. Section 8, "Expressions in Solitary Life," thus follows a path which is, from two points of view, parallel to that of the reduction to the monadic sphere of *Eigenheit* in the *Cartesian*

Meditations: the psychic is parallel to the transcendental, and the order of expressive experiences is parallel to the order of experiences in general.

> So far we have considered expressions as used in communication, which last depends essentially on the fact that they operate indicatively. But expressions also play a great part in uncommunicated, interior mental life. This change in function plainly has nothing to do with whatever makes an expression an expression. Expressions continue to have meanings (*Bedeutungen*) as they had before, and the same meanings as in dialogue. A word only ceases to be a word when our interest stops at its sensory contour, when it becomes a mere sound-pattern. But when we live in the understanding of a word, it expresses something and the same thing, whether we address it to anyone or not. It seems clear, therefore, that an expression's meaning (*Bedeutung*), and whatever else pertains to it essentially, cannot coincide with its feats of intimation (§ 8; ET, pp. 278–79).

The first advantage of this reduction to the interior monologue is that the physical event of language there seems absent. Insofar as the unity of the word—what lets it be recognized as a word, *the same* word, the unity of a sound-pattern and a sense—is not to be confused with the multiple sensible events of its employment or taken to depend on them, the *sameness* of the word is ideal; it is the ideal possibility of repetition, and it loses nothing by the reduction of *any* empirical event marked by its appearance, nor all of them. Although "what we are to use as an indication [the distinctive sign] must be perceived by us as *existent*," the unity of a word owes nothing to its *existence* (*Dasein, Existenz*). Its being an expression owes nothing to any worldly or empirical existence, etc.; it needs no empirical body but only the ideal and identical form of this body insofar as this form is animated by a meaning. Thus in "solitary mental life" the pure unity of expression as such should at last be restored to me.

Is this to say that in speaking to myself I communicate nothing to myself? Are the "*Kundgabe*" (the manifesting) and "*Kundnahme*" (the cognizance taken of the manifested) suspended then? Is nonpresence reduced and, with it, indication, the analogical detour, etc.? Do I not then modify myself? Do I learn nothing about myself?

Husserl considers the objection and then dismisses it: "Shall one say that in soliloquy one speaks to oneself, and employs words as signs (*Zeichen*), i.e., as indications (*Anzeichen*) of one's own inner experiences? I cannot think such a view acceptable" (§ 8; ET, p. 279).

Husserl's argumentation is decisive here; we must follow it closely. The whole theory of signification introduced in this first chapter devoted to essential distinctions would collapse if the *Kundgabe/Kundnahme* function could not be reduced in the sphere of my own lived experiences—in short, if the ideal or absolute solitude of subjectivity "proper" still needed indications to constitute its own relation to itself. We see unmistakably that in the end the need for indications simply means the need for signs. For it is more and more clear that, despite the initial distinction between an indicative sign and an expressive sign, only an indication is truly a sign for Husserl. The full expression—that is, as we shall see later on, the meaning-filled intention—departs in a certain manner from the concept of the sign. In the phrase just quoted, we can read: "as signs, i.e., as indications." But for the moment let us consider that as a slip of the tongue, the truth of which will be revealed only as we go on. Rather than say "as signs, i.e., as indications" (*als Zeichen, nämlich als Anzeichen*), let us say "signs, namely, signs in the form of indications." For on the surface of his text Husserl continues for the moment to respect the initial distinction between two kinds of signs.

To demonstrate that indication no longer functions in solitary mental life, Husserl begins by noting the difference between two kinds of "reference": reference as *Hinzeigen* (which we must avoid translating as "indication," for reasons of convention, as well as for fear of destroying the coherence of the text; let us say, arbitrarily, "showing"), and reference as *Anzeigen* (indication). If in the silent monologue, "as everywhere else, words function as signs," and if "everywhere they can be said to show something (*Hinzeigen*)," then in this case, Husserl tells us, the passage from expression to sense, from the signifier to the signified, is no longer indication. The *Hinzeigen* is not an *Anzeigen*, for this passage, or this reference, occurs without any existence (*Dasein, Existenz*), whereas in indication an existing sign or empirical event refers to a content whose existence is at least presumed, and it motivates our anticipation or conviction of the existence of what is indicated. An indicative sign cannot be conceived without the category of empirical, which is to say only probable, existence

(Husserl will thus define worldly existence in contrast to the existence of the *ego cogito*).

The reduction to the monologue is really a putting of empirical worldly existence between brackets. In "solitary mental life" we no longer use *real* (*wirklich*) words, but only imagined (*vorgestellt*) words. And lived experience—about which we were wondering whether it might not be "indicated" to the speaking subject by himself—does not have to be so indicated because it is immediately certain and present to itself. While in real communication existing signs *indicate* other existences which are only probable and mediately evoked, in the monologue, when expression is *full*,[3] nonexistent signs *show* significations (*Bedeutungen*) that are ideal (and thus nonexistent) and certain (for they are presented to intuition). The certitude of inner existence, Husserl thinks, has no need to be signified. It is immediately present to itself. It is living consciousness.

In the interior monologue, a word is thus only represented. It can occur in the imagination (*Phantasie*). We content ourselves with imagining the word, whose existence is thus neutralized. In this imagination, this imaginary representation (*Phantasievorstellung*) of the word, we no longer need the empirical

3. To avoid confusing and multiplying the difficulties, we shall here consider only the perfect expression, that by which the *"Bedeutungsintention"* is "filled." We can do this to the extent that this fullness is, as we shall see, the telos and completion of what Husserl wants to isolate here by the terms "meaning" and "expression." Nonfulfillment of expressions will give rise to new problems that we shall encounter later on.

Here is the passage we are referring to: "But if we reflect on the relation of expression to meaning (*Bedeutung*), and to this end break up our complex, intimately unified experience of the sense-filled expression, into the two factors of word and sense, the word comes before us as intrinsically indifferent, whereas the sense seems the thing aimed at by the verbal sign and meant by its means: the expression seems to direct interest away from itself towards its sense (*von sich ab und auf den Sinn hinzulenken*), and to point (*hinzuzeigen*) to the latter. But this pointing (*Hinzeigen*) is not an indication (*das Anzeigen*) in the sense previously discussed. The existence (*Dasein*) of the sign neither 'motivates' the existence of the meaning (*Bedeutung*), nor, properly expressed, our belief in the meaning's existence. What we are to use as an indication [the distinctive sign] must be perceived by us as existent (*als daseiend*). This holds also of expressions used in communication, but not for expressions used in soliloquy" (§ 8; ET, p. 279).

occurrence of the word; we are indifferent to its existence or nonexistence. For if we need the *imagination* of the word, we can do without the *imagined word*. The imagination of the word, the imagined, the word's being-imagined, its "image," is not the (imagined) word. In the same way as, in the perception of the word, the word (perceived or appearing) which is "in the world" belongs to a radically different order from that of the perception or appearing of the word, the word's being-perceived, so the (imagined) word is of a radically heterogeneous order from that of the imagination of the word. This simple and subtle difference shows what is irreducibly specific to phenomena; and unless one lends a constant and vigilant attention to differences such as these, one can understand nothing of phenomenology.

But why is Husserl not content with the difference between the existing (or perceived) word and the perception or being-perceived, the phenomenon, of the word? It is because in the phenomenon of perception reference is made, within its phenomenal being, to the existence of the word. The sense of "existence" thus belongs to the phenomenon. This is no longer the case in the phenomenon of imagination. In imagination the existence of the word is not implied, even by virtue of intentional sense. There *exists* only the imagination of the word, which is absolutely certain and self-present insofar as it is lived. This, then, is already a phenomenological reduction which isolates the subjective experience as the sphere of absolute certainty and absolute existence.

This absolute existence only appears by reducing the relative existence of the transcendent world. And the imagination, that "vital element of phenomenology" (*Ideas I*), already grants this move its privileged medium. Here, in solitary discourse,

we are in general content with imagined rather than with actual words. In imagination a spoken or printed word floats before us, though in reality it has no existence. We should not, however, confuse imaginative representations (*Phantasievorstellungen*), and still less the image-contents they rest on, with their imagined objects. The imagined verbal sound, or the imagined printed word, does not exist, only its imaginative representation does so. The difference is the difference between imagined centaurs and the imagination of such beings. The word's nonexistence (*Nicht-Existenz*) neither disturbs nor interests us, since it leaves the word's expressive function unaffected (§ 8; ET, p. 279, modified).

This argumentation would be fragile indeed if it merely appealed to a classical psychology of the imagination, but it would be most imprudent to understand it in this way. For such a psychology, the image is a picture-sign whose *reality* (whether it be physical or mental) would serve to indicate the imagined object. Husserl will show in *Ideas I* what problems such a conception leads to.[4] Although it belongs to the existent

4. Cf. *Ideas I*, § 90 and the whole of Chapter IV of Section III, particularly § § 99, 109, 111, and especially 112: "That attitude will not be changed until practice in general phenomenological analysis is more widespread than is the case at present. So long as one treats experiences as 'contents' or as mental 'elements,' which in spite of all the fashionable attacks against atomizing and hypostatizing psychology are still looked upon as a kind of minute matter (*Sächelchen*), so long as the belief accordingly prevails that it is possible to fix the difference between 'contents of sensation' and the corresponding 'contents of imagination' only through material characters of 'intensity,' 'fullness,' and the like, no improvement is to be looked for" (ET, p. 312).
The original phenomenological data that Husserl thus wants to respect lead him to posit an absolute heterogeneity between perception or primordial presentation (*Gegenwärtigung, Präsentation*) and representation or representative re-production, also translated as presentification (*Vergegenwärtigung*). Memory, images, and signs are representations in this sense. Properly speaking, Husserl is not *led* to recognize this heterogeneity, for it is this which constitutes the very possibility of phenomenology. For phenomenology can only make sense if a pure and primordial presentation is possible and given in the original. This distinction (to which we must add that between positional [*setzende*] re-presentation, which posits the having-been-present in memory, and the imaginary re-presentation [*Phantasie-Vergegenwärtigung*], which is neutral in that respect), part of a fundamental and complex system, which we cannot directly investigate here, is the indispensable instrument for a critique of classical psychology, and, in particular, the classical psychology of the imagination and the sign.
But can't one assume the necessity for this critique of naïve psychology only up to a certain point? What if we were to show, finally, that the theme or import of "pure presentation," pure and primordial perception, full and simple presence, etc., makes of phenomenology an accomplice of classical psychology—indeed constitutes their common metaphysical presupposition? In affirming that *perception does not exist* or that what is called perception is not primordial, that somehow everything "begins" by "re-presentation" (a proposition which can only be maintained by the elimination of these last two concepts: it means that there is no "beginning" and that the "re-presentation" we were talking about is not the modification of a "re-" that has *befallen* a primordial presentation) and by reintroducing the

and absolutely certain sphere of consciousness, an image, being an intentional or noematic sense, is not one reality duplicating another reality. This is not only because it is not a reality (*Realität*) in nature, but because the noema is a nonreal (*reell*) component of consciousness.

Saussure was also careful to distinguish between the real word and its image. He also saw the expressive value of a "signifier" only in the form of the "sound-image." [5] "Signifier"

---

difference involved in "signs" at the core of what is "primordial," we do not retreat from the level of transcendental phenomenology toward either an "empiricism" or a "Kantian" critique of the claim of having primordial intuition; we are here indicating the prime intention—and the ultimate scope—of the present essay.

5. This text of the *Logical Investigations* should be compared with the following passage from the *Course in General Linguistics*: "The linguistic sign unites, not a thing and a name, but a concept and a sound-image. The latter is not the material sound, a purely physical thing, but the psychological imprint of the sound, the impression that it makes on our senses. The sound-image is sensory, and if I happen to call it 'material,' it is only in that sense, and by way of opposing it to the other term of the association, the concept, which is generally more abstract. The psychological character of our sound-images becomes apparent when we observe our own speech. *Without moving our lips or tongue, we can talk to ourselves or recite mentally a selection of verse*" (*Cours de linguistique générale* [Paris: Payot, 1916], p. 98; italics added, ET, by Wade Baskin [New York: Philosophical Library, 1959], p. 66).

And Saussure adds this caution, which has been quickly forgotten: "Because we regard the words of our language as sound-images, we must avoid speaking of the 'phonemes' that make up the words. This term, which suggests vocal activity, is applicable to the spoken word only, to the realization of the inner image in discourse." This remark was no doubt forgotten because Saussure's proposed thesis only aggravates the difficulty: "We can avoid that misunderstanding by speaking of the *sounds* and *syllables* of a word provided we remember that the names refer to the sound-image." But that is easier to remember when speaking in terms of phonemes rather than sounds. Sounds are conceivable outside real vocal activity only insofar as they can be taken as objects in nature more easily than can phonemes.

To avoid other misunderstandings, Saussure concludes: "Ambiguity would disappear if the three notions involved here were designated by three names, each suggesting and opposing the others. I propose to retain the word *sign* to designate the whole and to replace *concept* and *sound-image* respectively by *signified* and *signifier*" (p. 67).

The equivalencies signifier/expression and signified/*Bedeutung* could be posited were not the *bedeuten/Bedeutung*/sense/object structure much more complex for Husserl than for Saussure. The operation means "sound-image." But, not taking the "phenomenological" precaution, Saussure makes the sound-image, the signifier as "mental impression," into a reality whose sole originality is to be internal, which is only to shift the problem without resolving it.

But if in the *Investigations* Husserl conducts his description within the realm of the mental rather than the transcendental, he nonetheless distinguishes the essential components of a structure that will be delineated in *Ideas I:* phenomenal experience does not belong to reality (*Realität*). In it, certain elements really (*reell*) belong to consciousness (*hylē, morphē,* and *noēsis*), but the noematic content, the sense, is a nonreal (*reell*) component of the experience.[6] The irreality of inner discourse is thus a most differentiated structure. Husserl writes with precision, though without emphasis: "a spoken or printed word floats before us, though in reality it has no existence. We should not, however, confuse imaginative representations (*Phantasievorstellungen*) *and still less* [our underlining] the image-contents they rest on, with their imagined objects." Not only, then, does the imagination of the word, which is not the word imagined, not exist, but the *content* (the noema) of this imagination exists *even less* than the act.

by which Husserl proceeds in the First Investigation would also have to be systematically compared with Saussure's delimitation of the "internal system" of language.

6. On the nonreality of the noema in the case of the image and the sign, cf., in particular, *Ideas I*, § 102.

4 / Meaning and Representation

LET US RECALL the object and crux of this demonstration: the pure function of expression and meaning is not to communicate, inform, or manifest, that is, to indicate. "Solitary mental life" would prove that such an expression without indication is possible. In solitary discourse the subject learns nothing about himself, manifests nothing to himself. To support this demonstration, whose consequences for phenomenology will be limitless, Husserl invokes two kinds of argument.

1. In inward speech, I communicate nothing to myself, I indicate nothing to myself. I can at most imagine myself doing so; I can only represent myself as manifesting something to myself. This, however, is only *representation* and *imagination*.

2. In inward speech I communicate nothing to myself *because there is no need of it;* I can only pretend to do so. Such an operation, the self-communication of the self, could not take place because it would make no sense, and it would make no sense because there would be *no finality* to it. The existence of mental acts does not have to be indicated (let us recall that in general only an existence can be indicated) because it is immediately present to the subject in the present moment.

Let us first read the paragraph that ties these two arguments together:

One of course *speaks,* in a certain sense, even in soliloquy, and it is certainly possible to think of oneself as speaking, and even as speaking to oneself, as, e.g., when someone says to himself: "You have gone wrong, you can't go on like that." But in the genuine sense of communication, there is no speech in such cases, nor does one tell oneself anything: one merely conceives of (*man stellt sich vor*) oneself as speaking and communicating. In a monologue words can perform no function of indicating the existence (*Dasein*) of mental acts, since such indication would there be quite purposeless (*ganz zwecklos wäre*). For the acts in question are themselves experienced by us at that very moment (*im selben Augenblick*) (First Investigation, § 8; ET, pp. 279–80).

These affirmations raise some very diverse questions, all concerned with the status of *representation* in language. Representation can be understood in the general sense of *Vorstellung*, but also in the sense of re-presentation, as repetition or re-production of presentation, as the *Vergegenwärtigung* which modifies a *Präsentation* or *Gegenwärtigung*. And it can be understood as what takes the place of, what occupies the place of, another *Vorstellung* (*Repräsentation, Repräsentant, Stellvertreter*).[1]

Let us consider the first argument. In monologue, nothing is communicated; one represents oneself (*man stellt sich vor*) as a speaking and communicating subject. Husserl thus seems here to apply the fundamental distinction between reality and representation to language. Between effective communication (indication) and "represented" communication there would be a difference in essence, a simple exteriority. Moreover, in order to reach inward language (in the sense of communication) as pure representation (*Vorstellung*), a certain fiction, that is, a particular type of representation, would have to be employed: the imaginary representation, which Husserl will later define as neutralizing representation (*Vergegenwärtigung*).

Can this system of distinctions be applied to language? From the start we would have to suppose that representation (in every sense of the term) is neither essential to nor constitutive of communication, the "effective" practice of language, but is only an accident eventually occurring in the practice of discourse. But there is every reason to believe that representation and reality are not merely added together here and there in language, for the simple reason that it is impossible in principle to rigorously distinguish them. And it doesn't help

1. Cf. on this subject the note by the French translators of the *Logical Investigations* (French ed., Vol. II, pt. I, p. 276) and that by the French translators of *The Phenomenology of Internal Time-Consciousness* (French ed., p. 26).

to say that this happens *in* language; language in general—and language alone—*is* this.

Husserl himself gives us the motives for the opposing position. When in fact I *effectively* use words, and whether or not I do it for communicative ends (let us consider signs in general, prior to this distinction), I must from the outset operate (within) a structure of repetition whose basic element can only be representative. A sign is never an event, if by event we mean an irreplaceable and irreversible empirical particular. A sign which would take place but "once" would not be a sign; a purely idiomatic sign would not be a sign. A signifier (in general) must be formally recognizable in spite of, and through, the diversity of empirical characteristics which may modify it. It must remain the *same*, and be able to be repeated as such, despite and across the deformations which the empirical event necessarily makes it undergo. A phoneme or grapheme is necessarily always to some extent different each time that it is presented in an operation or a perception. But, it can function as a sign, and in general as language, only if a formal identity enables it to be issued again and to be recognized. This identity is necessarily ideal. It thus necessarily implies representation: as *Vorstellung,* the locus of ideality in general, as *Vergegenwärtigung,* the possibility of reproductive repetition in general, and as *Repräsentation,* insofar as each signifying event is a substitute (for the signified as well as for the ideal form of the signifier). Since this representative structure is signification itself, I cannot enter into an "effective" discourse without being from the start involved in unlimited representation.

One might object that it is precisely this exclusively representative character of expression that Husserl wants to bring out by his hypothesis of solitary discourse, which would retain the essence of speech while dropping its communicative and indicative shell. Moreover, one might object that we have precisely formulated our question with Husserlian concepts. We have indeed. But according to Husserl's description, it is only expression and not signification in general that belongs to the order of representation as *Vorstellung.* However, we have just suggested that the latter—and its other representative modifications—is implied by any sign whatsoever. On the other hand, and more importantly, as soon as we admit that speech belongs

essentially to the order of representation, the distinction between "effective" speech and the representation of speech becomes suspect, whether the speech is purely "expressive" or
engaged in "communication." By reason of the primordially
repetitive structure of signs in general, there is every likelihood
that "effective" language is just as imaginary as imaginary speech
and that imaginary speech is just as effective as effective speech.
In both expression and indicative communication the difference
between reality and representation, between the veridical and the
imaginary, and between simple presence and repetition has
already begun to wear away. Does not the maintaining of this
difference—in the history of metaphysics and for Husserl as
well—answer to the obstinate desire to save presence and to
reduce or derive the sign, and with it all powers of repetition?
Which comes to living *in* the effect—the assured, consolidated,
constituted effect of repetition and representation, of the difference which removes presence. To assert, as we have been doing,
that within the sign *the difference does not take place* between
reality and representation, etc., amounts to saying that the
gesture that confirms this difference is the very obliteration of
the sign. But there are two ways of eliminating the primordiality of the sign; we must be attentive to the instability of all
these moves, for they pass quickly and surreptitiously into one
another. Signs can be eliminated in the classical manner in a
philosophy of intuition and presence. Such a philosophy elim-
inates signs by making them derivative; it annuls reproduction
and representation by making signs a modification of a simple
presence. But because it is just such a philosophy—which is,
in fact, *the* philosophy and history of the West—which has so
constituted and established the very concept of signs, the sign
is from its origin and to the core of its sense marked by this
will to derivation or effacement. Thus, to restore the original
and nonderivative character of signs, in opposition to classical
metaphysics, is, by an apparent paradox, at the same time to
eliminate a concept of signs whose whole history and meaning
belong to the adventure of the metaphysics of presence. This
also holds for the concepts of representation, repetition, difference, etc., as well as for the system they form. For the present
and for some time to come, the movement of that schema will
only be capable of working over the language of metaphysics
from within, from a certain sphere of problems inside that

language. No doubt this work has always already begun. We shall have to grasp what happens inside language when the closure of metaphysics is announced.

With the difference between real presence and presence in representation as *Vortstellung*, a whole system of differences involved in language is implied in the same deconstruction: the differences between the represented and the representative in general, the signified and signifier, simple presence and its reproduction, presentation as *Vorstellung* and re-presentation as *Vergegenwärtigung*, for what is represented in the re-presentation is a presentation (*Präsentation*) as *Vorstellung*. We thus come—against Husserl's express intention—to make the *Vorstellung* itself, and as such, depend on the possibility of re-presentation (*Vergegenwärtigung*). The presence-of-the-present is derived from repetition and not the reverse. While this is against Husserl's express intention, it does take into account what is implied by his description of the movement of temporalization and of the relation with the other, as will perhaps become clear later on.

The concept of *ideality* naturally has to be at the center of such a question. According to Husserl, the structure of speech can only be described in terms of ideality. There is the ideality of the sensible form of the signifier (for example, the word), which must remain *the same* and can do so only as an ideality. There is, moreover, the ideality of the signified (of the *Bedeutung*) or intended sense, which is not to be confused with the act of intending or with the object, for the latter two need not necessarily be ideal. Finally, in certain cases there is the ideality of the object itself, which then assures the ideal transparency and perfect univocity of language; this is what happens in the exact sciences.[2] But this ideality, which is but another name for the permanence of the same and the possibility of its repetition, *does not exist* in the world, and it does not come from another world; it depends entirely on the possibility of acts of repetition. It is constituted by this possibility. Its "being" is proportionate to the power of repetition; absolute ideality is the correlate of a possibility of indefinite repetition. It could therefore be said that being is determined by Husserl as ideality, that is, as repetition. For Husserl, historical progress always has

2. Cf. on this subject *The Origin of Geometry* and the Introduction to the French translation, pp. 60–69.

as its essential form the constitution of idealities whose repetition, and thus tradition, would be assured *ad infinitum,* where repetition and tradition are the transmission and reactivation of origins. And this determination of being as ideality is properly a *valuation,* an ethico-theoretical act that revives the decision that founded philosophy in its Platonic form. Husserl occasionally admits this; what he always opposed was a conventional Platonism. When he affirms the nonexistence or nonreality of ideality, it is always to acknowledge that ideality *is* a way of being that is irreducible to sensible existence or empirical reality and their fictional counterparts.[3] In determining the *ontōs on* as *eidos,* Plato himself was affirming the same thing.

Now (and here again the commentary must take its bearing from the interpretation) this determination of being as ideality is paradoxically one with the determination of being as presence. This occurs not only because pure ideality is always that of an ideal "ob-ject" which stands in front of, which is pre-sent before the act of repetition (*Vor-stellung* being the general form of presence as proximity to a viewing), but also because only a temporality determined on the basis of the living present as its source (the now as "source-point") can ensure the purity of ideality, that is, openness for the infinite repeatability of the same. For, in fact, what is signified by phenomenology's "principle of principles"? What does the value of primordial presence to intuition as source of sense and evidence, as the *a priori* of *a prioris,* signify? First of all it signifies the certainty, itself ideal and absolute, that the universal form of all experience (*Erlebnis*), and therefore of all life, has always been and will always be the *present.* The present alone is and ever will be. Being is presence or the modification of presence. The relation with the presence of the present as the ultimate form of being

3. The assertion implied by the whole of phenomenology is that the Being (*Sein*) of the *Ideal* is nonreality, nonexistence. This predetermination is the first word of phenomenology. Although it does not exist, ideality is anything but a nonbeing. "Each attempt to transform the being of what is ideal (*das Sein des Idealen*) into the possible being of what is real, must obviously suffer shipwreck on the fact that possibilities themselves are ideal objects. Possibilities can as little be found in the real world, as can numbers in general, or triangles in general" (*Logical Investigations,* Second Investigation, Chap. I, § 4; ET, p. 345). "It is naturally not our intention to put the *being of what is ideal* on a level with the *being-thought-of which characterizes the fictitious or the absurd* (*Widersinnigen*)" (*ibid.,* § 8; ET, p. 352).

and of ideality is the move by which I transgress empirical existence, factuality, contingency, worldliness, etc.—first of all, *my own* empirical existence, factuality, contingency, worldliness, etc. To think of presence as the universal form of transcendental life is to open myself to the knowledge that in my absence, beyond my empirical existence, before my birth and after my death, *the present is*. I can empty all empirical content, imagine an absolute overthrow of the *content* of every possible experience, a radical transformation of the world. I have a strange and unique certitude that this universal form of presence, since it concerns no determined being, will not be affected by it. The relationship with *my death* (my disappearance in general) thus lurks in this determination of being as presence, ideality, the absolute possibility of repetition. The possibility of the sign is this relationship with death. The determination and elimination of the sign in metaphysics is the dissimulation of this relationship with death, which yet produced signification.

If the possibility of my disappearance in general must somehow be experienced in order for a relationship with presence in general to be instituted, we can no longer say that the experience of the possibility of my absolute disappearance (my death) affects me, occurs to an *I am,* and modifies a subject. The *I am,* being experienced only as an *I am present,* itself presupposes the relationship with presence in general, with being as presence. The appearing of the *I* to itself in the *I am* is thus originally a relation with its own possible disappearance. Therefore, *I am* originally means *I am mortal. I am immortal* is an impossible proposition.[4] We can even go further: as a linguistic statement "I am he who am" is the admission of a mortal. The move which leads from the *I am* to the determination of my being as *res cogitans* (thus, as an immortality) is

4. Employing distinctions from "pure logical grammar" and the *Formal and Transcendental Logic,* this impossibility must be expressed as follows: this proposition certainly makes sense, it constitutes intelligible speech, it is not *sinnlos;* but within this intelligibility and for the reason indicated, it is "absurd" (with the absurdity of contradiction—*Widersinnigkeit*) and *a fortiori* "false." But as the classical idea of truth, which guides these distinctions, has itself issued from such a concealment of the relationship with death, this "falsity" is the very truth of truth. Hence, it is in other completely different "categories" (if such thoughts can still be labeled thus) that these movements have to be interpreted.

a move by which the origin of presence and ideality is concealed
in the very presence and ideality it makes possible.

The effacement (or derivation) of signs is thereby confused with the reduction of the imagination. Husserl's position
with respect to tradition is here ambiguous. No doubt he profoundly renewed the question of imagination, and the role he
reserves for fiction in the phenomenological method clearly
shows that for him imagination is not just one faculty among
others. Yet without neglecting the novelty and rigor of the
phenomenological description of images, we should certainly be
cognizant of their origin. Husserl continually emphasizes that,
unlike a memory, an image is not "positional"; it is a "neutralizing" re-presentation. While this gives it a privilege in "phenomenological" practice, both an image and a memory are
classified under the general concept "re-presentation" (*Vergegenwärtigung*), that is, the reproduction of a presence, even
if the product is a purely fictitious object. It follows that
imagination is not a simple "modification of neutrality," even if
it is neutralizing ("We must protect ourselves here against a
very closely besetting confusion, namely, that between
neutrality-modification and *imagination*" [*Ideas I*, Section III,
§ 111; ET, p. 309, modified]). Its neutralizing operation modifies a positional re-presentation (*Vergegenwärtigung*), which is
memory. "More closely stated, *imagination* in general is the
neutrality-modification applied to 'positional' presentification
(*Vergegenwärtigung*), and therefore of remembering in the
widest conceivable sense of the term" (*ibid.*). Consequently,
even if it is a good auxiliary instrument of phenomenological
neutralization, the image is not a pure neutralization. It retains a primary reference to a primordial presentation, that is,
to a perception and positing of existence, to a belief in general.

This is why pure ideality, reached through neutralization,
is not fictitious. This theme appears very early,[5] and it will
continually serve to feed the polemic against Hume. But it is no
accident that Hume's thought fascinated Husserl more and
more. The power of pure repetition that opens up ideality and
the power which liberates the imaginative reproduction of
empirical perception cannot be foreign to each other; nor can
their products.

5. Cf., particularly, *Logical Investigations*, Second Investigation,
Chap. II.

In this respect, the First Investigation also remains most disconcerting in more than one way:

1. Expressive phenomena in their expressive purity are, from the start, taken to be imaginative representations (*Phantasievorstellungen*).

2. In the inner sphere thus disengaged by this fiction, the communicative discourse that a subject may occasionally address to himself ("You have gone wrong") is called "fictitious." This leads one to think that a purely expressive and non-communicative discourse can *effectively* take place in "solitary mental life."

3. By the same token, it is supposed that in communication, where the same words, the same expressive cores are at work, where, consequently, pure idealities are indispensable, a rigorous distinction can be drawn between the fictitious and the effective and between the ideal and the real. It is consequently supposed that effectiveness comes like an empirical and exterior cloak to expression, like a body to a soul. And these are indeed the notions Husserl uses, even when he stresses the unity of the body and soul in intentional *animation*. This unity does not impair the essential distinction, for it always remains a unity of composition.

4. Inside the pure interior "representation," in "solitary mental life," certain kinds of speech could effectively take place, as *effectively* representative (this would be the case with expressive language and, we can already specify, language with a purely objective, theoretico-logical character), while certain others would remain purely *fictitious* (those fictions located in fiction would be the acts of indicative communication between the self and the self, between the self taken as other and the self taken as self, etc.).

However, if it is admitted that, as we have tried to show, every sign whatever is of an originally repetitive structure, the general distinction between the fictitious and effective usages of the sign is threatened. *The sign is originally wrought by fiction.* From this point on, whether with respect to indicative communication or expression, there is no sure criterion by which to distinguish an outward language from an inward language or, in the hypothesis of an inward language, an effective language from a fictitious language. Such a distinction, however, is indispensable to Husserl for proving that indication is exterior to expression, with all that this entails. In declaring this distinction illegitimate, we anticipate a whole chain of formidable consequences for phenomenology.

What we have just said concerning the sign holds, by the same token, for the act of the speaking subject. "But," as Husserl says, "in the genuine sense of communication, there is no speech in such cases, nor does one tell oneself anything: one merely conceives of oneself (*man stellt sich vor*) as speaking and communicating" (*LI*, § 8; ET, p. 280). This leads to the second argument proposed.

Between effective communication and the representation of the self as speaking subject, Husserl must suppose a difference such that the representation of the self can only be added on to the act of communication contingently and from the outside. But the primordial structure of repetition that we just evoked for signs must govern all acts of signification. The subject cannot speak without giving himself a representation of his speaking, and this is no accident. We can no more imagine effective speech without there being self-representation than we can imagine a representation of speech without there being effective speech. This representation may no doubt be modified, complicated, and be reflected in the primary modes that are studied by the linguist, the semiologist, the psychologist, the theoretician of literature or of art, or even the philosopher. They may be quite primary, but they all suppose the primordial unity of speech and the representation of speech. Speech represents itself; it *is* its representation. Even better, speech is *the* representation of itself.[6]

More generally, Husserl seems to allow that the subject as he is in his effective experience and the subject as he represents himself to be can be simply external to each other. The subject may think that he is talking to himself and communicating something; in truth he is doing nothing of the kind.

6. But if the *re-* of this re-presentation does not signify the simple —repetitive or reflexive—reduplication that *befalls* a simple presence (which is what the word *representation* has always *meant*), then what we are approaching or advancing here concerning the relation between presence and representation must be approached in other terms. What we are describing as primordial representation can be provisionally designated with this term only within the closure whose limits we are here seeking to trangress by setting down and demonstrating various contradictory or untenable propositions within it, attempting thereby to institute a kind of insecurity and to open it up to the outside. This can only be done from a certain inside.

Where consciousness is thus entirely overcome by the belief or illusion of speaking to itself, an entirely false consciousness, one might be tempted to conclude that the truth of experience would belong to the order of the nonconscious. Quite the contrary: consciousness is the self-presence of the living, the *Erleben*, of experience. Experience thus understood is simple and is in its essence free of illusion, since it relates only to itself in an absolute proximity. The illusion of speaking to oneself would float on the surface of experience as an empty, peripheral, and secondary consciousness. Language and its representation is added on to a consciousness that is simple and simply present to itself, or in any event to an experience which could reflect its own presence in silence.

As Husserl will say in *Ideas I*, § 111,

> every experience generally (every really living one, so to speak) is an experience according to the mode of "being present." It belongs to its very essence that it should be able to reflect upon that same essence in which it is necessarily characterized as *being* certain and present (ET, p. 310, modified).

Signs would be foreign to this self-presence, which is the ground of presence in general. It is because signs are foreign to the self-presence of the living present that they may be called foreign to presence in general in (what is currently styled) intuition or perception.

If the representation of indicative speech in the monologue is false, it is because it is useless; this is the ultimate basis of the argumentation in this section (§ 8) of the First Investigation. If the subject indicates nothing to himself, it is because he cannot do so, and he cannot do so because there is no need of it. Since lived experience is immediately self-present in the mode of certitude and absolute necessity, the manifestation of the self to the self through the delegation or representation of an indicative sign is impossible because it is superfluous. It would be, in every sense of the term, *without reason*—thus without cause. Without cause because without purpose: *zwecklos*, Husserl says.

This *Zwecklosigkeit* of inward communication is the nonalterity, the nondifference in the identity of presence as self-presence. Of course this concept of *presence* not only involves the enigma of a being appearing in absolute proximity to oneself; it also designates the temporal essence of this proximity—

which does not serve to dispel the enigma. The self-presence
of experience must be produced in the present taken as a now.
And this is just what Husserl says: if "mental acts" are not
announced to themselves through the intermediary of a *Kundgabe*," if they do not have to be informed about themselves
through the intermediary of indications, it is because they are
"lived by us in the same instant" (*im selben Augenblick*). The
present of self-presence would be as indivisible as the *blink of
an eye*.

5 / Signs and the Blink of an Eye

THE FORCE of this demonstration presupposes the instant as a point, the identity of experience instantaneously present to itself. Self-presence must be produced in the undivided unity of a temporal present so as to have nothing to reveal to itself by the agency of signs. Such a perception or intuition of self by self in presence would not only be the case where "signification" in general could not occur, but also would assure the general possibility of a primordial perception or intuition, i.e., of *nonsignification* as the "principle of principles." Later, whenever Husserl wants to stress the sense of primordial intuition, he will recall that it is the experience of the absence and uselessness of signs.[1]

1. For example, the whole of the Sixth Investigation continually points out that between intuitive acts and contents, on the one hand, and significative acts and contents, on the other, the phenomenological difference is "irreducible" (see, especially, § 26). And yet the possibility of a "mixture" is admitted there—which provokes questions. The whole of *The Phenomenology of Internal Time-Consciousness* is based upon the radical discontinuity between intuitive presentation and the symbolic representation "which not only represents the object voidly but also represents it 'by means of' signs or images" (Edmund Husserl, *Vorlesungen zur Phänomenologie des inneren Zeitbewusstseins* [Halle: Max Niemeyer, 1929]; English translation by James S. Churchill, *The Phenomenology of Internal Time-Consciousness* [Bloomington: Indiana University Press, 1964], Appendix II; ET, p. 134). [Hereafter abbreviated, in references, as *ITC*.—Translator.] In *Ideas I* we read that "between *perception* on the one hand and the *symbolic representation by means of images or signs* on the other, there exists an insurmountable eidetic difference." "We col-

The demonstration we are now concerned with was elaborated before his lectures on *The Phenomenology of Internal Time-Consciousness;* [2] for reasons that are as much historical as systematic, the temporality of experience is not a theme of the *Logical Investigations*. At this point, however, we cannot avoid noting that a certain concept of the "now," of the present as punctuality of the instant, discretely but decisively sanctions the whole system of "essential distinctions." If the punctuality of the instant is a myth, a spatial or mechanical metaphor, an inherited metaphysical concept, or all that at once, and if the present of self-presence is not *simple*, if it is constituted in a primordial and irreducible synthesis, then the whole of Husserl's argumentation is threatened in its very principle.

We cannot here go closely into the admirable analysis of *The Phenomenology of Internal Time-Consciousness*, which Heidegger, in *Sein und Zeit*, calls the first in the history of philosophy to break with a concept of time inherited from Aristotle's *Physics*, determined according to the basic notions of the "now," the "point," the "limit," and the "circle." Let us, however, assemble some references from the lectures that are relevant for our own point of view.

1. Whether or not it is a metaphysical presupposition, the concept of *punctuality*, of the *now* as *stigmē*, still plays a major role in *The Phenomenology of Internal Time-Consciousness*. Undoubtedly, no now can be isolated as a pure instant, a pure punctuality. Not only does Husserl recognize this ("it belongs to the essence of lived experiences that they must be extended in this fashion, that a punctual phase can never be for itself" [*ITC*, § 19; ET, p. 70], but his whole description is incomparably well adapted to the original modifications of this irreducible spreading-out. This spread is nonetheless thought and described on the basis of the self-identity of the now as point, as a "source-point." In phenomenology, the idea of primordial

---

lapse into nonsense when, as is ordinarily done, we completely mix up these modes of presentation with their essentially different constructions" (*Ideas I*, § 43; ET, pp. 136–37). And what Husserl says about the perception of sensible corporeal things also holds for perception in general, namely, that, by being given in person in presence, it is a "sign for itself" (*Ideas I*, § 52; ET, p. 161). Is being a sign of itself (*index sui*) the same as not being a sign? It is in this sense that, "in the very instant" it is perceived, experience is a sign of itself, present to itself without the indicative detour.

2. *ITC*, § 19; ET, p. 70.

presence and in general of "beginning," "absolute beginning" or *principium*,[3] always refers back to this "source-point." Although the flow of time is "not severable into parts which could be by themselves nor divisible into phases, points of the continuity, which could be by themselves," the "modes of running-off of an immanent temporal Object have a beginning, that is to say, a source-point. This is the mode of running-off with which the immanent Object begins to be. In its characterized as now" (*ITC*, § 10; ET, pp. 48–49).

Despite all the complexity of its structures, temporality has a nondisplaceable center, an eye or living core, the punctuality of the real now. The "now-apprehension is, as it were, the nucleus of a comet's tail of retentions" (*ibid.*, § 11; ET, p. 52) and "a punctual phase is actually present as now at any given moment, while the others are connected as a retentional train" (*ibid.*, § 16; ET, p. 61). "The actual *now* is necessarily something punctual (*ein Punktuelles*) and remains so, *a form that persists through continuous change of matter*" (*Ideas I*, § 81; ET, p. 237, modified).

It is to this self-same identity of the actual now that Husserl refers in the "*im selben Augenblick*" we began with. Moreover, within philosophy there is no possible objection concerning this privilege of the present-now; it defines the very element of philosophical thought, it is *evidence* itself, conscious thought itself, it governs every possible concept of truth and sense. No sooner do we question this privilege than we begin to get at the core of consciousness itself from a region that lies elsewhere than philosophy, a procedure that would remove every possible *security* and *ground* from discourse. In the last analysis,

3. It is perhaps opportune here to reread the definition of the "principle of principles." "But enough of such topsy-turvy theories! No theory we can conceive can mislead us in regard to the *principle of all principles*: that *every primordial dator Intuition is a source of authority* (*Rechtsquelle*) *for knowledge*, that *whatever presents itself in 'intuition' in primordial form* (as it were in its bodily reality), *is simply to be accepted as it gives itself out to be*, though *only within the limits in which it then presents itself*. Let our insight grasp this fact that the theory itself in its turn could not derive its truth except from primordial data. Every statement which does nothing more than give expression to such data through merely unfolding their meaning and adjusting it accurately is thus really, as we have put it in the introductory words of this chapter, an *absolute beginning*, called in a genuine sense to provide foundations, a *principium*" (*Ideas I*, § 24; ET, p. 92).

what is at stake is indeed the privilege of the actual present, the now. This conflict, necessarily unlike any other, is between philosophy, which is always a philosophy of presence, and a meditation on nonpresence—which is not perforce its contrary, or necessarily a meditation on a negative absence, or a theory of nonpresence *qua* unconsciousness.

The dominance of the now not only is integral to the system of the founding contrast established by metaphysics, that between *form* (or *eidos* or idea) and *matter* as a contrast between *act* and *potency* ("the actual *now* is necessarily something punctual and remains so, *a form that persists through continuous change of matter*") (*Ideas I*, § 81; ET, p. 237); it also assures the tradition that carries over the Greek metaphysics of presence into the "modern" metaphysics of presence understood as self-consciousness, the metaphysics of the idea as representation (*Vorstellung*). It therefore designates the locus of a problem in which phenomenology confronts every position centered on nonconsciousness that can approach what is ultimately at stake, what is at bottom decisive: the concept of time. It is no accident that *The Phenomenology of Internal Time-Consciousness* both confirms the dominance of the present and rejects the "after-event" of the becoming conscious of an "unconscious content" which is the structure of temporality implied throughout Freud's texts.[4] Husserl writes to this effect:

> It is certainly an absurdity to speak of a content of which we are "unconscious," one of which we are conscious only later (*nachträglich*). Consciousness (*Bewusstsein*) is necessarily a being-conscious (*bewusstsein*) in each of its phases. Just as the retentional phase was conscious of the preceding one without making it an object, so also are we conscious of the primal datum—namely, in the specific form of the "now"—without its being objective; . . . retention of a content of which we are not conscious is impossible; . . . if every "content" necessarily and in itself is "unconscious" then the question of an additional dator consciousness becomes senseless (*ITC*, Appendix IX; ET, pp. 162–63, modified).

2. Despite this motif of the punctual now as "primal form" (*Urform*) of consciousness (*Ideas I*), the body of the description in *The Phenomenology of Internal Time-Consciousness* and elsewhere prohibits our speaking of a simple self-identity of the

4. Cf., on this subject, our essay "Freud et la scène de l'écriture" in *L'Ecriture et la différence* (Paris: Seuil, 1967), pp. 293–340.

present. In this way not only is what could be called the meta-physical assurance par excellence shaken, but, closer to our concerns, the *"im selben Augenblick"* argument in the *Investigations* is undermined.

In its critical as well as descriptive work, *The Phenomenology of Internal Time-Consciousness* demonstrates and confirms throughout the irreducibility of re-presentation (*Vergegenwärtigung, Repräsentation*) to presentative perception (*Gegenwärtigen, Präsentieren*), secondary and reproductive memory to retention, imagination to the primordial impression, the re-produced now to the perceived or retained actual now, etc. Without being able, here, to follow the rigorous development of this text (and without its being necessary to question its demonstrative worth), we can still examine its foundation of evidence and the *context* of these distinctions, which relates the terms distinguished to one another and constitutes the very possibility of their *comparison.*

One then sees quickly that the presence of the perceived present can appear as such only inasmuch as it is *continuously compounded* with a nonpresence and nonperception, with primary memory and expectation (retention and protention). These nonperceptions are neither added to, nor do they *occasionally* accompany, the actually perceived now; they are essentially and indispensably involved in its possibility. Husserl admittedly says that retention is still a perception. But this is the absolutely unique case—Husserl never recognized any other —of a perceiving in which the perceived is not a present but a past existing as a modification of the present:

> . . . if we call perception *the act in which all "origination"* lies, which *constitutes originarily,* then *primary remembrance is perception.* For only in *primary remembrance do we see what is past;* only in it is the past constituted, i.e., *not in a representative but in a presentative way* (ITC, § 17, ET, p. 64).

Thus, in retention, the presentation that enables us to see gives a nonpresent, a past and unreal present. We might suspect, then, that if Husserl nonetheless calls it perception, this is because he holds to establishing a radical discontinuity between retention and reproduction, between perception and imagination, etc., and not between perception and retention. This is the *nervus demonstrandi* of his critique of Brentano. Husserl resolutely maintains that there is "no mention here of a continuous accommodation of perception to its opposite" (*ibid.*).

And yet, did not the preceding section quite explicitly entertain this very possibility?

> If we now relate what has been said about perception to the *differences of the givenness* with which temporal Objects make their appearance, then the *antithesis of perception* is *primary remembrance,* which appears here, and *primary expectation* (retention and protention), whereby *perception and non-perception continually* pass over into one another (*ITC,* § 16; ET, p. 62).

Further he writes:

> In an ideal sense, then, perception (impression) would be the phase of consciousness which constitutes the pure now, and memory every other phase of the continuity. But this is just an ideal limit, something abstract which can be nothing for itself. Moreover, it is also true that even this ideal now is not something *toto caelo* different from the not-now but continually accommodates itself thereto. The continual transition from perception to primary remembrance conforms to this accommodation. (*ITC,* § 16; ET, p. 63).

As soon as we admit this continuity of the now and the not-now, perception and nonperception, in the zone of primordiality common to primordial impression and primordial retention, we admit the other into the self-identity of the *Augenblick;* nonpresence and nonevidence are admitted into the *blink of the instant.* There is a duration to the blink, and it closes the eye. This alterity is in fact the condition for presence, presentation, and thus for *Vorstellung* in general; it precedes all the dissociations that could be produced in presence, in *Vorstellung.* The difference between retention and reproduction, between primary and secondary memory, is not the radical difference Husserl wanted between perception and nonperception; it is rather a difference between two modifications of nonperception. Whatever the phenomenological difference between these two modifications may be, and despite the immense problems it poses and the necessity of taking them into account, it only serves to separate two ways of relating to the irreducible nonpresence of another now. Once again, this relation to nonpresence neither befalls, surrounds, nor conceals the presence of the primordial impression; rather it makes possible its ever renewed upsurge and virginity. However, it radically destroys any possibility of a simple self-identity. And this holds in depth for the constituting flux itself:

> If . . . we now consider the *constitutive* phenomena, we find a *flux,* and every phase of this flux is a *continuity of shading.* However, in principle, no phase of this flux is to be broadened out to a continuous succession; therefore, the flux should not be thought to be so transformed that this phase is extended in identity with itself (*ITC,* § 35; ET, p. 99; italics added).

The fact that nonpresence and otherness are internal to presence strikes at the very root of the argument for the uselessness of signs in the self-relation.

3. Doubtless Husserl would refuse to assimilate the necessity of retention and the necessity of signs, for it is only the latter which (like the image) belong to the genus of representation and symbolism. Moreover, Husserl cannot give up this rigorous distinction without bringing into question the axiomatic *principium* of phenomenology itself. The force with which he maintains that retention and protention belong to the sphere of the primordial, provided it be understood "in the broad sense," and the insistence with which he contrasts the absolute validity of primary memory with the relative validity of secondary memory,[5] clearly indicate both his intent and his

5. Cf., for example, among many analogous texts, Appendix III to *The Phenomenology of Internal Time-Consciousness.* "Accordingly, we have as essential modes of time-consciousness: (1) 'sensation' as actual presentation and essentially entwined (*verflochtene*) with it but also capable of autonomy, retention, and protention (originary spheres in the broader sense); (2) positing presentification (memory), co-presentification, and re-presentification (expectation); (3) phantasy-presentification as pure phantasy, in which all the same modes occur in phantasy-consciousness" (ET, p. 142). Here again, it will be observed, the core of the problem assumes the form of an interweaving (*Verflechtung*) of threads whose essences phenomenology carefully unravels.

This extension of the primordial sphere is what permits us to distinguish between the absolute certainty attached to retention and the relative certainty dependent upon secondary memory or recall (*Wiedererinnerung*) in the form of re-presentation. Speaking of perceptions as primal experiences (*Urerlebnisse*), Husserl writes in *Ideas I:* "For closer inspection reveals in their concreteness only *one,* but that always a continuously flowing *absolute primordial phase,* that of the living *now.* . . . Thus, for instance, we grasp the *absolute right* of immanent *perceiving* reflexion, i.e., of immanent perception *simplici-*

uneasiness. His uneasiness stems from the fact that he is trying to retain two apparently irreconcilable possibilities: (*a*) The living now is constituted as the absolute perceptual source only in a state of continuity with retention taken as nonperception. Fidelity to experience and to "the things themselves" forbids that it be otherwise. (*b*) The source of certitude in general is the primordial character of the living now; it is necessary therefore to keep retention in the sphere of primordial certitude and to shift the frontier between the primordial and the nonprimordial. The frontier must pass not between the pure present and the nonpresent, i.e., between the actuality and inactuality of a living now, but rather between two forms of the re-turn or re-stitution of the present: re-tention and re-presentation.

Without reducing the abyss which may indeed separate retention from re-presentation, without hiding the fact that the problem of their relationship is none other than that of the history of "life" and of life's becoming conscious, we should be able to say *a priori* that their common root—the possibility of re-petition in its most general form, that is, the constitution of a trace in the most universal sense—is a possibility which not only must inhabit the pure actuality of the now but must constitute it through the very movement of differance it introduces. Such a trace is—if we can employ this language without immediately contradicting it or crossing it out as we proceed— more "primordial" than what is phenomenologically primordial. For the ideality of the form (*Form*) of presence itself implies that it be infinitely re-peatable, that its re-turn, as a return of the same, is necessary *ad infinitum* and is inscribed in presence itself. It implies that the re-turn is the return of a present which will be retained in a *finite* movement or retention and that primordial truth, in the phenomenological sense of the term, is only to be found rooted in the finitude of this retention. It is furthermore implied that the relation with infinity can be instituted only in the opening of the form of presence upon ideality, as the possibility of a re-turn *ad infinitum*. How can it be explained that

---

ter, and indeed in respect of that which it brings in its flow to real primordial givenness; likewise the *absolute right of immanent retention,* in respect of that in it of which we are conscious as 'still' living and having 'just' happened, but of course no further than the content of what is thus characterized reaches. . . . We likewise grasp the *relative* right of immanent recollection" (*Ideas I,* § 78; ET, pp. 221–22).

the possibility of reflection and re-presentation belongs by essence to every experience, without this nonself-identity of the presence called primordial? How could it be explained that this possibility belongs, like a pure and ideal freedom, to the essence of consciousness? Husserl ceaselessly emphasizes that it does, in speaking of reflection, especially in *Ideas I*,[6] and in speaking of re-presentation, already in *The Phenomenology of Internal Time-Consciousness*.[7] In all these directions, the presence of the present is thought of as arising from the bending-back of a return, from the movement of repetition, and not the reverse. Does not the fact that this bending-back is irreducible in presence or in self-presence, that this trace or differance is always older than presence and procures for it its openness, prevent us from speaking about a simple self-identity *"im selben Augenblick"*? Does this not compromise the usage Husserl wants to make of the concept of "solitary mental life," and consequently of the rigorous separation of indication from expression? Do indication and the several concepts on whose basis we have thus far tried to think it through (the concepts of existence, nature, mediation, the empirical, etc.) not have an ineradicable origin in the movement of transcendental temporalization? By the same token, does not everything that is announced already in this reduction to "solitary mental life" (the transcendental reduction in all its stages, and notably the reduction to the monadic sphere of "ownness"—*Eigenheit*— etc.) appear to be stricken in its very possibility by what we are calling time? But what we are calling time must be given a different name—for "time" has always designated a movement conceived in terms of the present, and can mean nothing else. Is not the concept of pure solitude—of the monad in the phenomenological sense—*undermined* by its own origin, by the very condition of its self-presence, that is, by "time," to be conceived anew on the basis now of difference within auto-affection, on the basis of identifying identity and nonidentity within the "sameness" of the *im selben Augenblick*? Husserl himself evoked the analogy between the relation with the *alter ego*,

6. Particularly in § 77, where the problem of the difference and relations between reflection and representation is posed, for example, in secondary memory.

7. Cf., for example, § 42: "But to every present and presenting consciousness there corresponds the ideal possibility of an exactly matching presentification of this consciousness" (ET, p. 115).

constituted within the absolute monad of the ego, and the relation with the other present, the past present, as constituted in the absolute actuality of the living present (*Cartesian Meditations*, § 52).

Does not this "dialectic"—in every sense of the term and before any speculative subsumption of this concept—open up living to differance, and constitute, in the pure immanence of experience, the *divergence* involved in indicative communication and even in signification in general? And we mean the divergence of indicative communication *and signification in general*, for Husserl not only intends to exclude indication from "solitary mental life"; he will consider language in general, the element of logos, in its expressive form itself, as a secondary event, superadded to a primordial and pre-expressive stratum of sense. Expressive language itself would be something supervenient upon the absolute silence of self-relationship.

6 / The Voice That Keeps Silence

Phenomenological "silence," then, can only be re-constituted by a double exclusion or double reduction: that of the relation to the other within me in indicative communication, and that of expression as a stratum that is subsequent to, above, and external to that of sense. It is in the relation be-tween these two exclusions that the strange prerogative of the vocal medium will become clear.

We shall start with a consideration of the first reduction as it figures in the "essential distinctions," to which we are here restricting our inquiry. One must admit that the criterion for the distinction between expression and indication in the end rests on an all too summary description of "inner life." It is argued that there is no indication in this inner life because there is no communication; that there is no communication because there is no *alter ego*. And when the second person does emerge in inner language, it is a fiction; and, after all, fiction is only fiction. "You have gone wrong, you can't go on like that"— this is only a false communication, a feigned communication.

Let us not formulate *from the outside* the questions that arise concerning the possibility and status of such fictions or feints and about the place from which this "you" can arise in monologue. Let us not ask these questions *yet;* their necessity will become even more evident when Husserl comes to note that, besides the *you,* personal pronouns in general, and es-pecially the *I,* are "essentially occasional" expressions, without "objective sense," and that in communicated speech they always function as indications. The *I* alone achieves its meaning within solitary speech and functions outside it as a "universally operative indication" (First Investigation, Chap. III, § 26; ET, p. 316).

For the moment let us ask in what sense, and in view of what, the structure of inner life is "simplified" here, and how the choice of examples is revelatory of Husserl's project. It is so in at least two respects.

1. These examples are of a *practical* order. In the propositions chosen the subject addresses himself as if to a second person whom he blames or exhorts, upon whom he enjoins a decision or a feeling of remorse. This doubtless proves that we are not here dealing with "indication." Nothing is shown, directly or indirectly; the subject learns nothing about himself; his language refers to nothing that "exists." The subject does not inform himself, in the sense of either *Kundgabe* or *Kundnahme*. Husserl has to choose his examples in the practical sphere in order to show both that nothing is "indicated" in them and that they are examples of false languages. Supposing that another kind of example could not be found, one might in fact be tempted to conclude from these examples that inner speech is always essentially practical, axiological, or axiopoietical. Even when one tells himself "you are thus and so," does not the predication envelop a valuative or productive act? But it is precisely this temptation that Husserl wants, above all and at all costs, to avoid. He always determined the model of language *in general*—indicative as well as expressive—on the basis of *theōrein*. Whatever care he subsequently took to respect the originality of the practical stratum of sense and expression, whatever the success and rigor of his analyses, he continued to affirm the reducibility of axiology to its logico-theoretical core.[1] Here again we find the necessity which pushed him to study language from a logical and epistemological point of view and pure grammar as pure *logical* grammar, governed more or less immediately by the possibility of a relationship with objects. Speech that is false is not speech, and contradictory (*widersinning*) speech avoids nonsense (*Unsinnigkeit*) only if its grammaticalness does not prohibit a meaning [*Bedeutung, vouloir-dire*] or meaning-intention, which in turn can be determined only as the aiming at an object.

1. Cf., particularly, Chapter IV, and especially § § 114–27 of *Ideas I* (Section III). Elsewhere we shall study them more closely and in their own right. Cf. "Form and Meaning."

It is therefore noteworthy that logical theory, *theōrein* in general, governs not only the determination of expression, of logical signification, but even that which is excluded from it, that is, indication—showing or pointing as *Weisen* or *Zeigen* in the *Hinweis* or *Anzeigen*. *It is also noteworthy that Husserl should, at a certain level, refer to an essentially theoretical core of indication so as to exclude it from expression—which is itself purely theoretical.* Perhaps at this level the determination of expression is contaminated by that very thing it seemed to exclude: *Zeigen*, the relation to the object as indicative showing, the pointing-out of what is before the eyes or what in its visibility is always capable of appearing to an intuition, *is only provisionally invisible*. *Zeigen* is always an intending (*Meinen*) that predetermines the profound essential unity between the *Anzeigen* proper to indication and the *Hinzeigen* proper to expression. And, in the final instance, signs (*Zeichen*) always refer to *Zeigen*, to the space, visibility, field, and compass of what is ob-jected and pro-jected; they refer to phenomenality as a state of encounter [*comme vis-à-vis*] and surface, as evidence or intuition, and first of all as light.

What, then, about speech [*voix*] and time? If showing is the unity of gesture and perception in signs, if signification is assigned to the pointing finger and the eye, and if this assignation is prescribed for every sign, whether indicative or expressive, discursive or nondiscursive, what can be said about speech and time? "If the invisible is the pro-visional, what about speech and time?" And why is Husserl bent upon separating indication from expression? Does uttering or hearing signs reduce the indicating spatiality or mediation? Let us be patient a little longer.

2. The example chosen by Husserl ("You have gone wrong, you can't go on like that") must then prove two things at once: that this proposition is not indicative (and thus is a fictitious communication) and that it does not give the subject any knowledge of himself. Paradoxically, it is not indicative because, as nontheoretical, nonlogical, and noncognitive, it is not expressive either. Thus it would be a phenomenon of completely fictitious signification. Thus we confirm the unity of *Zeigen* before its diffraction into indication and expression. However, the *temporal modality* of these propositions is not without importance. If these propositions are not cognitive propositions, it is because they are not immediately in the form of predication; they do not immediately utilize the verb *to be*. Their

sense, therefore, if not their grammatical form, is not in the present; they take note of a past in the form of a reproach, they are exhortations to remorse and amendment. *The present indicative of the verb "to be" is the pure and teleological form of expression insofar as it is logical*—or, better, we should say the present indicative of the verb "to be" in the *third person*. Better still, the pure, teleological form is a proposition of the type "S is *p*," in which S is not a person that one could replace by a personal pronoun, for in all real speech the personal pronoun has merely an indicating value.[2] The subject S must be a name, the name of an object. And we know that for Husserl "S is *p*" is the fundamental and primitive form, the primordial apophantic operation from which every logical proposition must be derivable by simple construction.[3] If we posit the identity of expression and logical *Bedeutung* (*Ideas I*, § 124), we then have to recognize that the third "person" present indicative of the verb *to be* is the pure and irreducible core of expression. Let us recall that, in Husserl's words, an expression is not primitively an "expressing oneself" but is, from the outset, an "expressing oneself about something" (*über etwas sich*

2. Cf. *Logical Investigations*, First Investigation, Chap. III, § 26: "Every expression, in fact, that includes a *personal pronoun* lacks an objective sense. The word 'I' names a different person from case to case. . . . In its case, rather, an indicative function mediates, crying as it were, to the hearer 'Your *vis-à-vis* intends himself'" (ET, pp. 315–16). The whole problem is whether, in solitary speech, where Husserl says, the *Bedeutung* of the I is filled and achieved, the element of universality proper to expressiveness as such does not forbid this fulfillment and dispossess the subject of the full intuition of the *Bedeutung* "I." The problem is whether solitary speech interrupts or only *interiorizes* the dialogue situation, in which, Husserl says, "since each person, in speaking of himself, says 'I,' the word has the character of a universally operative indication of this fact."

In this way we can better understand the difference between the *manifested*, which is always subjective, and the *expressed* as *named*. Each time the I appears, we have to do with propositions of indicative manifestation. The manifested and the named may sometimes partially overlap ("A glass of water, please" names the thing and manifests a desire), but they are *de jure* quite distinct, as in the example: $2 \times 2 = 4$. "This statement does not say what is said by 'I *judge that* $2 \times 2 = 4$.' They are not even equivalent statements, since the one can be true when the other is false" (First Investigation, § 25; ET, p. 313).

3. Cf., in particular, *Formal and Transcendental Logic*, Part I, Chapter 1, § 13; ET, by Dorion Cairns, pp. 52–53).

äussern, § 7). The "talking to oneself" that Husserl wants to re-establish here is not a "talking to oneself about oneself" unless this can take the form of a "telling oneself that *S* is *p.*"

It is here that *speech* is necessary. The sense of the verb "to be" (whose infinitive form, Heidegger tells us, has been enigmatically determined by philosophy on the basis of the third person present indicative) sustains an entirely singular connection with the *word,* that is, with the unity of the *phōnē* and sense. Evidently it is not a "mere word," since it can be translated into different languages. Moreover, it is not a conceptual generality.[4] But since its sense designates nothing, no thing, no state or ontic determination, since it is encountered nowhere outside the word, its irreducibility is that of the *verbum* or *legein,* the unity of thought and voice in logos. The prerogative of being cannot withstand the deconstruction of the word. *To be* is the first or the last word to withstand the deconstruction of a language of words. But why does using words get mixed up with the determination of being in general as presence? And why is there a privilege attached to the present indicative? Why is the epoch of the *phōnē* also the epoch of being in the form of presence, that is, of ideality?

Here we must *listen.* Let us return to Husserl. For him, pure expression, logical expression, must be an "unproductive" "medium" which "reflects" (*wiederzuspiegeln*) the pre-expressive stratum of sense. Its sole productivity consists in making sense pass into the ideality of conceptual and universal form.[5] There are essential reasons why all the sense is not completely repeated in expression, as well as why expressions bear dependent and incomplete significations (syncategorematic words, etc.). Nonetheless, the telos of perfect [*intégrale*] ex-

4. Whether it be demonstrated in the Aristotelian or the Heideggerian mode, the sense of being must precede the general concept of being. Concerning the singular nature of the relation between the word and the sense of being, and the problem of the present indicative, we refer to *Being and Time* and *An Introduction to Metaphysics.* Perhaps it is already apparent that, while we appeal to Heideggerian motifs in decisive places, we would especially like to raise the question whether, with respect to the relations between *logos* and *phōnē,* and with respect to the pretended irreducibility of certain word unities (the unity of the word *being* or of other "radical words"), Heidegger's thought does not sometimes raise the same questions as the metaphysics of presence.

5. *Ideas I,* § 124.

pression is the total restitution, in the form of presence of a sense actually given to intuition. Since sense is determined on the basis of a relation with an object, the element of expression consequently must protect, respect, and restore the *presence* of sense, *both as the object's being before us*, open to view, and *as a proximity to self in interiority*. The *pre* of the *present* *obj*ect now-before us is an *against* (*Gegen*wart, *Gegen*stand) both in the sense of the "up-against" [*tout-contre*] of proximity and as the *opposition* [*l'encontre*] of the op-posed.

There is an unfailing complicity here between idealization and speech [*voix*]. An ideal object is an object whose showing may be repeated indefinitely, whose presence to *Zeigen* is indefinitely reiterable precisely because, freed from all mundane spatiality, it is a pure noema that I can express without having, at least apparently, to pass through the world. In this sense the phenomenological voice, which seems to accomplish this operation "in time," does not break with the order of *Zeigen* but belongs to the same system and carries through its function. The passage to infinity characteristic of the idealization of objects is one with the historical advent of the *phōnē*. This does not mean that we can finally understand what the movement of idealization is on the basis of a determined "function" or "faculty," concerning which we would in turn know what it *is*, thanks to our familiarity with experience, the "phenomenology of our body," or with some objective science (phonetics, phonology, or the physiology of phonation). Quite the contrary, what makes the history of the *phōnē* fully enigmatic is the fact that it is inseparable from the history of idealization, that is, from the "history of mind," or history as such.

In order to really understand where the power of the voice lies, and how metaphysics, philosophy, and the determination of being as presence constitute the epoch of speech as *technical* mastery of objective being, to properly understand the unity of *technē and phōnē*, we must think through the objectivity of the object. The ideal object is the most objective of objects; independent of the here-and-now acts and events of the empirical subjectivity which intends it, it can be repeated infinitely while remaining the same. Since its presence to intuition, its being-before the gaze, has no essential dependence on any worldly or empirical synthesis, the re-establishment of its sense in the form of presence becomes a universal and unlimited possibility. But, being *nothing* outside the world, this ideal being must be constituted, repeated, and expressed in a medium that does not impair the presence and self-presence of the acts that aim at it, a medium which both preserves the *presence of the object* before intuition and *self-presence*, the absolute proximity of the acts to themselves. The ideality of the object, which is only its being-for a nonempirical consciousness, can only be expressed in an element whose phenomenality does not have worldly form. *The name of this element is the voice. The voice is heard.* Phonic signs ("acoustical images" in Saussure's sense, or the phenomenological voice) are heard [*entendus* = "heard" plus "understood"] by the subject who proffers them in the absolute proximity of their present. The subject does not have to pass forth beyond himself to be immediately affected by his expressive activity. My words are "alive" because they seem not to leave me: not to fall outside me, outside my breath, at a visible distance; not to cease to belong to me, to be at my disposition "without further props." In any event, the phenomenon of speech, the phenomenological voice, *gives itself out* in this manner. The objection will perhaps be raised that this interiority belongs to the phenomenological and ideal aspect of every signifier. The ideal form of a written signifier, for example, is not in the world, and the distinction between the grapheme and the empirical body of the corresponding graphic sign separates an inside from an outside, phenomenological consciousness from the world. And this is true for every visual or spatial signifier. And yet every nonphonic signifier involves a spatial reference in its very "phenomenon," in the phenomenological (nonworldly) sphere of experience in which it is given. The sense of being "outside," "in the world," is an essential component of its phenomenon. Apparently there is nothing like this in the phenomenon of speech. In phenomenological interiority, hearing oneself and seeing oneself are two radically different orders of self-relation. Even before a description of this difference is sketched out, we can understand why the hypothesis of the "monologue" could have sanctioned the distinction between indication and expression only by presupposing an essential tie between expression and *phōnē*. Between the phonic element (in the phenomenological sense and not that of a real sound) and expression, taken as the logical character of a signifier that is *animated* in view of the ideal presence of a *Bedeutung* (itself related to an object), there must be a necessary bond. Husserl is unable to bracket what in glossamatics is called the "substance of expression" without menacing his whole enterprise. The appeal to this substance thus plays a major philosophical role.

Let us try, then, to question the phenomenological value of the voice, its transcendent dignity with regard to every other signifying substance. We think, and will try to show, that this transcendence is only apparent. But this "appearance" is the very essence of consciousness and its history, and it determines an epoch characterized by the philosophical idea of truth and the opposition between truth and appearance, as this opposition still functions in phenomenology. It can therefore not be called "appearance" or be named within the sphere of metaphysical conceptuality. One cannot attempt to deconstruct this transcendence without descending, across the inherited concepts, toward the unnamable.

The "apparent transcendence" of the voice thus results from the fact that the signified, which is always ideal by essence, the "expressed" *Bedeutung*, is immediately present in the act of expression. This immediate presence results from the fact that the phenomenological "body" of the signifier seems to fade away at the very moment it is produced; it seems already to belong to the element of ideality. It phenomenologically reduces itself, transforming the worldly opacity of its body into pure diaphaneity. This effacement of the sensible body and its exteriority is *for consciousness* the very form of the immediate presence of the signified.

Why is the phoneme the most "ideal" of signs? Where does this complicity between sound and ideality, or rather, between voice and ideality, come from? (Hegel was more attentive to this than any other philosopher, and, from the point of view of the history of metaphysics, this is a noteworthy fact, one we will examine elsewhere.) When I speak, it belongs to the phenomenological essence of this operation that *I hear myself* [je m'entende] *at the same time* that I speak. The signifier, animated by my breath and by the meaning-intention (in Husserl's language, the expression animated by the *Bedeutungsintention*), is in absolute proximity to me. The living act, the life-giving act, the *Lebendigkeit*, which animates the body of the signifier and transforms it into a meaningful expression, the soul of language, seems not to separate itself from itself, from its own self-presence. It does not risk death in the body of a signifier that is given over to the world and the visibility of space. It can *show* the ideal object or ideal *Bedeutung* connected to it without venturing outside ideality, outside the interiority of self-present life. The system of *Zeigen*, the finger and eye movements (concerning which we earlier wondered whether they were not inseparable from phenomenality) are not absent here; but they are interiorized. The phenomenon continues to be an object for the voice; indeed, insofar as the ideality of the object seems to depend on the voice and thus becomes *absolutely accessible* in it, the system which ties phenomenality to the possibility of *Zeigen* functions better than ever in the voice. *The phoneme is given as the dominated ideality of the phenomenon.*

This self-presence of the animating act in the transparent spirituality of what it animates, this inwardness of life with itself, which has always made us say that speech [*parole*] is alive, supposes, then, that the speaking subject hears himself [*s'entende*] in the present. Such is the essence or norm of speech. It is implied in the very structure of speech that the speaker *hears himself:* both that he perceives the sensible form of the phonemes and that he understands his own expressive intention. If accidents occur which seem to contradict this teleological necessity, either they will be overcome by some supplementary operation or there will be no speech. Deaf and dumb go hand in hand. He who is deaf can engage in colloquy only by shaping his acts in the form of words, whose telos requires that they be heard by him who utters them.

Considered from a purely phenomenological point of view, within the reduction, the process of speech has the originality of presenting itself already as pure phenomenon, as having already suspended the natural attitude and the existential thesis of the world. The operation of "hearing oneself speak" is an auto-affection of a unique kind. On the one hand, it operates within the medium of universality; what appears as signified therein must be idealities that are *idealiter* indefinitely repeatable or transmissible as the same. On the other hand, the subject can hear or speak to himself and be affected by the signifier he produces, without passing through an external detour, the world, the sphere of what is not "his own." Every other form of auto-affection must either pass through what is outside the sphere of "ownness" or forego any claim to universality. When I see myself, either because I gaze upon a limited region of my body or because it is reflected in a mirror, what is outside the sphere of "my own" has already entered the field of this auto-affection, with the result that it is no longer pure. In the experience of touching and being touched, the same thing happens. In both cases, the surface of my body, as something external, must begin by being exposed in the world. But, we could ask, are there not forms of pure auto-affection in the inwardness of one's own body which do not require the intervention of any surface displayed in the world and yet are not of the order of the voice? But then these forms remain purely empirical, for they could not belong to a medium of universal signification. Now, to account for the phenomenological power of the voice, we shall have to specify the concept of pure auto-affection more precisely and describe what, in it, makes it open to universality. As pure auto-affection, the operation of hearing oneself speak seems to reduce even the inward surface of one's own body; in its phenomenal being it seems capable of dispensing with this exteriority within interiority, this interior space in which our experience or image of our own body is spread forth. This is why hearing oneself speak [*s'entendre parler*] is experienced as an absolutely pure auto-affection, occurring in a self-proximity that would in fact be the absolute reduction of space in general. It is this purity that makes it fit for universality. Requiring the intervention of no determinate surface in the world, *being produced in the world as pure auto-affection*, it is a signifying substance absolutely at our disposition. For the voice meets no obstacle to its emission in the world precisely because it is produced *as pure auto-affection*. This auto-affection is no doubt the possibility for what is called *subjectivity* or the *for-itself*, but, without it, no world *as such* would appear. For its basis involves the unity of sound (which is in the world) and *phŏnē* (in the phenomenological sense). An objective "worldly" science surely can teach us nothing about the essence of the voice. But the unity of sound and voice, which allows the voice to be produced in the world as pure auto-affection, is the sole case to escape the distinction between what is worldly and what is transcendental; by the same token, it makes that distinction possible.

It is this universality which dictates that, *de jure* and by virtue of its structure, no consciousness is possible without the voice. The voice is the being which is present to itself in the form of universality, as con-sciousness; the voice *is* con-sciousness. In colloquy, the propagation of signs does not *seem* to meet any obstacles because it brings together two *phenomenological* origins of pure auto-affection. To speak to someone is doubtless to hear oneself speak, to be heard by oneself; but, at the same time, if one is heard by another, to speak is to make him *repeat immediately* in himself the hearing-oneself-speak in the very form in which I effectuated it. This immediate repetition is a reproduction of pure auto-affection without the help of anything external. This possibility of reproduction, whose structure is absolutely unique, *gives itself out* as the phenomenon of a mastery or limitless power over the signifier, since the signifier itself has the form of what is not external. Ideally, in the teleological essence of speech, it would then be possible for the signifier to be in absolute proximity to the signified aimed at in intuition and governing the meaning. The signifier would become perfectly diaphanous due to the absolute proximity to the signified. This proximity is broken when, instead of hearing myself speak, I see myself write or gesture.

This absolute proximity of the signifier to the signified, and its effacement in immediate presence, is the condition for Husserl's being able to consider the medium of expression as "unproductive" and "reflective." Paradoxically, it is also on this condition that he will be able to reduce it without loss and assert that there exists a pre-expressive stratum of sense. It is again on this condition that Husserl will accord himself the right to reduce the totality of language, be it indicative or expressive, in order to recover sense in its primordiality.

How can we understand this reduction of language when Husserl, from the *Logical Investigations* to *The Origin of Geometry*, continually thought that scientific truth, i.e., absolutely ideal objects, can be found only in "statements" and that not only spoken language but *inscription* as well was indispensable for the constitution of ideal objects, that is, objects capable of being transmitted and repeated as the same?

First, we should recognize that the more evident aspect of the movement which, for a long time under way, terminates in *The Origin of Geometry* confirms the underlying limitation of language to a secondary stratum of experience and, in the consideration of this secondary stratum, confirms the traditional phonologism of metaphysics. If writing brings the constitution of ideal objects to completion, it does so through phonetic writing: [6] it proceeds to fix, inscribe, record, and incarnate an already prepared utterance. To reactivate writing is always to reawaken an expression in an indication, a word in the body of a letter, which, as a symbol that may always remain empty, bears the threat of crisis in itself. Already speech was playing the same role by first constituting the identity of sense in thought. For example, the "protogeometer" must produce the pure ideality of the pure geometrical object in thought by a passage to the limit, assuring its transmissibility by speech, and must finally commit it to writing. By means of this written inscription, one can always repeat the original sense, that is, the act of *pure thought* which created the ideality of sense. With the possibility of progress that such an incarnation allows, there goes the ever growing risk of "forgetting" and loss of sense. It becomes more and more difficult to reconstitute the presence of the act buried under historical sedimentations. The moment of crisis is always the moment of signs.

Moreover, despite the minute detail, the rigor, and the absolute novelty of his analyses, Husserl always describes all these movements in a metaphysical conceptual system. What governs here is the absolute difference between body and soul. Writing is a body that expresses something only if we actually pronounce the verbal expression that animates it, if its space is temporalized. The word is a body that means something only if an actual intention animates it and makes it pass from the state of inert sonority (*Körper*) to that of an animated body (*Leib*). This body proper to words expresses something only if it is animated (*sinnbelebt*) by an act of meaning (*bedeuten*) which transforms it into a spiritual flesh (*geistige Leiblichkeit*). But only the *Geistigkeit* or *Lebendigkeit* is independent and primordial.[7] As such, it needs no signifier to be present to itself. Indeed, it is as much in spite of its signifiers as thanks to them that it is awakened or maintained in life. Such is the traditional side of Husserl's language.

But if Husserl had to recognize the necessity of these "in-

6. It is strange that, despite the formalist motif and fidelity to Leibniz affirmed continually in his work, Husserl never placed the problem of writing in the center of his reflection and, in *The Origin of Geometry*, did not take into account the difference between phonetic and nonphonetic writing.

7. Cf. the Introduction to *The Origin of Geometry*, French ed., translated by Jacques Derrida (Paris, 1962), pp. 83–100.

carnations," even as beneficial threats, it is because an underlying motif was disturbing and contesting the security of these traditional distinctions from within and because the possibility of writing dwelt within speech, which was itself at work in the inwardness of thought.

And here again we find all the incidences of primordial nonpresence whose emergence we have already noted on several occasions. Even while repressing difference by assigning it to the exteriority of the signifiers, Husserl could not fail to recognize its work at the origin of sense and presence. Taking auto-affection as the exercise of the voice, auto-affection supposed that a pure difference comes to divide self-presence. In this pure difference is rooted the possibility of everything we think we can exclude from auto-affection: space, the outside, the world, the body, etc. As soon as it is admitted that auto-affection is the condition for self-presence, no pure transcendental reduction is possible. But it was necessary to pass through the transcendental reduction in order to grasp this difference in what is closest to it—which cannot mean grasping it in its identity, its purity, or its origin, for it has none. We come closest to it in the movement of differance.[8]

This movement of differance is not something that happens to a transcendental subject; it produces a subject. Auto-affection is not a modality of experience that characterizes a being that would already be itself (*autos*). It produces sameness as self-relation within self-difference; it produces sameness as the nonidentical.

8. [Derrida introduces a neologism here; from the French "*différence*" he derives the term "*différance*." As in the Latin "*differre*," the French "*différer*" bears two quite distinct significations. One has a reference to spatiality, as the English "to differ"—to be at variance, to be unlike, apart, dissimilar, distinct in nature or quality from something. This is even more evident in its cognate form, "to differentiate." The other signification has a reference to temporality, as in the English "to defer"—to put off action to a future time, to delay or postpone.

I have thus chosen to follow Derrida's employment of *différance* by rendering it as "differance" in English. This should not be too disconcerting a translation, for it incorporates the common origin of the two relevant English verbs, "to defer" and "to differ," namely, the Latin *differre*. While Derrida briefly explains this term in the first paragraph of Chapter 7, he devotes an article of considerable length and importance to it later on. This has been included in the present volume as an additional essay; see below, pp. 129–60.—Translator.]

Shall we say that the auto-affection we have been talking about up until now concerns only the operation of the voice? Shall we say that difference concerns only the order of the phonic "signifier" or the "secondary strata" of expression? Can we always hold out for the possibility of a pure and purely self-present identity at the level Husserl wanted to disengage as a level of pre-expressive experience, that is, the level of sense prior to *Bedeutung* and expression?

It would be easy to show that such a possibility is excluded at the very root of transcendental experience.

Why, in fact, is the concept of auto-affection incumbent on us? What constitutes the originality of speech, what distinguishes it from every other element of signification, is that its substance seems to be purely temporal. And this temporality does not unfold a sense that would itself be nontemporal; even before being expressed, sense is through and through temporal. According to Husserl, the omnitemporality of ideal objects is but a mode of temporality. And when Husserl describes a sense that seems to escape temporality, he hastens to make it clear that this is only a provisional step in analysis and that he is considering a constituted temporality. However, as soon as one takes the movement of temporalization into account, as it is already analyzed in *The Phenomenology of Internal Time-Consciousness*, the concept of pure auto-affection must be employed as well. This we know is what Heidegger does in *Kant and the Problem of Metaphysics*, precisely when he is concerned with the subject of time. The "source point" or "primordial impression," that out of which the movement of temporalization is produced, is already pure auto-affection. First it is a pure production, since temporality is never the real predicate of a being. The intuition of time itself cannot be empirical; it is a receiving that receives nothing. The absolute novelty of each now is therefore engendered by nothing; it consists in a primordial impression that engenders itself:

> The primal impression is the absolute beginning of this generation —the primal source, that from which all others are continuously generated. In itself, however, it is not generated; it does not come into existence as that which is generated but through *spontaneous generation*. It does not grow up (it has no seed): it is primal creation (*The Phenomenology of Internal Time-Consciousness*, Appendix I; ET, p. 131; italics added).

This pure spontaneity is an impression; it creates nothing. The new now is not a being, it is not a produced object; and every language fails to describe this pure movement other than by metaphor, that is, by borrowing its concepts from the order of the objects of experience, an order this temporalization makes possible. Husserl continually warns us against these metaphors.[9]

9. See, e.g., the admirable § 36 of *The Phenomenology of Internal Time-Consciousness* which proves the absence of a proper noun for this strange "movement," which, furthermore, is not a movement. "For all this," concludes Husserl, "names fail us." We would still have to radicalize Husserl's intention here in a specific direction. For it is not by chance that he still designates this unnamable as an "absolute subjectivity," that is, as a being conceived on the basis of presence as substance, *ousia, hypokeimenon:* a self-identical being in self-presence which forms the substance of a subject. What is said to be unnamable in this paragraph is not exactly something we know to be a *present* being in the form of self-presence, a substance modified into a subject, into an absolute subject whose self-presence is pure and does not depend on any external affection, any outside. *All this is present, and we can name it, the proof being that its being as absolute subjectivity is not questioned.* What is unnamable, according to Husserl, are only the "absolute properties" of this subject; the subject therefore is indeed designated in terms of the classical metaphysical schema which distinguishes substance (present being) from its attributes. Another schema that keeps the incomparable depth of the analysis within the closure of the metaphysics of presence is the subject-object opposition. This being whose "absolute properties" are indescribable is present as *absolute* subjectivity, is an *absolutely* present and *absolutely* self-present being, only in its opposition to the object. The object is relative; what is absolute is the subject: "We can only say that *this flux is something which we name in conformity with what is constituted,* but it is nothing temporally 'Objective.' It is absolute subjectivity and has the absolute properties of something to be denoted metaphorically as 'flux,' as a point of actuality, primal source-point, that from which springs the 'now,' and so on. In the lived experience of actuality, we have the primal source-point and a continuity of moments of reverberation (*Nachhallmomenten*). For all this, names are lacking" (*ITC*, § 36; ET, p. 100; italics added). This determination of "absolute subjectivity" would also have to be crossed out as soon as we conceive the present on the basis of difference, and not the reverse. The concept of *subjectivity* belongs a *priori and in general* to the order of the *constituted*. This holds a *fortiori* for the analogical appresentation that constitutes intersubjectivity. Intersubjectivity is inseparable from temporalization taken as the openness of the present upon an outside of itself, upon *another* absolute present. This being outside itself proper to time is its *spacing:* it is a proto-stage [*archi-scène*]. This stage, as the relation of one present to another present *as such,* that is, as a nonderived re-presentation (*Verge-*

The process by which the living now, produced by spontaneous generation, must, in order to be a now and to be retained in another now, affect itself without recourse to anything empirical but with a new primordial actuality in which it would become a non-now, a past now—this process is indeed a pure auto-affection in which the same is the same only in being affected by the other, only by becoming the other of the same. This auto-affection must be pure since the primordial impression is here affected by nothing other than itself, by the absolute "novelty" of another primordial impression which is another now. We speak metaphorically as soon as we introduce a determinate being into the description of this "movement"; we talk about "movement" in the very terms that movement makes possible. But we have been always already adrift in ontic metaphor; temporalization here is the root of a metaphor that can only be primordial. The word "time" itself, as it has always been understood in the history of metaphysics, is a metaphor which *at the same time* both indicates and dissimulates the "movement" of this auto-affection. All the concepts of metaphysics—in particular those of activity and passivity, will and nonwill, and therefore those of affection or auto-affection, purity and impurity, etc.—*cover up* the strange "movement" of this difference.

But this pure difference, which constitutes the self-presence of the living present, introduces into self-presence from the beginning all the impurity putatively excluded from it. The living present springs forth out of its nonidentity with itself and from the possibility of a retentional trace. It is always already a trace. This trace cannot be thought out on the basis of a simple present whose life would be within itself; the self of the living present is primordially a trace. The trace is not an attribute; we cannot say that the self of the living present "primordially is" it. Being-primordial must be thought on the basis of the trace, and not the reverse. This protowriting is at work at the origin of sense. Sense, being temporal in nature, as Husserl recognized, is never simply present; it is always already engaged in the "movement" of the trace, that is, in the order of "signification." It has always already issued forth from

---

genwärtigung or *Repräsentation*), produces the structure of signs in general as "reference," as being-for-something (*für etwas sein*), and radically precludes their reduction. There is no constituting subjectivity. The very concept of constitution itself must be deconstructed.

itself into the "expressive stratum" of lived experience. Since the trace is the intimate relation of the living present with its outside, the openness upon exteriority in general, upon the sphere of what is not "one's own," etc., *the temporalization of sense is, from the outset, a "spacing."* As soon as we admit spacing both as "interval" or difference and as openness upon the outside, there can no longer be any absolute inside, for the "outside" has insinuated itself into the movement by which the inside of the nonspatial, which is called "time," appears, is constituted, is "presented." Space is "in" time; it is time's pure leaving-itself; it is the "outside-itself" as the self-relation of time. The externality of space, externality as space, does not overtake time; rather, it opens as pure "outside" "within" the movement of temporalization. If we recall now that the pure inwardness of phonic auto-affection supposed the purely temporal nature of the "expressive" process, we see that the theme of a pure inwardness of speech, or of the "hearing oneself speak," is radically contradicted by "time" itself. The going-forth "into the world" is also primordially implied in the movement of temporalization. "Time" cannot be an "absolute subjectivity" precisely because it cannot be conceived on the basis of a present and the self-presence of a present being. Like everything thought under this heading, and like all that is excluded by the most rigorous transcendental reduction, the "world" is primordially implied in the movement of temporalization. As a relation between an inside and an outside in general, an existent and a nonexistent in general, a constituting and a constituted in general, temporalization is at once the very power and limit of phenomenological reduction. Hearing oneself speak is not the inwardness of an inside that is closed in upon itself; it is the irreducible openness in the inside; it is the eye and the world within speech. *Phenomenological reduction is a scene, a theater stage.*

Also, just as expression is not added like a "stratum" [10] to

10. Moreover, in the important § § 124–27 of *Ideas I*, which we shall elsewhere follow step by step, Husserl invites us—while continually speaking of an underlying stratum of pre-expressive experience —not to "hold too hard by the metaphor of stratification (*Schichtung*); expression is not of the nature of an overlaid varnish or covering garment; it is a mental formation, which exercises new intentional influences on the intentional substratum (*Unterschicht*)" (*Ideas I*, § 124; ET, p. 349).

the presence of a pre-expressive sense, so, in the same way, the inside of expression does not accidentally happen to be affected by the outside of indication. Their intertwining (*Verflechtung*) is primordial; it is not a contingent association that could be undone by methodic attention and patient reduction. The analysis, necessary as it is, encounters an absolute limit at this point. If indication is not added to expression, which is not added to sense, we can nonetheless speak in regard to them, of a primordial "supplement": their *addition* comes to *make up for* a deficiency, it comes to compensate for a primordial nonself-presence. And if indication—for example, writing in the everyday sense—must necessarily be "added" to speech to complete the constitution of the ideal object, if speech must be "added" to the thought identity of the object, it is because the "presence" of sense and speech had already from the start fallen short of itself.

7 / The Supplement of Origin

THUS UNDERSTOOD, what is supplementary is in reality *differance*, the operation of differing which at one and the same time both fissures and retards presence, submitting it simultaneously to primordial division and delay. *Differance* is to be conceived prior to the separation between deferring as delay and differing as the active work of difference. Of course this is inconceivable if one begins on the basis of consciousness, that is, presence, or on the basis of its simple contrary, absence or nonconsciousness. It is also inconceivable as the mere *homogeneous* complication of a diagram or line of time, as a complex "succession." The supplementary difference vicariously stands in for presence due to its primordial self-deficiency. Going *through* the First Investigation, we must try to ascertain how far these concepts respect the relations between signs in general (indicative as well as expressive) and presence in general. When we say *through* Husserl's text, we mean a reading that can be neither simple commentary nor simple interpretation.

Let us note first that this concept of primordial supplementation not only implies nonplenitude of presence (or, in Husserl's language, the nonfulfillment of an intuition); it designates this function of substitutive supplementation [*suppléance*] in general, the "in the place of" (*für etwas*) structure which belongs to every sign in general. We were surprised, above, that Husserl did not submit the possibility of this structure to any critical questioning, that he assumed it as a matter of course when he distinguished between indicative and expressive signs. What we would ultimately like to draw attention to is that the for-itself of self-presence (*für-sich*)—traditionally determined in its dative dimension as phenomenological self-giving, whether reflexive or prereflexive—arises in the role of supplement as primordial substitution, in the form "in the place of" (*für etwas*), that is, as we have seen, in the very operation of significance in general. The *for-itself* would be an *in-the-place-of-itself*: put *for itself,* instead of itself. The strange structure of the supplement appears here: by delayed reaction, a possibility produces that to which it is said to be added on.

This structure of supplementation is quite complex. As a supplement, the signifier does not represent first and simply the absent signified. Rather, it is substituted for another signifier, for another type of signifier that maintains another relation with the deficient presence, one more highly valued by virtue of the play of difference. It is more highly valued because the play of difference is the movement of idealization and because, the more ideal the signifier is, the more it augments the power to repeat presence, the more it keeps, reserves, and capitalizes on its sense. Thus an indication is not merely a substitute that makes up for [*supplée*] the absence or invisibility of the indicated term. The latter, it will be remembered, is always an *existent.* An indicative sign also replaces another kind of signifier, an expressive sign, a signifier whose signified (*Bedeutung*) is ideal. In real communicative speech, expression gives way to indication because, we saw, the sense aimed at by the other and, more generally, his experience are not presented to me in person and never can be. This is why Husserl says that, in such cases, expression functions "like indication."

It now remains to be seen—and this is most important—in what respect expression itself implies, in its very structure, a nonplenitude. It is known as being more full than indication, since the appresentational detour is no longer necessary here, and since it can function as such in the alleged self-presence of solitary speech.

It is important to see how from a distance—an articulated distance—an intuitionistic theory of knowledge determines the Husserl's conception of language. The whole originality of this conception lies in the fact that its ultimate subjection to intuitionism does not oppress what might be called the freedom of language, the candor of speech, even if it is false and contradictory. One can speak without knowing. And against the whole philosophical tradition Husserl shows that in that case speech is still genuinely speech, provided it obeys certain rules which do not immediately figure as rules for knowledge. Pure logical grammar, pure formal semantic theory, must tell us *a priori* on what conditions speech can be speech, even where it makes no knowledge possible.

We must here consider the last exclusion—or reduction—to which Husserl invites us, so as to isolate the specific purity of expression. It is the most audacious one; it consists in putting out of play, as "nonessential components" of expression, the acts of intuitive cognition which "fulfill" meaning.

We know that the act of meaning, the act that confers *Bedeutung* (*Bedeutungsintention*), is always the aim of a relation with an object. But it is enough that this intention animates the body of a signifier for speech to take place. The fulfillment of the aim by an intuition is not indispensable. It belongs to the original structure of expression to be able to dispense with the full presence of the object aimed at by intuition. Once again evoking the confusion that arises from the intertwining (*Verflechtung*) of relations, Husserl writes in the First Investigation, § 9:

> If we seek a foothold in pure description, the concrete phenomenon of the sense-informed (*sinnebelebten*) expression breaks up, on the one hand, into the *physical phenomenon* forming the physical side of the expression, and, on the other hand, into the *acts* which give it *meaning* and possibly also *intuitive fulness*, in which its relation to an expressed object is constituted. In virtue of such acts, the expression is more than a merely sounded word. It *means* something, and in so far as it means something, it relates to what is objective (ET, p. 280).[1]

Fullness therefore is only contingent. The absence of the object aimed at does not compromise the meaning, does not reduce the expression to its unanimated, and in itself meaningless, physical side.

> This objective somewhat [i.e., what was meant or intended] can either be actually present (*aktuell gegenwärtig*), through accompanying intuitions, or may at least appear in representation (*vergegenwärtigt*) e.g., in a mental image, and where this happens

1. [Unless otherwise indicated, all quotations from Husserl in this chapter are from the First Investigation.—Translator.]

the relation to an object is realized. Alternatively this need not occur: the expression functions significantly (*fungiert sinnvoll*), it remains more than mere sound of words, but it lacks any basic intuition that will give it its object (ET, p. 280).

The "fulfilling" intuition therefore is not essential to expression, to what is aimed at by the meaning. The latter part of this chapter is wholly devoted to accumulating proofs of this difference between intention and intuition. Because they were blind in this respect, all the classical theories of language were unable to avoid aporias or absurdities,[2] which Husserl locates along the way. In the course of subtle and decisive analyses, which we cannot follow up here, he demonstrates the ideality of *Bedeutung* and the noncoincidence between the *expression*, the *Bedeutung* (both as ideal unities), and the *object*. Two identical expressions may have the same *Bedeutung*, may mean the same thing, and yet have different objects (for example, the two propositions, "Bucephalus is a *horse*" and "This steed is a *horse*"). Two different expressions may have different *Bedeutungen* but refer to the same object (for example, the two expressions, "The victor at Jena" and "The vanquished at Waterloo"). Finally, two different expressions may have the same *Bedeutung* and the same object (London, *Londres; zwei, two, duo,* etc.).

Without such distinctions, no pure logical grammar would be possible. The possibility of a theory of the pure forms of judgments, which supports the entire structure of the *Formal and Transcendental Logic,* would be blocked. We know that pure logical grammar depends entirely on the distinction between *Widersinnigkeit* and *Sinnlosigkeit*. If it obeys certain rules, an expression may be *widersinnig* (contradictory, false, absurd according to a certain kind of absurdity) without ceasing to have an intelligible sense that permits normal speech to occur, without becoming nonsense (*Unsinn*). It may have no possible object for empirical reasons (a golden mountain) or for *a priori* reasons (a square circle) without ceasing to have an intelligible sense, without being *sinnlos*. The absence of an object (*Gegenstandslosigkeit*) is hence not the absence of

2. That is, according to Husserl. No doubt this is more true of the modern theories he refutes than, for example, certain mediaeval attempts which he hardly ever refers to. One exception to this is a brief allusion to Thomas of Erfurt's *Grammatica speculativa* in the *Formal and Transcendental Logic*.

meaning (*Bedeutungslosigkeit*). Pure logical grammar, then, excludes from normal discourse only what is nonsense in the sense of *Unsinn* ("Abracadabra," "Green is where"). If we were not able to understand what a "square circle" or "golden mountain" means, how could we come to a conclusion about the absence of a possible object for such expressions? It is this modicum of comprehension that is denied us in the *Unsinn*, in the ungrammaticalness of nonsense.

Following the logic and necessity of these distinctions, we might be tempted to maintain not only that meaning does not imply the intuition of the object but that it essentially excludes it. What is structurally original about meaning would be the *Gegenstandslosigkeit*, the absence of any object given to intuition. In the full presence that comes to fill the meaning's aim, intuition and intention are melted together, "forming an intimately blended unity (*eine innig verschmolzene Einheit*) of an original character." [3] This is to say that the language that speaks in the presence of its object effaces its own originality or lets it melt away; the structure peculiar to language alone, which allows it to function entirely *by itself* when its intention is cut off from intuition, here dissolves. Here, instead of suspecting that Husserl began his analysis and dissociation too soon, we could ask if he does not unify them too much and too soon. Are not two possibilities excluded from the start, namely, that the unity of intuition and intention can ever be homogeneous at all and that meaning can be fused into intuition without disappearing? And are they not excluded for reasons that are essential and structural, reasons that Husserl himself has adduced? To take up Husserl's language, are we not in principle excluded from ever "cashing in the draft made on intuition" *in expression*?

Let us consider the extreme case of a "statement about perception." Let us suppose that it is produced at the very moment of the perceptual intuition: I say, "I see a particular person by the window" while I really do see him. It is structurally implied in my performance that the content of this

3. "In the realized relation of the expression to its objective correlate, the sense-informed expression becomes one (*eint sich*) with the act of meaning-fulfilment. The sounded word is first made one with (*ist einst mit*) the meaning-intention, and this in its turn is made one (as intentions in general are made one with their fulfilments) with its corresponding meaning-fulfilment" (§ 9; ET, p. 281).

expression is ideal and that its unity is not impaired by the absence of perception here and now.[4] Whoever hears this proposition, whether he is next to me or infinitely removed in space and time, should, by right, understand what I mean to say. Since this possibility is constitutive of the possibility of speech, it should structure the very act of him who speaks while perceiving. My nonperception, my nonintuition, my *hic et nunc* absence are expressed by that very thing that I say, by *that* which I say and *because* I say it. This structure will never form an "intimately blended unity" with intuition. The absence of intuition—and therefore of the subject of the intuition—is not only *tolerated* by speech; it is *required* by the general structure of signification, when considered *in itself*. It is radically requisite: the total absence of the subject and object of a statement —the death of the writer and/or the disappearance of the objects he was able to describe—does not prevent a text from "meaning" something. On the contrary, this possibility gives birth to meaning as such, gives it out to be heard and read.

Let us go further. How is writing—the common name for signs which function despite the total absence of the subject because of (beyond) his death—involved in the very act of signification in general and, in particular, in what is called "living" speech? How does writing inaugurate and complete idealization when it itself is neither real nor ideal? And why, finally, are death, idealization, repetition, and signification intelligible, as pure possibilities, only on the basis of one and the same openness? This time let us take the example of the personal pronoun *I*. Husserl classes it among "essentially occasional" expressions. It shares this character with a whole "conceptually unified group of possible meanings (*Bedeutungen*), in whose case it is essential [each time] to orient actual meaning (*Bedeutung*) to the occasion, the speaker and the situation" (§ 26; ET, p. 315). This group is to be distinguished both from the group of expressions whose multiplicity of meanings is contingent and reducible by a convention (the word "rule," for example, means both a wooden instrument and a prescription) and from the group of "objective" expressions where the circumstances of the utterance, the context, and the situation of

4. "We distinguish, in a perceptual statement, as in every statement, between *content* and *object;* by the 'content' we understand the self-identical meaning that the hearer can grasp even if he is not a percipient" (§ 14; ET, p. 290).

the speaking subject do not affect their univocal meaning (for example, "all expressions in theory, expressions out of which the principles and theorems, the proofs and theories of the 'abstract' sciences are made up" [ET, p. 315]. Mathematical expression would be the model for such expressions.) Objective expressions alone are absolutely pure expressions, free from all indicative contamination. An essentially occasional expression is recognizable in that it cannot in principle be replaced in speech by a permanent objective conceptual representation without distorting the meaning (*Bedeutung*) of the statement. If, for example, I tried to substitute, for the word *I* as it appears in a statement, what I take to be its objective conceptual content ("whatever speaker is designating himself"), I would end up in absurdities. Instead of "I am pleased," I would have "Whatever speaker is now designating himself is pleased." Whenever such a substitution distorts the statement, we have to do with an essentially subjective and occasional expression which functions indicatively. Indication thus enters into speech whenever a reference to the subject's situation is not reducible, wherever this subject's situation is designated by a personal pronoun, a demonstrative pronoun, or a "subjective" adverb such as *here, there, above, below, now, yesterday, tomorrow, before, after,* etc. This massive return of indication into expression forces Husserl to conclude:

> An essentially indicating character naturally spreads to all expressions which include these and similar presentations as parts: this includes all the manifold speech-forms where the speaker gives normal expression to something concerning himself, or which is thought of in relation to himself. All expressions for percepts, beliefs, doubts, wishes, fears, commands belong here (§ 26; ET, p. 318).

We quickly see that the root of all these expressions is to be found in the zero-point of the subjective origin, the *I*, the *here*, the *now*. The meaning (*Bedeutung*) of these expressions is carried off into indication whenever it animates real intended speech for someone else. But Husserl seems to think that this *Bedeutung*, as a relationship with the object (*I, here, now*), is "realized" *for the one who is speaking.*[5] "In solitary

5. "In solitary speech the meaning (*Bedeutung*) of 'I' is essentially realized in the immediate idea of one's own personality, which is also the meaning (*Bedeutung*) of the word in communicated speech. Each

speech the meaning of 'I' is essentially realized in the immediate idea of one's own personality" (ET, p. 316).

Is this certain? Even supposing that such an immediate representation is possible and actually given, does not the appearance of the word *I* in solitary speech (a supplement whose *raison d'être* is not clear if immediate representation is possible) already function as an ideality? Doesn't it give itself out as capable of remaining *the same* for an I-here-now in general, keeping its sense even if my empirical presence is eliminated or radically modified? When I say *I*, even in solitary speech, can I give my statement meaning without implying, there as always, the possible absence of the object of speech—in this case, myself? When I tell myself "I am," this expression, like any other according to Husserl, has the status of speech only if it is intelligible in the absence of its object, in the absence of intuitive presence—here, in the absence of myself. Moreover, it is in this way that the *ergo sum* is introduced into the philosophical tradition and that a discourse about the transcendental ego is possible. Whether or not I have a present intuition of myself, "I" expresses something; whether or not I am alive, *I am* "means something." Here also the fulfilling intuition is not an "essential component" of expression. Whether or not the *I* functions in solitary speech, with or without the self-presence of the speaking subject, it is *sinnvoll*. And there is no need to know who is speaking in order to understand or even utter it. Once again the border seems less certain between solitary speech and communication, between the reality and the representation of speech. Does not Husserl contradict the difference he established between *Gegenstandslosigkeit* and *Bedeutungslosigkeit* when he writes, "The word 'I' names a different person from case to case, and does so by way of an ever altering meaning (*Bedeutung*)"? Does not speech and the ideal nature of every *Bedeutung* exclude the possibility that a *Bedeutung* is "ever altering"? Does not Husserl contradict what he has

---

man has his own I-presentation (and with it his individual notion of I) and this is why the word's meaning (*Bedeutung*) differs from person to person." One can't help being astonished at this *individual concept* and this *"Bedeutung"* which differs with each individual. And it is Husserl's premises themselves that give rise to this astonishment. Husserl continues, "But since each person, in speaking of himself, says 'I,' the word has the character of a universally operative indication of this fact" (§ 27; ET, p. 316).

asserted about the independence of the intention and fulfilling intuition when he writes,

> What its meaning [*Bedeutung*—that of the word "I"] is at the moment can be gleaned only from the living utterance and from the intuitive circumstances which surround it. If we read this word without knowing who wrote it, it is perhaps not meaningless (*bedeutungslos*) but is at least estranged from its normal meaning (*Bedeutung*) (ET, p. 315).

Husserl's premises should sanction our saying exactly the contrary. Just as I need not perceive in order to understand a statement about perception, so there is no need to intuit the object *I* in order to understand the word *I*. The possibility of this nonintuition constitutes the *Bedeutung* as such, the *normal Bedeutung* as such. When the word *I* appears, the ideality of its *Bedeutung*, inasmuch as it is distinct from its "object," puts us in what Husserl describes as an abnormal situation— just as if *I* were written by someone unknown. This alone enables us to account for the fact that we understand the word *I* not only when its "author" is unknown but when he is quite fictitious. And when he is dead. The ideality of the *Bedeutung* here has by virtue of its structure the value of a testament. And just as the import of a statement about perception did not depend on there being actual or even possible perception, so also the signifying function of the *I* does not depend on the life of the speaking subject. Whether or not perception accompanies the statement about perception, whether or not life as self-presence accompanies the uttering of the *I*, is quite indifferent with regard to the functioning of meaning. My death is structurally necessary to the pronouncing of the *I*. That I am also "alive" and certain about it figures as something that comes over and above the appearance of the meaning. And this structure is operative, it retains its original efficiency, even when I say "I am alive" at the very moment when, if such a thing is possible, I have a full and actual intuition of it. The *Bedeutung* "I am" or "I am alive" or "my living present is" is what it is, has the ideal identity proper to all *Bedeutung*, only if it is not impaired by falsity, that is, if I can be dead at the moment when it is functioning. No doubt it will be different from the *Bedeutung* "I am dead," but not necessarily from the *fact* that "I am dead." The statement "I am alive" is accompanied by my being dead, and its possibility requires the possibility that I be dead; and conversely. This is not an extraordinary tale by Poe but the ordinary story of language. Earlier we reached the "I am mortal" from the "I am"; here we understand the "I am" out of the "I am dead." The anonymity of the written *I*, the impropriety of the *I am writing*, is, contrary to what Husserl says, the "normal situation." The autonomy of meaning with regard to intuitive cognition, what Husserl established and we earlier called the freedom or "candor" [*franc-parler*] of language, has its norm in writing and in the relationship with death. This writing cannot be added to speech because, from the moment speech awakens, this writing has duplicated it by animating it. Here indication neither degrades nor diverts expression; it dictates it. We draw this conclusion, then, from the idea of a pure logical grammar, from the sharp distinction between the meaning-intention (*Bedeutungsinten-tion*), which can always function "emptily," and its "eventual" fulfillment by the intuition of the object. This conclusion is again reinforced by the supplementary distinction, equally sharp, between fulfillment by "sense" and the fulfillment by the "object." The former does not necessarily demand the latter, and one could draw the same lesson from an attentive reading of § 14 ("Content as Object, Content as Fulfilling Sense, and Content as Sense or Meaning *Simpliciter*").

From the same premises, why does Husserl refuse to draw these conclusions? It is because the theme of full "presence," the intuitionistic imperative, and the project of knowledge continue to command—at a distance, we said—the whole of the description. Husserl describes, and in one and the same movement effaces, the emancipation of speech as nonknowing. The originality of meaning as an aim is limited by the telos of vision. To be radical, the difference that separates intention from intuition would nonetheless have to be *pro-visional*. And yet this provision would constitute the essence of meaning. The *eidos* is determined in depth by the *telos*. The "symbol" always points to [*fait signe vers*] "truth"; it is itself constituted as a lack of "truth."

> If "possibility" or "truth" is lacking, an assertion's intention can only be carried out symbolically: it cannot derive any "fulness" from intuition or from the categorial functions performed on the latter, in which "fulness" its value for knowledge consists. It then lacks, as one says, a "true," a "genuine" meaning (*Bedeutung*) (§ 11; ET, pp. 285–86).

In other words, the genuine and true meaning is the will to say the truth. This subtle shift incorporates the *eidos* into the *telos*, and language into knowledge. A speech could well be in conformity with its essence as speech when it was false; it nonetheless attains its entelechy when it is true. One can well *speak* in saying "The circle is square"; one speaks *well*, however, in saying that it is not. There is already sense in the first proposition, but we would be wrong to conclude from this that sense *does not wait upon* truth. It does not await truth as expecting it; it only precedes truth as its anticipation. *In truth*, the telos which announces the fulfillment, promised for "later," has already and beforehand opened up sense as a relation with the object. This is what is meant by the concept of *normality* each time it occurs in Husserl's description. The norm is knowledge, the intuition that is adequate to its object, the evidence that is not only distinct but also "clear." It is the full presence of sense to a consciousness that is itself self-present in the fullness of its life, its living present.

Thus, without disregarding the rigor and boldness of "pure logical grammar," without forgetting the advantages it has over the classical projects of rational grammar, we must clearly recognize that its "formality" is limited. We could say as much about the pure morphology of *judgments*, which, in the *Formal and Transcendental Logic*, determines pure logical grammar or pure morphology of *significations*. The purification of the formal is guided by a concept of *sense* which is itself determined on the basis of a *relation with an object*. Form is always the form of a sense, and sense opens up only in the knowing intentionality relating to an object. Form is but the emptiness and pure intention of this intentionality. Perhaps no project of pure grammar can escape this object-related intentionality, perhaps the telos of knowing rationality is the irreducible origin of the idea of pure grammar, and perhaps the semantic theme, "empty" as it is, always limits the formalist project. In any case transcendental intuitionism still weighs very heavily upon the formalist theme in Husserl. Apparently independent from fulfilling intuitions, the "pure" forms of signification, as "empty" or canceled sense, are always governed by the epistemological criterion of the relation with objects. The difference between "The circle is square" and "Green is where" or "Abracadabra" (and Husserl links up these last two examples somewhat hastily; he is perhaps not attentive enough to their difference) is that the form of the relation with an object and of a unitary intuition appears only in the first example. Here this aim will always be disappointed, yet this proposition makes *sense* only because *another content,* put in this form (*S* is *p*), *would be able* to let us know and see an object. "The circle is square," an expression that has sense (*sinnvoll*), has no possible object, but it makes sense only insofar as its grammatical form tolerates the possibility of a relation with the object. The efficiency and the form of signs that do not obey these rules, that is, that do not promise any knowledge, can be determined as nonsense (*Unsinn*) only if one has antecedently, and according to the most traditional philosophical move, defined sense in general on the basis of truth as objectivity. Otherwise we would have to relegate to absolute nonsense all poetic language that transgresses the laws of this grammar of cognition and is irreducible to it. In the forms of nondiscursive signification (music, nonliterary arts generally), as well as in utterances such as "Abracadabra" or "Green is where," there are modes of sense which do not point to any possible objects. Husserl would not deny the signifying force of such formations: he would simply refuse them the formal quality of being expressions endowed with *sense,* that is, of being logical, in the sense that they have a relation with an *object.* All of which amounts to recognizing an initial limitation of sense to knowledge, of logos to objectivity, of language to reason.

WE HAVE EXPERIENCED the systematic interdependence of the concepts of sense, ideality, objectivity, truth, intuition, perception, and expression. Their common matrix is being as *presence:* the absolute proximity of self-identity, the being-in-front of the object available for repetition, the maintenance of the temporal present, whose ideal form is the self-presence of transcendental *life,* whose ideal identity allows *idealiter* of infinite repetition. The living present, a concept that cannot be broken down into a subject and an attribute, is thus the conceptual foundation of phenomenology as metaphysics.

While everything that is *purely* thought in this concept is thereby determined as *ideality,* the living present is nevertheless *in fact,* really, effectively, etc., deferred *ad infinitum.* This *differance* is the difference between the ideal and the nonideal. Indeed, this is a proposition which could already have been verified at the start of the *Logical Investigations,* from the point of view we are advancing. Thus, after having proposed an essential distinction between objective expressions and essentially subjective expressions, Husserl shows that absolute ideality can only be on the side of objective expressions. There is nothing surprising in that. But he immediately adds that, even in essentially subjective expressions, the fluctuation is not in the objective content of the expression (the *Bedeutung*) but only in the act of meaning (*bedeuten*). This allows him to conclude, apparently against his former demonstration, that, in a subjective expression, the *content* may always be replaced by an objective and therefore ideal content: only the act then is lost for ideality. But this substitution (which, let us note in passing, would again confirm what we said about the play of life and death in the *I*) is ideal. As the ideal is always thought by Husserl in the form of an Idea in the Kantian sense, this substitution of ideality for nonidentity, of objectivity for nonobjectivity, is infinitely *deferred*. Assigning a subjective origin to fluctuation, and contesting the theory which claims it would belong to the objective content of *Bedeutung* and so impair its ideality, Husserl writes:

> We shall have to look on such a notion as invalid. The content meant by the subjective expression, with sense oriented to the occasion, is an ideal unit of meaning (*Bedeutung*) in precisely the same sense as the content of a fixed expression. This is shown by the fact that, *ideally* speaking, each subjective expression is replaceable by an objective expression which will preserve the identity of each momentary meaning (*Bedeutung*) intention.
>
> *We shall have to concede that such replacement is not only impracticable, for reasons of complexity, but that it cannot in the vast majority of cases, be carried out at all, will, in fact, never be so capable.*
>
> Clearly, in fact, to say that each subjective expression could be replaced by an objective expression, is no more than to assert the *unbounded range* (*Schrankenlosigkeit*) *of objective reason*. Everything that is, can be known "in itself." Its being is a being definite in content, and documented in such and such "truths in themselves." . . . But what is objectively quite definite, must permit *objective* determination, and what permits objective determination, must, ideally speaking, permit expression through wholly determinate word-meanings (*Bedeutungen*). . . .
>
> *We are infinitely removed from this ideal.* . . . *Strike out the essentially occasional expressions from one's language, try to de-*

scribe any subjective experience in unambiguous, objectively fixed
fashion: such an attempt is always plainly vain (§ 28; ET, pp. 321–
22; italics added).

These theses concerning the unambiguous objective expression
as an inaccessible ideal will be taken up again in *The Origin of
Geometry* in a literally identical form.

*In its ideal value, then, the whole system of "essential dis-
tinctions" is a purely teleological structure.* By the same token,
the possibility of distinguishing between the sign and the non-
sign, linguistic sign and nonlinguistic sign, expression and indication, ideality and nonideality, subject and object, grammaticalness and nongrammaticalness, pure grammaticalness and
empirical grammaticalness, pure general grammaticalness and
pure logical grammaticalness, intention and intuition, etc., is
deferred *ad infinitum*. Thus these "essential distinctions" are
caught up in the following aporia: *de facto* and *realiter* they
are never respected, and Husserl recognizes this. *De jure* and
idealiter they vanish, since, as distinctions, they live only from
the difference between fact and right, reality and ideality.
Their possibility is their impossibility.

But how can we conceive this difference? What does *"ad
infinitum"* mean here? What does presence mean, taken as *differance ad infinitum*? What does the life of the living present
mean as *differance ad infinitum*?

That Husserl always thought of infinity as an Idea in the
Kantian sense, as the indefiniteness of an *"ad infinitum,"* leads
one to believe that he never *derived* difference from the fullness of a *parousia*, from the full presence of a positive infinite,
that he never believed in the accomplishment of an "absolute
knowledge," as the self-adjacent presence of an infinite concept in Logos. What he shows us of the movement of temporalization leaves no room for doubt on this subject: although he
had not made a theme of "articulation," of the "diacritical"
work of difference in the constitution of sense and signs, he at
bottom recognized its necessity. And yet, the whole phenomenological discourse is, we have sufficiently seen, caught up
within the schema of a metaphysics of presence which relent-
lessly exhausts itself in trying to make difference derivative.
Within this schema Hegelianism seems to be more radical, especially at the point where it makes clear that the positive

infinite must be thought through (which is possible only if it thinks *itself*) in order that the indefiniteness of *differance* appear *as such*. Hegel's critique of Kant would no doubt also hold against Husserl. But this appearing of the Ideal as an infinite *differance* can only be produced within a relationship with death in general. Only a relation to my-death could make the infinite differing of presence appear. By the same token, compared to the ideality of the positive infinite, this relation to my-death becomes an accident of empirical finitude. The appearing of the infinite *differance* is itself finite. Consequently, *differance*, which does not occur outside this relation, becomes the finitude of life as an essential relation with oneself and one's death. *The infinite* differance *is finite*. It can therefore no longer be conceived within the opposition of finiteness and infinity, absence and presence, negation and affirmation.

In this sense, *within* the metaphysics of presence, within philosophy as knowledge of the presence of the object, as the being-before-oneself of knowledge in consciousness, we believe, quite simply and literally, in absolute knowledge as the *closure* if not the end of history. And we believe *that such a closure has taken place*. The history of being as presence, as self-presence in absolute knowledge, as consciousness of self in the infinity of *parousia*—this history is closed. The history of presence is closed, for "history" has never meant anything but the presentation (*Gegenwärtigung*) of Being, the production and recollection of beings in presence, as knowledge and mastery. Since absolute self-presence in con-sciousness is the infinite *vocation* of full presence, the achievement of absolute knowledge is the end of the infinite, which could only be the unity of the concept, logos, and consciousness in a voice without *differance. The history of metaphysics therefore can be expressed as the unfolding of the structure or schema of an absolute will-to-hear-oneself-speak*. This history is closed when this infinite absolute appears to itself as its own death. *A voice without differance, a voice without writing, is at once absolutely alive and absolutely dead.*

As for what "begins" then—"beyond" absolute knowledge —*unheard-of* thoughts are required, sought for across the memory of old signs. As long as we ask if the concept of differing should be conceived on the basis of presence or antecedent to it, it remains one of these old signs, enjoining us to continue indefinitely to question presence within the closure of knowledge. It must indeed be so understood, but also understood differently: it is to be heard in the openness of an un-heard-of question that opens neither upon knowledge nor upon some nonknowledge which is a knowledge to come. In the open-ness of this question *we no longer know*. This does not mean that we know nothing but that we are beyond absolute knowledge (and its ethical, aesthetic, or religious system), approaching that on the basis of which its closure is announced and decided. Such a question will legitimately be understood as *meaning* nothing, as no longer belonging to the system of meaning.

Thus we no longer know whether what was always presented as a derived and modified re-presentation of simple presentation, as "supplement," "sign," "writing," or "trace," "is" not, in a neces-sarily, but newly, ahistorical sense, "older" than presence and the system of truth, older than "history." Or again, whether it is "older" than sense and the senses: older than the primordial dator intuition, older than the present and full perception of the "thing itself," older than seeing, hearing, and touching, even prior to the distinction between their "sensible" literalness and their metaphorical elaboration staged throughout the history of philosophy. We therefore no longer know whether what has always been reduced and abased as an accident, modification, and re-turn, under the old names of "sign" and "re-presentation," has not repressed that which related truth to its own death as it related it to its origin. We no longer know whether the force of the *Vergegenwärtigung,* in which the *Gegenwärtigung* is de-pre-sented so as to be re-presented as such, whether the repetitive force of the living present, which is re-presented in a *supplement,* because it has never been present to itself, or whether what we call with the old names of force and *differance* is not more "ancient" than what is "primordial."

In order to conceive of this age, in order to "speak" about it, we will have to have other names than those of sign or re-presentation. New names indeed will have to be used if we are to conceive as "normal" and preprimordial what Husserl believed he could isolate as a particular and accidental experience, something dependent and secondary—that is, the indefinite drift of signs, as errance and change of scene (*Verwand-lung*), linking re-presentations (*Vergegenwärtigungen*) one to another without beginning or end. There never was any "per-ception"; and "presentation" is a representation of the repre-sentation that yearns for itself therein as for its own birth or its death.

Everything has, no doubt, begun in the following way:

A name on being mentioned reminds us of the Dresden gallery.
. . . We wander through the rooms. . . . A painting by Teniers
. . . represents a gallery of paintings. . . . The paintings of this
gallery would represent in their turn paintings, which on their part
exhibited readable inscriptions and so forth (*Ideas I*, § 100; ET, p.
293, modified).

Certainly nothing has preceded this situation. Asssuredly
nothing will suspend it. It is not *comprehended,* as Husserl
would want it, by intuitions or presentations. Of the broad day-
light of presence, outside the gallery, no perception is given us
or assuredly promised us. The gallery is the labyrinth which
includes in itself its own exits: we have never come upon it as
upon a particular *case* of experience—that which Husserl believes he is describing.

It remains, then, for us to *speak,* to make our voices *resonate* throughout the corridors in order to make up
for [*suppléer*] the breakup of presence. The phoneme, the
akoumenon, is the *phenomenon of the labyrinth.* This is the
case with the *phōnē.* Rising toward the sun of presence, it is
the way of Icarus.

And contrary to what phenomenology—which is always
phenomenology of perception—has tried to make us believe,
contrary to what our desire cannot fail to be tempted into believing, the thing itself always escapes.

Contrary to the assurance that Husserl gives us a little further on, "the look" cannot "abide."

Other Essays

Form and Meaning:
A Note on the
Phenomenology of Language

Τὸ γὰρ ἴχνος τοῦ ἀμόρφου μορφή.

Plotinus

PHENOMENOLOGY HAS CRITICIZED metaphysics as it is in fact only in order to restore it. It has informed metaphysics about its actual state of affairs in order to reawaken it to the essence of its task, to its original and authentic purpose. This is recalled in the latter pages of the *Cartesian Meditations:* against "adventurous" speculation, against "naïve" and "degenerate" metaphysics, we must return to the critical project of "first philosophy." If certain metaphysical systems awaken suspicion, even if the whole of existing metaphysics is "suspended" by phenomenology, this does not exclude "metaphysics in general."

To follow this movement of critical purification in phenomenology, the concept of *form* could be used as a guiding thread. If the word "form" translates several Greek terms in a highly equivocal way, we can be sure nonetheless that all these terms themselves refer back to founding metaphysical concepts. By reinscribing the Greek terms (*eidos, morphē,* etc.) into the language of phenomenology, by playing upon the differences between the Greek, Latin, and German, Husserl clearly wanted to disengage the original concepts from the later and supervenient metaphysical interpretations, which, he declared, charged the word with an invisible sedimentation.[1] But Husserl labors al-

This essay was published originally as "La Forme et le vouloir-dire: Note sur la phénoménologie du langage," in the *Revue internationale de philosophie,* LXXXI (September, 1967), 277–99.

1. Cf. the Introduction to *Ideas: General Introduction to Pure Phenomenology I* (*Ideas I*), trans. W. R. Boyce Gibson (New York: Humanities Press, 1969). [Unless otherwise indicated, all quotations from Husserl in this essay are from *Ideas I.*—Translator.]

ways to restore a *primordial* sense to these terms, a sense which *began* to be perverted at the time of its inscription into the tradition; thus Husserl often goes against the *first* thinkers, against Plato and Aristotle. Whether it is a question of determining the *eidos* against "Platonism," the form (*Form*) (in the problem of formal logic and ontology) or *morphē* (in the problem of transcendental constitution and in its relations with *hylē*) against Aristotle, the force, vigilance, and efficacy of the critique remains intrametaphysical in its motives. How could it be otherwise?

As soon as we use the concept of form—even to criticize *another* concept of form—we must appeal to the evidence of a certain source of sense. And the medium of this evidence can only be the language of metaphysics. For that language we know what "form" means, how the possibility of its variations is ordered, what its limits are, and the field of all conceivable disputes concerning it. The system of oppositions in which something like form can be considered, the formality of form, is a finite system. Furthermore, it is not enough to say that "form" has a *sense* for us, a center of *evidence*, or that its *essence* is given to us as such: indeed, this concept is, and always has been, indissociable from the concepts of appearance, sense, evidence, or essence. Only a form is *evident*, only a form has or is an essence, only a form *presents itself* as such. This is a point of certainty that no interpretation of the Platonic or Aristotelian conceptual system can dislodge.

All the concepts by which *eidos* or *morphē* could be translated and determined refer back to the theme of *presence in general*. Form is presence itself. Formality is what is presented, visible, and conceivable of the thing in general. That metaphysical thought—and consequently phenomenology—is the thought of being as form, that in it thought is conceived as the thought of form and the formality of form, is nothing less than necessary; the fact that Husserl determines the *living present* (*lebendige Gegenwart*) as the ultimate, universal, and absolute "*form*" of transcendental experience in general is a final indication of this.

Although the privilege of *theōria* is not, in phenomenology, as simple as has sometimes been claimed, although the classical theories are profoundly re-examined therein, the metaphysical domination of the concept of form cannot fail to effectuate a certain subjection to the look. This subjection would always be a subjection of *sense* to seeing, of sense to the sense of

sight, since sense in general is in fact the concept of every phe-
nomenological field. The implications of such a *putting-on-view* could be unfolded in many directions and by proceeding from what would appear to be the most diverse places within the text and problems of phenomenology. It could be shown, for example, how this putting-on-view and this concept of form permit a movement between the project of formal ontology, the description of time or of intersubjectivity, the latent theory of the work of art, etc.

But if sense is not speech, their relationship with regard to this *putting-on-view* no doubt deserves some particular atten-
tion. Thus we have here chosen to narrow our perspective and address ourselves particularly to a text that concerns the status of language in *Ideas I*. Among the determination of this status, the privilege of the formal, and the predominance of the the-
oretical there is a certain systematic interchange. And yet the coherence of this system seems to be worked over by something outside that relation to the outside which is the relation to form. It is out of this circularity and uneasiness that we want only to raise some preliminary indications, with the conviction that not only does *Ideas I* not contradict the *Logical Investigations* on this point but, on the contrary, continually makes it explicit and that no text posterior to *Ideas I* has ever expressly re-
considered its analyses.

MEANING IN THE TEXT

FOR MORE than two-thirds of the book, transcendental experience is presented as though it were silent, as though it were inhabited by no language whatever, or rather, as though it were deserted by *expression* as such, for, since the *Investigations*, Husserl had in fact determined the essence or telos of language as *expression (Ausdruck)*. The transcendental de-
scription of the fundamental structures of all experience is fol-
lowed up until the end of the next-to-last section without the problem of language even being touched upon. The cultural world and the world of science are indeed evoked, but even though in fact the predicates of culture and science are inconceivable outside a world of language, Husserl takes himself to be justified, for methodological reasons, in not considering

the "stratum" of expression, in provisionally putting it between brackets.

Husserl can assume he is justified in so doing only by supposing that expression constitutes an original and strictly delimited "stratum" (*Schicht*) of experience. What the *Investigations* had proposed an emphatic demonstration of, and what remains presupposed in *Ideas I*, is that acts of expression are original and irreducible in their nature. Thus at a certain moment of the descriptive itinerary, we can come to consider linguistic expression as a circumscribed problem. And we already know from the moment we approach it that the "stratum of logos" will be included *in the most general structure* of experience, whose poles or correlations were just described: the parallel opposition of the noesis and the noema. Thus it is already assumed that, however original its nature may be, the stratum of logos has to be organized according to the noetic-noematic parallelism.

The problem of "meaning" (*bedeuten*) [2] is broached in *Ideas I* in § 124, entitled "The Noetic-Noematic Stratum of the 'Logos.' Meaning and Meaning Something (*Bedeuten und Bedeutung*)." The metaphor of the *stratum* (*Schicht*) has two implications: on the one hand, meaning is founded on something other than itself, and this dependence will be continually confirmed by Husserl's analysis. On the other hand, it constitutes a layer whose unity can be strictly delimited. But if the metaphor of the stratum is approved throughout the section, in the last few lines it will nonetheless be held suspect. This suspicion is not purely rhetorical; it translates a profound uneasiness over the descriptive fidelity of speech. If the metaphor of the stratum does not answer to the structure to be described, how could it have been used so long?

> For we should not hold too hard by the metaphor of stratification (*Schichtung*); expression is not of the nature of an overlaid varnish (*übergelagerter Lack*) or covering garment; it is a mental formation (*geistige Formung*), which exercises new intentional influences (*Funktionen*) on the intentional substratum (*an der*

2. We have tried to justify this translation in *Speech and Phenomena: Introduction to the Problem of Signs in Husserl's Phenomenology*, which refers particularly to the first of the *Logical Investigations*. The present essay is thus dependent upon it at every moment.

intentionalen Unterschicht) and experiences from the latter cor-relative intentional influences (ET, p. 349).[3]

This distrust of a metaphor manifests itself at the mo-ment when a new complication of the analysis becomes neces-sary. We would like only to note here that, *before* encounter-ing *thematic difficulties,* the effort to isolate the logical "stratum" of expression encounters difficulties in its *enuncia-tion.* The discourse on *the logic* of speech becomes caught up in the play of metaphors; that of the stratum, as we shall see, is far from being the only one.

From the start of the analysis the concern to bring out what it is that assures the properly *logical* function of speech is manifest. We find that the essence or telos of language is determined as *logical* and that, as in the *Investigations,* the theory of speech reduces the considerable mass of what is not purely *logical* in language to *extrinsic value.* One metaphor already betrays the difficulty of this first reduction, a difficulty which, having been only deferred and not resolved at the end of the paragraph, will require new explanations and new dis-tinctions.

> Acts of expression, act-strata in the specific "logical" sense, are interwoven (*verweben sich*) with all the acts hitherto considered, and in their case no less than in the others the parallelism of no-esis and noema must be clearly brought out. The prevalent and unavoidable ambiguity of our ways of speaking, which is caused by this parallelism and is everywhere operative where the con-comitant circumstances are mentioned, operates also of course when we talk of expression and meaning (§ 124; ET, p. 345).

The *interweaving* (*Verwebung*) of language, of what is purely linguistic in language with the other threads of experi-ence, constitutes one fabric. The term *Verwebung* refers to this metaphorical zone. The "strata" are "woven"; their intermixing is such that the warp cannot be distinguished from the woof. If the stratum of logos were simply *founded,* one could set it aside so as to let the underlying substratum of nonexpressive acts and contents appear beneath it. But since this superstruc-

3. We refer the French reader to the translation and valuable commentary on *Ideas I* by Paul Ricoeur. For reasons in keeping with the intention of our analysis, we have had to underline certain Ger-man terms and insist upon their metaphorical import.

ture reacts in an essential and decisive way upon the *Unterschicht* [substratum], one is obliged, from the start of the
description, to associate the geological metaphor with a properly *textual* metaphor, for *fabric* or *textile* means *text*.
Verweben here means *texere*. The discursive refers to the
nondiscursive, the linguistic "stratum" is intermixed with the
prelinguistic "stratum" according to the controlled system of a
sort of *text*. We already know—and Husserl does recognize it
—that, at least in fact, the secondary threads are going to act
on the primary threads; with what is woven [*ourdit*] in such
a way, it is precisely the operation of beginning (*ordiri*) which
can no longer be recaptured. In the spinning-out of language
the discursive woof is rendered unrecognizable as a woof and
takes the place of a warp; it takes the place of something that
has not really preceded it. This texture is all the more inextricable in that it is wholly signifying: *the nonexpressive
threads are not without signification*. In the *Investigations* Husserl has showed that their signification is simply of an *indicative* nature. In the section we are now concerned with, he
recognizes that the terms *bedeuten* and *Bedeutung* can well
exceed the "expressive" field:

> We restrict our glance exclusively to "the meaning content"
> (*Bedeutung*), and "the act of meaning" (*Bedeuten*). Originally
> these words relate only to the sphere of speech (*sprachliche
> Sphäre*), that of "expression" (*des Ausdrückens*). But it is almost
> inevitable, and at the same time an important step for knowledge,
> to extend the meaning of these words, and to modify them suitably
> so that they may be applied in a certain way to the whole noetico-
> noematic sphere, to all acts, therefore, whether these are inter-
> woven (*verflochten*) with expressive acts or not (§ 124; ET, p. 346,
> modified).

Before this inextricable texture, this interweaving (*Verflechtung*)[4] that seems to defy analysis, the phenomenologist
does not become discouraged; his patience and attention to
detail should, at least theoretically, disentangle the confusion.
This is what follows from phenomenology's "principle of principles." If the description does not bring out a ground that would
absolutely and plainly found signification in general, if an
intuitive and perceptual ground, a base of silence, does not

4. Concerning the sense and importance of *Verflechtung* and
the functioning of this concept in the *Investigations*, see "The Reduction of Indication" in *Speech and Phenomena*.

found speech in the primordially given presence of the thing itself, if, in short, the texture of the text is irreducible, then, not only will the phenomenological description have failed, but the descriptive "principle" itself will have to be re-examined. What is at stake in this disentanglement is thus the phenomenological motif itself.

Mirrored Writing

Husserl begins by delimiting the problem, simplifying or purifying its given data. He proceeds to a double exclusion or, if one likes, a double reduction, complying with a necessity he had established in the *Investigations* and which will never again be re-examined. *On the one hand,* the *sensible aspect* of language, its sensible and nonmaterial aspect, what could be called the animated "proper body" (*Leib*) of language is put out of play. Since, for Husserl, expression supposes a meaning-intention (*Bedeutungsintention*), its essential condition therefore is the pure act of the animating intention and not the body to which, in a mysterious way, it is united and gives life. Husserl accords himself the right to dissociate this enigmatic unity of the informing intention and the informed matter in its very principle. This is why, *on the other hand,* he defers—forever, it seems—the problem of the unity of the two aspects, the problem of the union of soul and body:

> Let us start from the familiar distinction between the sensory, the so to speak bodily aspect (*leiblichen Seite*) of expression, and its non-sensory "mental" aspect. There is no need for us to enter more closely into the discussion of the first aspect, nor upon the way of uniting the two aspects, though we clearly have title-headings here indicated for phenomenological problems that are not unimportant (§ 124; ET, p. 346).[5]

5. These precautions had been taken and were justified at great length in the *Investigations*. Of course, to be demonstrative, these justifications nonetheless had to keep within the system of traditional metaphysical oppositions (body/soul, physical/mental, living/non-living, intentionality/unintentionality, form/matter, signified/signifying, intelligible/sensible, ideality/empiricality, etc.). These precautions will be particularly met with in the First Investigation (which is in fact but a long explication of them), and in the Fifth (Chap. XI, § 19) and the Sixth (Chap. I, § 7). They will continually be confirmed in *Formal and Transcendental Logic* and *The Origin of Geometry*.

After Husserl takes this double precaution, the contours of the problem appear more clearly. What distinctive traits separate the essentially expressive stratum from the pre-expressive stratum, and how can the effects of one on the other be subjected to an eidetic analysis? This question will receive its full formulation only after a certain progress made in the analysis:

> . . . how to interpret the "expressing" of "what is expressed," how expressed experiences stand in relation to those that are not expressed, and what changes the latter undergo when expression supervenes; one is then led to the question of their "intentionality," of their "immanent meaning," of their "content" (*Materie*) and quality (i.e., the act-character of the thesis), of the distinction of this meaning and these phases of the essence which lie in the pre-expressive from the meaning of the expressing phenomenon itself and its own phases, and so forth. One gathers still in various ways from the writings of the day how little justice is apt to be done to the great problems here indicated in their full and deep-lying significance (§ 124; ET, p. 348).

This problem had, of course, already been posed, especially at the beginning of the sixth *Logical Investigation*. But the path which leads up to it is different here, not only for very general reasons (the access to an explicitly transcendental problem, the appeal to the notion of the noema, the acknowledged generality of the noetic-noematic structure), but in particular by virtue of the distinction that has come to be added, in the interim, between the concepts of *Sinn* and *Bedeutung*. Not that Husserl now accepts the distinction proposed by Frege, which he had contested in the *Investigations;* [6] he simply finds it convenient to reserve the *bedeuten-Bedeutung* ["to mean," "meaning"] terms for the order of expressive meaning, for speech in the strict sense, and to extend the concept of *sense* (*Sinn*) to the totality of the noematic side of experience, whether or not it is expressive. [7]

As soon as the extension of *sense* exceeds that of *meaning,*

6. *Logical Investigations I*, Chap. I, § 15, trans. J. N. Findlay (New York: Humanities Press, 1970), I, 291.
7. *Ideas I*, § 124; ET, p. 346. It goes without saying that, by "speech in the strict sense," we do not understand the effectively and physically uttered speech but, following Husserl's intentions, the animation of verbal expression by a meaning, by an "intention," that, without thereby being essentially affected, can remain physically silent.

speech will always have to "draw its sense"; it will only be able somehow to *repeat or reproduce* a sense content, which does not wait for speech in order to be what it is.[8] If it is as we have described it, speech can only be the outward transfer of a sense that is constituted without it and before it. This is one of the reasons why the essence of logical meaning is determined as expression (*Ausdruck*). Speech is in essence expressive because it consists in carrying outside, in *exteriorizing,* a content of interior thought. It cannot operate without this *sich äussern* [expressing oneself] that was spoken of in the First Investigation (§ 7).

Thus we are already in possession of the first distinctive trait of the expressive stratum. If, physically or not, it only *proffers* a constituted sense, it is essentially re-productive, that is, *unproductive.* The first stage of Husserl's analysis proceeds toward this definition:

> The stratum of expression—and this constitutes its peculiarity— apart from the fact that it lends expression to all other intentionalities, is not productive. Or if one prefers: *its productivity, its noematic service, exhausts itself in expressing,* and in the *form of the conceptual* which first comes with the expressing (§ 124; ET, pp. 348–49).

This unproductiveness of the logos becomes, so to speak, *incorporated* [*prend corps*] in Husserl's description. And it becomes *seduced* by two metaphors which cannot escape our attention.

8. From this point of view we could question the entire aesthetics latent in phenomenology, the whole theory of the work of art that appears throughout the didactics of the examples, whether it is a question of exposing the problem of the imagination or the status of ideality, and the creation "once upon a time" of the work of art, whose ideal identity can be infinitely reproduced as *the same.* A system and a classification of the arts are prefigured in this description of the relation between the archetype and the reproductions. Can Husserl's theory of the ideality of the work of art and its relations with perception account for the differences between the musical and plastic works of art, between the literary and nonliterary work of art in general? And do Husserl's (even revolutionary) precautions with regard to what is original in imagination suffice to protect the work of art from a whole metaphysics of art as reproduction, from a *mimetics*? It could be shown that art, according to Husserl, always refers to perception as its absolute source. And is it not already an aesthetic and metaphysical decision to give works of art as examples in a theory of the *imaginary*?

The first seems to have passed unperceived by Husserl. It shifts between a kind of writing and a mirror; or, rather, it tells of mirrored writing. Let us follow its constitution.

To explain the difference between sense and meaning, Husserl resorts to a perceptual example, the silent perception of a "this white." In a way the statement "This is white" is quite independent of perceptual experience. It is intelligible even for someone who does not have this perception; this had been forcefully demonstrated in the *Investigations*. This independence of the expressive function implies the independence of the perceptual *sense*. We can make this *sense* explicit:

> The process makes no call whatsoever on "expression," neither on expression in the sense of verbal sound nor on the like as verbal meaning, and here the latter can also be present independently of the verbal sound (as in the case when this sound is "forgotten") (§ 124; ET, p. 347).

The passage to the enunciation consequently adds nothing to the sense; in any event, it adds no sense content to it. And yet, despite this sterility, or rather because of it, the appearance of expression is something quite new. It is somehow quite new, because it only restates the noematic sense. Since it neither adds nor deforms anything, expression can always in principle repeat the sense by bringing it to "conceptual form":

> . . . if we have *"thought"* or *stated* "This is white," a new stratum is there with the rest, and unites with the "meant as such" in its pure perceptive form. On these lines everything remembered or fancied can, as such, have its meaning made more explicit and expressible (*explizierbar und ausdrückbar*). Whatever is "meant (*Gemeint*) as such," every meaning (*Meinung*) in the noematic sense (and indeed as noematic nucleus) of any act whatsoever *can be expressed conceptually* (*durch "Bedeutungen"*) (§ 124; ET, p. 347).

Husserl then declares, as a universal rule, that logical meaning is an act of expression: "Logische Bedeutung ist ein Ausdruck." Everything therefore is in principle capable of being said; everything must be able to be brought to the conceptual generality that properly constitutes the logicality of logos. And this must be so, not despite but thanks to the originality of the medium of logical expression, which consists in not introducing anything new, in effacing itself like an unproductive transparency before the passage of sense.

But this transparency must have some consistency, not only in order to *express,* but first of all to be *impressed* with, what it will then present to be read:

> From the noetic standpoint the rubric "expressing" should indicate a special act-stratum to which all other acts must adjust themselves in their own way, and with which they must blend remarkably in such wise that every noematic act-sense, and consequently the relation to objectivity which lies in it, *impresses itself* (*sich ausprägt:* strikes or stamps itself) "conceptually" (*begrifflich*) in the noematic phase of the expressing (§ 124; ET, p. 347, modified).

Thus the pre-expressive noema, the prelinguistic sense, must be impressed on the expressive noema; it must acquire its conceptual determination in the meaning-content. To be limited to bearing outwardly an already constituted sense, at the same time bringing it to conceptual generality without altering it, expressing what has already been thought—we should almost say written—and faithfully reduplicating it, expression must let itself be impressed by sense at the same time that it impresses the sense. The sense must be inscribed in the meaning. The expressive noema must present itself (and here is the new image of its unproductiveness) as a blank page or a clean slate, at least as a palimpsest restored to its pure receptivity. As soon as the inscription of sense upon the expressive noema makes it readable, the logical order of conceptuality as such will be constituted. The expressive noema then will present itself *begrifflich,* in a discernible, workable, conceivable, and conceptual way. The conceptual order is inaugurated by expression, but this inauguration reduplicates a pre-existing conceptuality, since it must have been from the start impressed upon the blank page of meaning. Production and revelation are unified in the impression-expression proper to speech. And since what Husserl is considering here is not the verbal order, with all its interwoven (physical and intentional) complexity, but the still silent meaning-intention (i.e., the moment *meaning,* which is more than *sense,* has appeared but has not yet been effectively and physically offered), we must conclude that sense in general, the noematic sense of every experience, is something which, by its very nature, must be already able to *be impressed* on a meaning, to leave or receive its formal determination in a meaning. Sense would therefore already be a kind of blank and mute writing which is reduplicated in meaning.

The stratum of meaning then would have only the kind of originality of the *tabula rasa*. This metaphor will bring on serious problems, as we can already foresee. If, in particular, there is an original history and permanence proper to concepts (such as they are already inscribed in the meaning alone, and even with the supposition that the meaning can be separated from the history of a language and of its signifiers), they are always older than the sense, and constitute a text also. Even if we could, in principle, suppose some virginal text that had received, *in illo tempore*, the first production of sense, it is *in fact* necessary that the systematic order of meaning somehow impose its own sense on that sense, dictate its own form to it, and oblige it to be imprinted according to syntactic or other rules. And this "in fact" is not one empirical necessity among others; we cannot put it in brackets in order to ask questions that are transcendental in principle, since the status of meaning cannot be fixed without, at the same time, determining the status of sense. The putting of this "fact" in brackets is a decision about the status of sense in general in its relation to speech. *It does not depend on phenomenology; rather it opens up phenomenology in a noncritical movement.* And although, in what followed, Husserl never again questioned this *de jure* "anteriority" of sense in relation to meaning (of *Sinn* in relation to *bedeuten*), it is difficult to see how it is reconcilable with the subsequent thematic—for example, with that of *The Origin of Geometry*. This thematic is just what we are following at this moment, *at the same time* that we are following the theme of a sedimented history of meaning. And even if we considered only the egological history, how could we ever conceive of the perpetual restoration of meaning in its virginal state?

Husserl's attention is not held by the scriptural analogy; it is drawn away by another metaphor.

The medium that receives the imprint will be neutral. After having discussed the conceptual *Ausprägung* [impression], Husserl describes its medium as neutral, without a color of its own, without any determinate opacity, without refractive power. But this neutral character of the medium is less that of transparency than of a mirror reflection:

A peculiar intentional instrument lies before us which essentially possesses the outstanding characteristic of reflecting back as from a mirror (*widerzuspiegeln*) every other intentionality according to its form and content, of copying (*abzubilden*) it whilst colouring it in its own way, and thereby of working into (*einzubilden*) it its own form of "conceptuality" (§ 124; ET, pp. 347–48).

There is a double effect of the medium, a double relation between logos and sense: on the one hand, it is a pure and simple *reflexion*, a *reflection* which respects what it receives and returns, *de-picts* the sense as such in its original colors and re-presents it in person. This is language as *Abbildung* (copy, portrait, figuration, representation). But, on the other hand, this reproduction imposes the blank imprint of the concept. It forms the sense in the meaning, it produces a specific nonproduction, which, without changing anything in the sense, *pictures* something in it. The concept is produced without adding anything to the sense. We could speak here, in a certain sense, of conceptual *fiction* and a kind of *imagination* that would take up the intuition of sense into conceptual generality. This would be language as *Einbildung*. The two terms do not enter into Husserl's description fortuitously: what is peculiar to the unproductive production of the logical would be just this strange concurrence of *Abbildung* and *Einbildung*.

Is this conception self-contradictory? Husserl in any event betrays a certain uneasiness. And we shall have to think over the fact that he attributes the indecisiveness of his description to the incidentally metaphorical character of language, which he precisely calls the *Bildlichkeit* of speech. It is because speech must occasionally use images, figures, and analogies —linguistic debris, so to speak—that *logos* must be described both as the unproductivity of *Abbildung* and as the productivity of *Einbildung*. If we were to eliminate the *Bildlichkeit* in descriptive speech, we would, by the same token, eliminate the apparent contradiction between *Abbildung* and *Einbildung*. But Husserl does not ask how this nucleic *bilden* [to construct, to form, to fashion] operates in its relations with logos. The passage we just quoted continues:

> Yet these figures of speech which here thrust themselves upon us, those of mirroring and copying, must be adopted with caution, as the imaginativeness [*Bildlichkeit:* metaphorical representation, depiction, pictorial representation] which colours their application might easily lead one astray (*irreführen*).

Thus the metaphor, in every sense of this term, is seductive. Phenomenological speech should resist this seduction.

THE LIMITING POWER OF FORM

IF HUSSERL QUESTIONS all the *predicates* related to the medium of logos, he never criticizes the concept of *medium* itself. The expressive stratum is a *medium*, that is, both an *element* and a *means*, an ether that accepts the sense, and a means of giving it conceptual form. The term "medium" often appears on the following pages. It enters into the formulation of the problem of the history of concepts, whose difficulties we mentioned earlier in relation with the subsequent themes of *The Origin of Geometry*. Even at this point Husserl formulates the difficulty [9] that will constitute the central theme of that work:

> Problems of exceptional difficulty beset the phenomena which find their place under the headings "to mean" (*Bedeuten*) and "meaning" (*Bedeutung*). Since every science, viewed from the side of its theoretical content, of all that constitutes its "doctrine" (*Lehre*) (theorem, proof, theory), is objectified in a specific "logical" medium, the medium of expression, it follows that for philosophers and psychologists who are guided by general logical interests the problems of expression and meaning (*Bedeutung*) lie nearest of all, and are also the first, generally speaking, which, so soon as one seeks seriously to reach their foundations, compel towards phenomenological inquiry into the essential nature of things (§ 124; ET, p. 348).

Theory, therefore, can neither dispense with objectification in the medium nor tolerate the least deformation in the submission to it. While there is no scientific sense (*Sinn*) without meaning (*bedeuten*), it belongs to the essence of science to demand a strict univocity, an absolute transparency of speech. Science would thus require that what it needs (speech as pure meaning) serve for nothing but to guard and preserve the sense that science has conferred upon it. Nowhere can speech be both more productive and more unproductive than as an element of theory.

If this unproductive productivity is the telos of expression, then it is clearly confirmed that logico-scientific speech has been continually functioning here as the model for all possible speech.

9. This problem had already been formulated in the Introduction to the *Logical Investigations* (§ 2).

The whole analysis will henceforth have to shift between two concepts, two values. On the one hand, ideal speech will have to achieve an overlapping or *coincidence* (*Deckung*) of the nonexpressive stratum of sense with the expressive stratum of meaning. But for reasons we have already recognized, this overlapping must never be a *confusion*. And the work of clarification, distinction, and articulation, etc., must bear upon these two strata as such. The difference between coincidence and confusion leads us back, then, to the very opening of our problem. But perhaps this formulation will allow us to progress.

In the best of cases, in the perfect overlapping of the two strata, there would thus be a *parallelism*. The concept of the parallel would respect both the perfect correspondence and the nonconfusion. And according to an analogy that must be examined, it would have to play as decisive a role here as in the case where Husserl explicitly brings it in to describe the relations between the purely psychic and transcendental.

Only if the sense of the underlying substratum is *completely* reproduced by the meaning (if not by effective speech) can the parallelism of the two strata be a perfect overlapping. There is always a certain overlapping of the two strata, for without this the phenomenon of expression would not even occur. This overlapping, however, can be incomplete:

> We must further lay stress on the difference between *complete* (*vollständigem*) and *incomplete* (*unvollständigem*) *expression*. The unity of the expressing and the expressed in the phenomenon is indeed that of a certain overlapping (*Deckung*), but the upper layer need not extend its expressing function over the entire lower layer. Expression is complete when the *stamp of conceptual meaning has been impressed* (*ausprägt*) *upon all the synthetic forms and matter* (*Materien*) *of the lower layer*; incomplete when this is only partially effected: as when, in regard to a complex process, the arrival of the carriage, perhaps, bringing guests that have been long expected; we call out: the carriage! the guests! This difference of completeness will naturally cut across that of relative clearness and distinctness (§ 126; ET, p. 352, modified).

Up until this point we might have thought that the incompleteness of expression and the nonparallelism of the two strata figure only as facts or accidents and that, even if such a *fact* occurs frequently, if it nearly always affects the entirety of our speech, *it does not belong to the essence of expression.* The example just cited by Husserl does in fact belong to the language of everyday life, and one can still suppose that the mission and power of scientific expression consists in mastering these ambiguities and restoring the completeness of the sense intended in expression.

However, at the risk of compromising an axiom (the unproductive and reflective function of expression), Husserl also brings to light an *essential* incompleteness of expression, an inadequacy that no effort can ever surmount, precisely because it belongs to the *conceptual form,* to formality itself, without which expression would not be what it is. It seemed, above, that Husserl wanted to insist upon the reflective, reproductive, repetitive nature of expression, on its *Abbilden,* but to neutralize its effects and its marks, its power of deformation or refraction, its *Einbilden.* He now insists, on the contrary, upon an essential shift of expression that would prevent it from ever bringing out the stratum of sense. Meaning (*bedeuten*) will never be the duplicate of sense (*Sinn*): and this difference is nothing less than that of the concept. We must read the whole of this paragraph:

> An incompleteness of a totally different kind (*Eine total andere Unvollständigkeit*) from the one just discussed is that which belongs to the essential nature of the expression as such, namely, to its *generality* (*Allgemeinheit*). "I would like," expresses the wish in a general form; the form of command, the command; "might very well be" the presumption, or the likely as such, and so forth. Every closer determination in the unity of the expression is itself again expressed in general form. It lies in the meaning of the generality which belongs to the essential nature of the expressing function that it would not ever be possible for all the specifications of the expressed to be reflected (*sich reflektieren*) in the expression. The stratum of the meaning function is not, and in principle is not, a sort of duplication (*Reduplikation*) of the lower stratum. (§ 126; ET, p. 352).

Referring back to the whole problem of complete and incomplete expressions in the *Logical Investigations,* Husserl then evokes the functions of the underlying substratum, which in principle cannot be repeated in expression (the qualities of clarity, distinctness, attentional modifications, etc.).

This impoverishment is the condition for scientific formalization. There is univocity to the extent that the complete repetition of sense in the meaning is given up. We cannot even say, therefore, that *de facto* incompleteness (taken as inessential or accidental) is reduced by a teleology of scientific speech or that it is included, as a provisional obstacle, within the horizon of an infinite task. The telos of scientific speech itself, and *as such,* involves an eschewing of completeness. Difference here is not a provisional deficiency of *epistēmē* taken as speech; it is its own means, the positive condition of its activity and productivity. It is as much the limit of scientific power as the power of the scientific limit; it is the limiting power of its formality.

THE FORM "IS"—ITS ELLIPSIS

THESE REMARKS apparently concerned, above all, the relationship of the form of statements with their sense-content, the order of meaning with the noematic order in general. But they now imply an essential decision concerning *the relationship between statements themselves,* within the general system of expression. To be able to determine the relationship between expression and sense as we have, did we not already have to have taken a certain type of statement as absolutely privileged? Is there not an essential relationship between formal import and a certain sentence structure? By the same token, is there not an *easy movement* from a certain type of noema (or experience of sense) to the order of meaning, a movement that somehow makes the whole of this phenomenology of logos possible?

With this question we retrace our first steps: what about the concept of form? How does it inscribe phenomenology within the closure of metaphysics? How does it determine the sense of being as presence, indeed, as the present? What secretly connects it with that delimitation of the sense of being that makes us think of it particularly in the verbal form of the present and, more narrowly still, in the third person present indicative? What does the complicity between form in general (*eidos, morphē*) and the "is" (*esti*) suggest for our thought?

Let us bring these questions back into contact with Husserl's text at the point where the formal impoverishment comes to be recognized as an essential rule. Then the problem of the relationship between the different types of statements arises quite naturally. Is the statement in the form of the judgment, the form "It *is* thus," one statement among others? Is not some particular excellence reserved for it in the stratum of expressiveness?

> We must be clear about all these points if one of the oldest and hardest problems of the sphere of meaning (*Bedeutungssphäre*) is to be solved, a problem which hitherto, precisely because it lacked the requisite phenomenological insight, has remained without solution: the problem, namely, as to *how statement as the expression of judgment is related to the expressions of other acts* (§ 127; ET, p. 353).

The answer to such a question had been prepared, and its necessity announced, at a step in the analysis which was not yet concerned with the stratum of expression. There it was a question of bringing forth the evidence, in practical or affective experience, in the acts of aesthetic or moral evaluation, etc., for a "doxic" core which, still allowing us to think of values as states of being (the wished-for as the being-wished-for, the agreeable as the being-agreeable, etc. [§114]), constitutes, so to speak, the *logicality* of the pre-expressive stratum. It is because this silent stratum always carries with it a relation to form (or always has the power to restore such a relation), it is because it can always convert its affective or axiological experience, its relation to what is not a being-present, into an experience that has the form being-present (the beautiful as being-beautiful, the desired as being-desired, the dreaded future as the being-dreaded-future, the inaccessible as being-inaccessible, and, as the limiting case, the absent as being-absent), that it gives itself unreservedly to logical speech, speech controlled by the predicative form, that is, by the present indicative of the verb "to be." [10] For Husserl, not only will this conver-

10. Husserl wants to respect the novelty or originality of the (practical, affective, axiological) sense, which supervenes upon the nucleus of sense of the bare thing as such (*Sache*), and yet to bring out the "founded," superstructural character of this sense. "The new sense introduces a *totally new dimension of sense:* with it there is constituted no new determining marks of the mere '*material*' (*Sachen*), but *values of the materials*—qualities of value (*Wertheiten*), or concrete objectified values (*Wertobjektitäten*): beauty and ugliness, goodness and badness; or the object for use, the work of art, the machine, the book, the action, the deed, and so forth. . . . Further, the consciousness in respect of this new character is once again a *positional* consciousness: the 'valuable' can be doxically posited as being valuable (*als wert seiend*). The 'state of being' (*seiend*) which

sion not diminish the originality of practical, affective, axiological experiences and speech, but it will assure them the possibility of an unlimited formalization.[11]

Having brought out that *"every act, as also every act-correlate, harbours explicitly or implicitly a 'logical' factor"* (§ 117; ET, p. 332), Husserl has only to draw forth the consequences with regard to the expressive reworking of these acts and thus to confirm rather than discover the privilege of the "is" or predicative statement. The moment he repeats [12] the question for the order of meaning, the answer, really, is al-

---

belongs to the 'valuable' as *its* characterization can be thought of also as *modalized,* as can every 'state of being' " (§ 116; ET, p. 327, modified).

"We can therefore also say: *Every act, as also every act-correlate, harbours explicitly or implicitly a 'logical' factor (ein Logisches). . . .* It results from all this *that all acts generally—even the acts of feeling and will—are 'objectifying' ('objektivierende') acts, original factors in the 'constituting' of objects,* the necessary sources of different regions of being and of the ontologies that belong therewith. . . . Here lies the deepest of the sources for shedding light on the *universality of the logical,* in the last resort that of the predicative judgment (to which we must add the stratum of meaningful expression [*des bedeutungsmässigen Ausdrückens*] which we have not yet subjected to closer study) (§ 117; ET, pp. 332–33).

11. "But therein in the last resort are grounded those analogies which have at all times been felt to hold between general logic, general theory of value, and ethics, which, when pursued into their farthest depths, lead to the constituting of general *formal* disciplines on lines parallel to the above, formal logic, formal axiology, and the formal theory of practice (*Praktik*)" (§ 117; ET, p. 330). Cf. also, *Formal and Transcendental Logic,* § 50.

12. "We have expressive predications in which a 'thus it is!' (*So ist es!*) comes to expression. We have expressive presumptions, questions, doubts, expressive wishes, commands, and so forth. Linguistically we have here forms of sentence whose structure is in part distinctive, while yet they are of ambiguous interpretation: by the side of sentences that embody statements we have sentences embodying questions, presumptions, wishes, commands and so forth. The original debate bore on the issue whether, disregarding the grammatical wording and its historical forms, we had here to do with coordinate types of meaning (*gleichgeordnete Bedeutungsarten*), or whether the case was not rather this, that all these sentences, so far as their meaning is concerned, are not in truth sentences that state. If the latter, then all act-constructions, such, for instance, as those of the sphere of feeling, which in themselves are not acts of judgment, can achieve 'expression' only in a roundabout way (*Umweg*) through the mediation of an act of judging which is grounded in them" (§ 127; ET, p. 353).

ready required. We should be neither surprised nor deceived
by this. We find, like a rule of speech or textual rule, that the
question can be inscribed only in the form dictated by the
answer which awaits it, that is, which did not wait for it. It
need only be asked how the answer has prescribed the form of
the question—not according to the necessary, conscious, and
calculated anticipation of someone who is conducting a systematic exposé but somehow unawares. Thus we can ask to what
extent the reference to the expressive stratum, even before
it has become thematic, has secretly guided the analyses of
the pre-expressive stratum and has allowed us to discover in
it a core of logical sense under the universal and allegedly
silent form of being-present.

And we can ask whether, between being as being-present in
the form of meaning (*bedeuten*) and being as being-present in
what is called the pre-expressive form of sense (*Sinn*), some
irreducible complicity has not functioned throughout this
whole problem, fusing the two strata, thereby also enabling the
one to relate to the other, articulating them. Is not this the
locus of decision for all the problems we have pointed out
thus far? [13] With this question, does not the very idea of an

13. Although the answer has prescribed the form of the question, or, if one likes, is itself prescribed in it, its thematic articulation
is not a mere redundancy. It engages new concepts and meets new
difficulties, as when, toward the end of § 127, there is the question of
direct or *indirect* expressions of sense and the roundabout (*Umweg*)
status of periphrasis. Let us note certain points of reference in this
paragraph:

"Is the medium for the expressing of meaning, this unique medium of the Logos, *specifically doxic?* . . . This would not of course
exclude the possibility of there being various ways of expressing such
experiences, those of feeling, for instance. A single one of these would
be the *direct* [*schlicht;* our italics] plain expression of the experience
(or of its noema, in the case of the correlative meaning of the term
'expression') through the *immediate* [our italics] adjustment of an
articulated expression to the articulated experience of feeling whereby
doxic and doxic tally together. Thus it would have been the *doxic* form
dwelling in respect of all its component aspects within the experience
of feeling that made possible the adjustability of the expression, as an
exclusively doxothetic (*doxothetischen*) experience, to the experience
of feeling. . . . To speak more accurately, this *direct* expression,
if it would be true and complete, should be applied only to the *doxic
nonmodalized* experiences. . . . There exist at all times *a number
of alternative indirect expressions* involving 'roundabout phrases'
(*mit 'Umwegen'*)" (ET, pp. 354–55).

expressive language become problematic, as well as the possibility of a distinction between the stratum of sense and the stratum of meaning? Most important of all, can the relationships between the two strata be conceived with the category of expression? To say that the description of the infrastructure (of sense) has been secretly guided by the superstructural possibility of meaning is not to contest, against Husserl, the duality of the strata and the unity of a certain passage that relates them. Nor is it to wish to reduce one stratum to the other, or to judge the complete recapture of sense into meaning to be impossible. Nor is it to reconstruct experience (of sense) as a *language*—especially if we understand this to be *speech,* a verbal fabric—or to produce a critique of language based on the ineffable richness of sense. It is simply to ask a question about *another relationship* between what is, problematically, called *sense* and *meaning.*

That is, it is to question the unity of sense and word in the "is"—which *de jure* could have assured the incorporation of all language into *theoretical* predication only by already having teleologically destined all sense to meaning. And it is also to question the relationship between the *is* and formality in general. It is through the evidence of the (present) *is,* in *evidence itself,* that the whole of transcendental phenomenology is put forth in its supreme ambition: aiming to achieve both the constitution of an absolutely *formal* logic and ontology and a transcendental description of self-*presence* or primordial consciousness.

It might then be thought that the *sense of being* has been limited by the imposition of *form*—which in its most overt function, and ever since the origin of philosophy, would, with the authority of the *is,* have assigned to the sense of being the closure of presence, the form-of-presence, presence-in-form, or form-presence.[14] It might, on the contrary, be thought that

14. Form (presence, evidence) would not be the final recourse, the last instance, to which every possible sign would refer—the *archē* or the *telos;* but rather, in a perhaps unheard-of way, the *morphē, archē,* and *telos* would still turn out to be signs. In a sense—or a non-sense—that metaphysics would have excluded from its field, while nonetheless being secretly and incessantly related to it, the form would already and in itself be the *trace* (*ichnos*) of a certain non-presence, the vestige of the formless, announcing and recalling its other to the whole of metaphysics—as Plotinus perhaps said. The trace would not be the mixture or passage between form and the

formality—or formalization—is limited by the sense of being which in fact, throughout its whole history, has never been separated from its determination as presence, under the fine control of the *is*, and, therefore, that thought, controlled by the concept of form, has the power to extend itself beyond the thought devoted to being. But perhaps what Husserl's enterprise illustrates is that these two limits are *the same*. Phenomenology has been able to push the *formalist demand* to its extreme limit and to criticize all the preceding formalisms only on the basis of conceiving being as *self-presence*, only on the basis of a transcendental *experience* of pure consciousness.

There is, then, probably no choice to be made between two lines of thought; our task is rather to reflect on the circularity which makes the one pass into the other indefinitely. And, by strictly repeating this *circle* in its own historical possibility, we allow the production of some *elliptical* change of site, within the difference involved in repetition; this displacement is no doubt deficient, but with a deficiency that is not yet, or is already no longer, absence, negativity, nonbeing, lack, silence. Neither matter nor form, it is nothing that any philosopheme, that is, any dialectic, however determinate, can capture. It is an ellipsis of both meaning and form; it is neither plenary speech nor perfectly circular. More and less, neither more nor less—it is perhaps an entirely different question.

---

amorphous, between presence and absence, etc., but that which, in escaping this opposition, renders it possible because of its irreducible excess. Then the closure of metaphysics, which certain bold statements of the *Enneads* seem to have indicated by transgressing metaphysical thought (but other texts, too, could be cited), would not move *around* the homogeneous and continuous field of metaphysics. The closure of metaphysics would crack the structure and history of this field, by *organically* inscribing and systematically *articulating* from within the traces of the *before*, the *after*, and the *outside* of metaphysics. In this way we are offered an infinite and infinitely surprising reading of this structure and history. An irreducible rupture and excess may always occur within a given epoch, at a certain point in its text (for example in the "Platonic" fabric of "Neo-Platonism") and, no doubt, already in Plato's text.

Differance

THE VERB "to differ" [*différer*] seems to differ from itself. On the one hand, it indicates difference as distinction, inequality, or discernibility; on the other, it expresses the interposition of delay, the interval of a *spacing* and *temporalizing* that puts off until "later" what is presently denied, the possible that is presently impossible. Sometimes the *different* and sometimes the *deferred* correspond [in French] to the verb "to differ." This correlation, however, is not simply one between act and object, cause and effect, or primordial and derived.

In the one case "to differ" signifies nonidentity; in the other case it signifies the order of the *same*. Yet there must be a common, although entirely differant [1] [*différante*], root within the sphere that relates the two movements of differing to one another. We provisionally give the name *difference* to this *sameness* which is not *identical:* by the silent writing of

This essay appeared originally in the *Bulletin de la Société française de philosophie*, LXII, No. 3 (July–September, 1968), 73–101. Derrida's remarks were delivered as a lecture at a meeting of the Société at the Sorbonne, in the Amphithéâtre Michelet, on January 27, 1968, with Jean Wahl presiding. Professor Wahl's introductory and closing remarks have not been translated. The essay was reprinted in *Théorie d'ensemble*, a collection of essays by Derrida and others, published by Editions Seuil in 1968. It is reproduced here by permission of Editions Seuil.
    1. [The reader should bear in mind that "differance," or difference with an *a*, incorporates two significations: "to differ" and "to defer." See also above, footnote 8, p. 82.—Translator.]

[129]

its *a*, it has the desired advantage of referring to differing, *both* as spacing/temporalizing and as the movement that structures every dissociation.

As distinct from difference, differance thus points out the irreducibility of temporalizing (which is also temporalization —in transcendental language which is no longer adequate here, this would be called the constitution of primordial temporality—just as the term "spacing" also includes the constitution of primordial spatiality). Differance is not simply active (any more than it is a subjective accomplishment); it rather indicates the middle voice, it precedes and sets up the opposition between passivity and activity. With its *a*, differance more properly refers to what in classical language would be called the origin or production of differences and the differences between differences, the *play* [*jeu*] of differences. Its locus and operation will therefore be seen wherever speech appeals to difference.

Differance is neither a *word* nor a *concept*. In it, however, we shall see the juncture—rather than the summation—of what has been most decisively inscribed in the thought of what is conveniently called our "epoch": the difference of forces in Nietzsche, Saussure's principle of semiological difference, differing as the possibility of [neurone] facilitation,[2] impression and delayed effect in Freud, difference as the irreducibility of the trace of the other in Levinas, and the ontic-ontological difference in Heidegger.

Reflection on this last determination of difference will lead

2. [For the term "facilitation" (*frayage*) in Freud, cf. "Project for a Scientific Psychology I" in *The Complete Psychological Works of Sigmund Freud,* 24 vols. (New York and London: Macmillan, 1964), I, 300, note 4 by the translator, James Strachey: "The word 'facilitation' as a rendering of the German '*Bahnung*' seems to have been introduced by Sherrington a few years after the *Project* was written. The German word, however, was already in use." The sense that Derrida draws upon here is stronger in the French or German; that is, the opening-up or clearing-out of a pathway. In the context of the "Project for a Scientific Psychology I," facilitation denotes the conduction capability that results from a difference in resistance levels in the memory and perception circuits of the nervous system. Thus, lowering the resistance threshold of a contact barrier serves to "open up" a nerve pathway and "facilitates" the excitatory process for the circuit. Cf. also J. Derrida, *L'Ecriture et la différence*, Chap. VII, "Freud et la scène de l'écriture" (Paris: Seuil, 1967), esp. pp. 297–305.—Translator.]

us to consider differance as the *strategic* note or connection
—relatively or provisionally *privileged*—which indicates the
closure of presence, together with the closure of the conceptual
order and denomination, a closure that is effected in the
functioning of traces.

I SHALL SPEAK, THEN, OF A LETTER—the first one,
if we are to believe the alphabet and most of the speculations
that have concerned themselves with it.

I shall speak then of the letter *a,* this first letter which it
seemed necessary to introduce now and then in writing the
word "difference." This seemed necessary in the course of
writing about writing, and of writing within a writing whose
different strokes all pass, in certain respects, through a gross
spelling mistake, through a violation of the rules governing
writing, violating the law that governs writing and regulates
its conventions of propriety. In fact or theory we can always
erase or lessen this spelling mistake, and, in each case, while
these are analytically different from one another but for practical purposes the same, find it grave, unseemly, or, indeed,
supposing the greatest ingenuousness, amusing. Whether or
not we care to quietly overlook this infraction, the attention
we give it beforehand will allow us to recognize, as though
prescribed by some mute irony, the inaudible but displaced
character of this literal permutation. We can always act as
though this makes no difference. I must say from the start
that my account serves less to justify this silent spelling mistake, or still less to excuse it, than to aggravate its obtrusive
character.

On the other hand, I must be excused if I refer, at least
implicitly, to one or another of the texts that I have ventured
to publish. Precisely what I would like to attempt to some
extent (although this is in principle and in its highest degree
impossible, due to essential *de jure* reasons) is to bring together an *assemblage* of the different ways I have been able
to utilize—or, rather, have allowed to be imposed on me—what
I will provisionally call the word or concept of differance in
its new spelling. It is literally neither a word nor a concept, as
we shall see. I insist on the word "assemblage" here for two
reasons: on the one hand, it is not a matter of describing a
history, of recounting the steps, text by text, context by context, each time showing which scheme has been able to impose

this graphic disorder, although this could have been done as well; rather, we are concerned with the *general system of all these schemata*. On the other hand, the word "assemblage" seems more apt for suggesting that the kind of bringing-together proposed here has the structure of an interlacing, a weaving, or a web, which would allow the different threads and different lines of sense or force to separate again, as well as being ready to bind others together.

In a quite preliminary way, we now recall that this particular graphic intervention was conceived in the writing-up of a question about writing; it was not made simply to shock the reader or grammarian. Now, in point of fact, it happens that this graphic difference (the *a* instead of the *e*), this marked difference between two apparently vocalic notations, between vowels, remains purely graphic: it is written or read, but it is not heard. It cannot be heard, and we shall see in what respects it is also beyond the order of understanding. It is put forward by a silent mark, by a tacit monument, or, one might even say, by a pyramid—keeping in mind not only the capital form of the printed letter but also that passage from Hegel's *Encyclopaedia* where he compares the body of the sign to an Egyptian pyramid. The *a* of differance, therefore, is not heard; it remains silent, secret, and discreet, like a tomb.[3]

It is a tomb that (provided one knows how to decipher its legend) is not far from signaling the death of the king.

It is a tomb that cannot even be made to resonate. For I cannot even let you know, by my talk, now being spoken before the Société Française de Philosophie, which difference I am talking about at the very moment I speak of it. I can only talk about this graphic difference by keeping to a very indirect speech about writing, and on the condition that I specify each time that I am referring to difference with an *e* or differance with an *a*. All of which is not going to simplify matters today, and will give us all a great deal of trouble when we want to understand one another. In any event, when I do specify which difference I mean—when I say "with an *e*" or "with an *a*"--this will refer irreducibly to a *written text*, a text governing my talk, a text that I keep in front of me, that I will read, and toward which I shall have to try to lead

3. [On "pyramid" and "tomb" see J. Derrida, "Le Puits et la pyramide" in *Hegel et la pensée moderne* (Paris: Presses Universitaires de France, 1970), esp. pp. 44–45.—Translator.]

your hands and eyes. We cannot refrain here from going by way of a written text, from ordering ourselves by the disorder that is produced therein—and this is what matters to me first of all.

Doubtless this pyramidal silence of the graphic difference between the *e* and the *a* can function only within the system of phonetic writing and within a language or grammar historically tied to phonetic writing and to the whole culture which is inseparable from it. But I will say that it is just this—this silence that functions only within what is called phonetic writing—that points out or reminds us in a very opportune way that, contrary to an enormous prejudice, there is no phonetic writing. There is no purely and strictly phonetic writing. What is called phonetic writing can only function —in principle and *de jure,* and not due to some factual and technical inadequacy—by incorporating nonphonetic "signs" (punctuation, spacing, etc.); but when we examine their structure and necessity, we will quickly see that they are ill described by the concept of signs. Saussure had only to remind us that the play of difference was the functional condition, the condition of possibility, for every sign; and it is itself silent. The difference between two phonemes, which enables them to exist and to operate, is inaudible. The inaudible opens the two present phonemes to hearing, as they present themselves. If, then, there is no purely phonetic writing, it is because there is no purely phonetic phone. The difference that brings out phonemes and lets them be heard and understood [*en-tendre*] itself remains inaudible.

It will perhaps be objected that, for the same reasons, the graphic difference itself sinks into darkness, that it never constitutes the fullness of a sensible term, but draws out an invisible connection, the mark of an inapparent relation between two spectacles. That is no doubt true. Indeed, since from this point of view the difference between the *e* and the *a* marked in "differance" eludes vision and hearing, this happily suggests that we must here let ourselves be referred to an order that no longer refers to sensibility. But we are not referred to intelligibility either, to an ideality not fortuitously associated with the objectivity of *theōrein* or understanding. We must be referred to an order, then, that resists philosophy's founding opposition between the sensible and the intelligible. The order that resists this opposition, that resists it because it sustains it, is designated in a movement of differance (with an *a*) between two differences or between two letters. This differance belongs neither to the voice nor to writing in the ordinary sense, and it takes place, like the strange space that will assemble us here for the course of an hour, *between* speech and writing and beyond the tranquil familiarity that binds us to one and to the other, reassuring us sometimes in the illusion that they are two separate things.

Now, HOW AM I TO SPEAK OF the *a* of differance? It is clear that it cannot be *exposed*. We can expose only what, at a certain moment, can become *present*, manifest; what can be shown, presented as a present, a being-present in its truth, the truth of a present or the presence of a present. However, if differance ⌐is⌐ (I also cross out the "is") what makes the presentation of being-present possible, it never presents itself as such. It is never given in the present or to anyone. Holding back and not exposing itself, it goes beyond the order of truth on this specific point and in this determined way, yet is not itself concealed, as if it were something, a mysterious being, in the occult zone of a nonknowing. Any exposition would expose it to disappearing as a disappearance. It would risk appearing, thus disappearing.

Thus, the detours, phrases, and syntax that I shall often have to resort to will resemble—will sometimes be practically indiscernible from—those of negative theology. Already we had to note that *differance is not*, does not exist, and is not any sort of being-present (*on*). And we will have to point out everything *that* it *is not*, and, consequently, that it has neither existence nor essence. It belongs to no category of being, present or absent. And yet what is thus denoted as differance is not theological, not even in the most negative order of negative theology. The latter, as we know, is always occupied with letting a supraessential reality go beyond the finite categories of essence and existence, that is, of presence, and always hastens to remind us that, if we deny the predicate of existence to God, it is in order to recognize him as a superior, inconceivable, and ineffable mode of being. Here there is no question of such a move, as will be confirmed as we go along. Not only is differance irreducible to every ontological or theological—onto-theological—reappropriation, but it opens up the very space in which onto-theology—philosophy—produces its system and its history. It thus encompasses and irrevocably surpasses onto-theology or philosophy.

For the same reason, I do not know where *to begin* to mark out this assemblage, this graph, of differance. Precisely what is in question here is the requirement that there be a *de jure* commencement, an absolute point of departure, a responsibility arising from a principle. The problem of writing opens by questioning the *archē*. Thus what I put forth here will not be developed simply as a philosophical discourse that operates on the basis of a principle, of postulates, axioms, and definitions and that moves according to the discursive line of a rational order. In marking out differance, everything is a matter of strategy and risk. It is a question of strategy because no transcendent truth present outside the sphere of writing can theologically command the totality of this field. It is hazardous because this strategy is not simply one in the sense that we say that strategy orients the tactics according to a final aim, a *telos* or the theme of a domination, a mastery or an ultimate reappropriation of movement and field. In the end, it is a strategy without finality. We might call it blind tactics or empirical errance, if the value of empiricism did not itself derive all its meaning from its opposition to philosophical responsibility. If there is a certain errance in the tracing-out of differance, it no longer follows the line of logico-philosophical speech or that of its integral and symmetrical opposite, logico-empirical speech. The concept of *play* [*jeu*] remains beyond this opposition; on the eve and aftermath of philosophy, it designates the unity of chance and necessity in an endless calculus.

By decision and, as it were, by the rules of the game, then, turning this thought around, let us introduce ourselves to the thought of differance by way of the theme of strategy or stratagem. By this merely strategic justification, I want to emphasize that the efficacy of this thematics of differance very well may, and even one day must, be sublated, i.e., lend itself, if not to its own replacement, at least to its involvement in a series of events which in fact it never commanded. This also means that it is not a theological thematics.

I will say, first of all, that differance, which is neither a word nor a concept, seemed to me to be strategically the theme most proper to think out, if not master (thought being here, perhaps, held in a certain necessary relation with the structional limits of mastery), in what is most characteristic of *decouvre the epoch us a finite context*

Greek Latin

our "epoch." I start off, then, strategically, from the place and time in which "we" are, even though my opening is not justifiable in the final account, and though it is always on the basis of differance and its "history" that we can claim to know who and where "we" are and what the limits of an "epoch" can be.

Although "differance" is neither a word nor a concept, let us nonetheless attempt a simple and approximative semantic analysis which will bring us in view of what is at stake [*en vue de l'enjeu*].

We do know that the verb "to differ" [*différer*] (the Latin verb *differre*) has two seemingly quite distinct meanings; in the *Littré* dictionary, for example, they are the subject of two separate articles. In this sense, the Latin *differre* is not the simple translation of the Greek *diapherein*; this fact will not be without consequence for us in tying our discussion to a particular language, one that passes for being less philosophical, less primordially philosophical, than the other. For the distribution of sense in the Greek *diapherein* does not carry one of the two themes of the Latin *differre,* namely, the action of postponing until later, of taking into account, the taking-account of time and forces in an operation that implies an economic reckoning, a detour, a respite, a delay, a reserve, a representation—all the concepts that I will sum up here in a word I have never used but which could be added to this series: *temporalizing.* "To differ" in this sense is to temporalize, to resort, consciously or unconsciously, to the temporal and temporalizing mediation of a detour that suspends the accomplishment or fulfillment of "desire" or "will," or carries desire or will out in a way that annuls or tempers their effect. We shall see, later, in what respects this temporalizing is also a temporalization and spacing, is space's becoming-temporal and time's becoming-spatial, is "primordial constitution" of space and time, as metaphysics or transcendental phenomenology would call it in the language that is here criticized and displaced.

The other sense of "to differ" [*différer*] is the most common and most identifiable, the sense of not being identical, of being other, of being discernible, etc. And in "differents," whether referring to the alterity of dissimilarity or the alterity of allergy or of polemics, it is necessary that interval, distance, *spacing* occur among the different elements and occur actively, dynamically, and with a certain perseverence in repetition.

But the word "difference" (with an *e*) could never refer to differing as temporalizing or to difference as *polemos*. It is this loss of sense that the word differance (with an *a*) will have to schematically compensate for. Differance can refer to the whole complex of its meanings at once, for it is immediately and irreducibly multivalent, something which will be important for the discourse I am trying to develop. It refers to this whole complex of meanings not only when it is supported by a language or interpretive context (like any signification), but it already does so somehow of itself. Or at least it does so more easily by itself than does any other word: here the *a* comes more immediately from the present participle [*différant*] and brings us closer to the action of "differing" that is in progress, even before it has produced the effect that is constituted as different or resulted in difference (with an *e*). Within a conceptual system and in terms of classical requirements, differance could be said to designate the productive and primordial constituting causality, the process of scission and division whose differings and differences would be the constituted products or effects. But while bringing us closer to the infinitive and active core of differing, "differance" with an *a* neutralizes what the infinitive denotes as simply active, in the same way that "parlance" does not signify the simple fact of speaking, of speaking to or being spoken to. Nor is resonance the act of resonating. Here in the usage of our language we must consider that the ending *-ance* is undecided between active and passive. And we shall see why what is designated by "differance" is neither simply active nor simply passive, that it announces or rather recalls something like the middle voice, that it speaks of an operation which is not an operation, which cannot be thought of either as a passion or as an action of a subject upon an object, as starting from an agent or from a patient, or on the basis of, or in view of, any of these *terms*. But philosophy has perhaps commenced by distributing the middle voice, expressing a certain intransitiveness, into the active and the passive voice, and has itself been constituted in this repression.

How are differance as temporalizing and differance as spacing conjoined?

Let us begin with the problem of signs and writing—since we are already in the midst of it. We ordinarily say that a sign is put in place of the thing itself, the present thing—"thing" holding here for the sense as well as the referent. Signs represent the present in its absence; they take the place of the present. When we cannot take hold of or show the thing, let us say the present, the being-present, when the present does not present itself, then we signify, we go through the detour of signs. We take up or give signs; we make signs. The sign would thus be a deferred presence. Whether it is a question of verbal or written signs, monetary signs, electoral delegates, or political representatives, the movement of signs defers the moment of encountering the thing itself, the moment at which we could lay hold of it, consume or expend it, touch it, see it, have a present intuition of it. What I am describing here is the structure of signs as classically determined, in order to define —through a commonplace characterization of its traits—signification as the differance of temporalizing. Now this classical determination presupposes that the sign (which defers presence) is conceivable only *on the basis of* the presence that it defers and *in view of* the deferred presence one intends to reappropriate. Following this classical semiology, the substitution of the sign for the thing itself is both *secondary* and *provisional*: it is second in order after an original and lost presence, a presence from which the sign would be derived. It is provisional with respect to this final and missing presence, in view of which the sign would serve as a movement of mediation.

In attempting to examine these secondary and provisional aspects of the substitute, we shall no doubt catch sight of something like a primordial differance. Yet we could no longer even call it primordial or final, inasmuch as the characteristics of origin, beginning, *telos*, *eschaton*, etc., have always denoted presence—*ousia*, *parousia*, etc. To question the secondary and provisional character of the sign, to oppose it to a "primordial" differance, would thus have the following consequences:

1. Differance can no longer be understood according to the concept of "sign," which has always been taken to mean the representation of a presence and has been constituted in a system (of thought or language) determined on the basis of and in view of presence.

2. In this way we question the authority of presence or its simple symmetrical contrary, absence or lack. We thus interrogate the limit that has always constrained us, that always constrains us—we who inhabit a language and a system of thought—to form the sense of being in general as presence or absence, in the categories of being or beingness (*ousia*). It already appears that the kind of questioning we are thus led back to is, let us say, the Heideggerian kind, and that differance *seems* to lead us back to the ontic-ontological difference. But permit me to postpone this reference. I shall only note that between differance as temporalizing-temporalization (which we can no longer conceive within the horizon of the present) and what Heidegger says about temporalization in *Sein und Zeit* (namely, that as the transcendental horizon of the question of being it must be freed from the traditional and metaphysical domination by the present or the now)— between these two there is a close, if not exhaustive and irreducibly necessary, interconnection.

But first of all, let us remain with the semiological aspects of the problem to see how differance as temporalizing is conjoined with differance as spacing. Most of the semiological or linguistic research currently dominating the field of thought (whether due to the results of its own investigations or due to its role as a generally recognized regulative model) traces its genealogy, rightly or wrongly, to Saussure as its common founder. It was Saussure who first of all set forth the *arbitrariness of signs* and the *differential character* of signs as principles of general semiology and particularly of linguistics. And, as we know, these two themes—the arbitrary and the differential—are in his view inseparable. Arbitrariness can occur only because the system of signs is constituted by the differences between the terms, and not by their fullness. The elements of signification function not by virtue of the compact force of their cores but by the network of oppositions that distinguish them and relate them to one another. "Arbitrary and differential" says Saussure "are two correlative qualities."

As the condition for signification, this principle of difference affects the *whole sign*, that is, both the signified and the signifying aspects. The signified aspect is the concept, the ideal sense. The signifying aspect is what Saussure calls the material or physical (e.g., acoustical) "image." We do not here have to enter into all the problems these definitions pose. Let us only cite Saussure where it interests us:

> The conceptual side of value is made up solely of relations and differences with respect to the other terms of language, and the same can be said of its material side. . . . Everything that has been said up to this point boils down to this: in language there are only differences. Even more important: a difference generally implies positive terms between which the difference is set up; but in language there are only differences *without positive terms.* Whether we take the signified or the signifier, language has neither ideas nor sounds that existed before the linguistic system, but only conceptual and phonic differences that have issued from the system. The idea or phonic substance that a sign contains is of less importance than the other signs that surround it.[4]

The first consequence to be drawn from this is that the signified concept is never present in itself, in an adequate presence that would refer only to itself. Every concept is necessarily and essentially inscribed in a chain or a system, within which it refers to another and to other concepts, by the systematic play of differences. Such a play, then—differance—is no longer simply a concept, but the possibility of conceptuality, of the conceptual system and process in general. For the same reason, differance, which is not a concept, is not a mere word; that is, it is not what we represent to ourselves as the calm and present self-referential unity of a concept and sound [*phonie*]. We shall later discuss the consequences of this for the notion of a word.

The difference that Saussure speaks about, therefore, is neither itself a concept nor one word among others. We can say this *a fortiori* for differance. Thus we are brought to make the relation between the one and the other explicit.

Within a language, within the *system* of language, there are only differences. A taxonomic operation can accordingly undertake its systematic, statistical, and classificatory inventory. But, on the one hand, these differences *play a role* in language, in speech as well, and in the exchange between language and speech. On the other hand, these differences are

4. Ferdinand de Saussure, *Cours de linguistique générale,* ed. C. Bally and A. Sechehaye (Paris: Payot, 1916); English translation by Wade Baskin, *Course in General Linguistics* (New York: Philosophical Library, 1959), pp. 117–18, 120.

themselves *effects*. They have not fallen from the sky ready made; they are no more inscribed in a *topos noētos* than they are prescribed in the wax of the brain. If the word "history" did not carry with it the theme of a final repression of differance, we could say that differences alone could be "historical" through and through and from the start.

What we note as *differance* will thus be the movement of play that "produces" (and not by something that is simply an activity) these differences, these effects of difference. This does not mean that the differance which produces differences is before them in a simple and in itself unmodified and indifferent present. Differance is the nonfull, nonsimple "origin"; it is the structured and differing origin of differences.

Since language (which Saussure says is a classification) has not fallen from the sky, it is clear that the differences have been produced; they are the effects produced, but effects that do not have as their cause a subject or substance, a thing in general, or a being that is somewhere present and itself escapes the play of difference. If such a presence were implied (quite classically) in the general concept of cause, we would therefore have to talk about an effect without a cause, something that would very quickly lead to no longer talking about effects. I have tried to indicate a way out of the closure imposed by this system, namely, by means of the "trace." No more an effect than a cause, the "trace" cannot of itself, taken outside its context, suffice to bring about the required transgression.

As there is no presence before the semiological difference or outside it, we can extend what Saussure writes about language to signs in general: "Language is necessary in order for speech to be intelligible and to produce all of its effects; but the latter is necessary in order for language to be established; historically, the fact of speech always comes first." [5]

Retaining at least the schema, if not the content, of the demand formulated by Saussure, we shall designate by the term *differance* the movement by which language, or any code, any system of reference in general, becomes "historically" constituted as a fabric of differences. Here, the terms "constituted," "produced," "created," "movement," "historically," etc., with all they imply, are not to be understood only in terms

5. *Course in General Linguistics*, p. 18.

of the language of metaphysics, from which they are taken. It would have to be shown why the concepts of production, like those of constitution and history, remain accessories in this respect to what is here being questioned; this, however, would draw us too far away today, toward the theory of the representation of the "circle" in which we seem to be enclosed. I only use these terms here, like many other concepts, out of strategic convenience and in order to prepare the deconstruction of the system they form at the point which is now most decisive. In any event, we will have understood, by virtue of the very circle we appear to be caught up in, that differance, as it is written here, is no more static than genetic, no more structural than historical. Nor is it any less so. And it is completely to miss the point of this orthographical impropriety to want to object to it on the basis of the oldest of metaphysical oppositions—for example, by opposing some generative point of view to a structuralist-taxonomic point of view, or conversely. These oppositions do not pertain in the least to differance; and this, no doubt, is what makes thinking about it difficult and uncomfortable.

If we now consider the chain to which "differance" gets subjected, according to the context, to a certain number of nonsynonymic substitutions, one will ask why we resorted to such concepts as "reserve," "protowriting," "prototrace," "spacing," indeed to "supplement" or *"pharmakon,"* and, before long, to "hymen," etc.[6]

Let us begin again. Differance is what makes the movement of signification possible only if each element that is said to be "present," appearing on the stage of presence, is related to something other than itself but retains the mark of a past element and already lets itself be hollowed out by the mark of its relation to a future element. This trace relates no less to what is called the future than to what is called the past, and it constitutes what is called the present by this very relation

6. [On "supplement" see above, *Speech and Phenomena*, Chap. 7, pp. 88–104. Cf. also Derrida, *De la grammatologie* (Paris: Editions de Minuit, 1967). On *"pharmakon"* see Derrida, "La Pharmacie de Platon," *Tel Quel*, No. 32 (Winter, 1967), pp. 17–59; No. 33 (Spring, 1968), pp. 4–48. On "hymen" see Derrida, "La Double séance," *Tel Quel*, No. 41 (Spring, 1970), pp. 3–43; No. 42 (Summer, 1970), pp. 3–45. "La Pharmacie de Platon" and "La Double séance" have been reprinted in a recent text of Derrida, *La Dissémination* (Paris: Editions du Seuil, 1972).—Translator.]

to what it is not, to what it absolutely is not; that is, not even to a past or future considered as a modified present. In order for it to be, an interval must separate it from what it is not; but the interval that constitutes it in the present must also, and by the same token, divide the present in itself, thus dividing, along with the present, everything that can be conceived on its basis, that is, every being—in particular, for our metaphysical language, the substance or subject. Constituting itself, dynamically dividing itself, this interval is what could be called *spacing;* time's becoming-spatial or space's becoming-temporal (*temporalizing*). And it is this constitution of the present as a "primordial" and irreducibly nonsimple, and, therefore, in the strict sense nonprimordial, synthesis of traces, retentions, and protentions (to reproduce here, analogically and provisionally, a phenomenological and transcendental language that will presently be revealed as inadequate) that I propose to call protowriting, prototrace, or differance. The latter (is) (both) spacing (and) temporalizing.[7]

Given this (active) movement of the (production of) differance without origin, could we not, quite simply and without any neographism, call it *differentiation*? Among other confusions, such a word would suggest some organic unity, some primordial and homogeneous unity, that would eventually come to be divided up and take on difference as an event. Above all, formed on the verb "to differentiate," this word would annul the economic signification of detour, temporalizing delay, "deferring." I owe a remark in passing to a recent reading of one of Koyré's texts entitled "Hegel at Jena."[8] In that text, Koyré cites long passages from the Jena *Logic* in German and gives

7. [Derrida often brackets or "crosses out" certain key terms taken from metaphysics and logic, and in doing this, he follows Heidegger's usage in *Zur Seinsfrage*. The terms in question no longer have their full meaning, they no longer have the status of a purely signified content of expression—no longer, that is, after the deconstruction of metaphysics. Generated out of the play of differance, they still retain a vestigial trace of sense, however, a trace that cannot simply be gotten around (*incontourable*). An extensive discussion of all this is to be found in *De la grammatologie*, pp. 31–40.—Translator.]

8. Alexandre Koyré, "Hegel à Iéna," *Revue d'histoire et de philosophie religieuse*, XIV (1934), 420–58; reprinted in Koyré, *Etudes d'histoire de la pensée philosophique* (Paris: Armand Colin, 1961), pp. 135–73.

his own translation. On two occasions in Hegel's text he encounters the expression *"differente Beziehung."* This word (*different*), whose root is Latin, is extremely rare in German and also, I believe, in Hegel, who instead uses *verschieden* or *ungleich*, calling difference *Unterschied* and qualitative variety *Verschiedenheit*. In the Jena *Logic,* he uses the word *different* precisely at the point where he deals with time and the present. Before coming to Koyré's valuable remark, here are some passages from Hegel, as rendered by Koyré:

> The infinite, in this simplicity is—as a moment opposed to the self-identical—the negative. In its moments, while the infinite presents the totality to (itself) and in itself, (it is) excluding in general, the point or limit; but in this, its own (action of) negating, it relates itself immediately to the other and negates itself. The limit or moment of the present (*der Gegen-wart*), the absolute "this" of time or the now, is an absolutely negative simplicity, absolutely excluding all multiplicity from itself, and by this very fact is absolutely determined; it is not an extended whole or *quantum* within itself (and) which would in itself also have an undetermined aspect or qualitative variety, which of itself would be related, indifferently (*gleichgültig*) or externally to another, but on the contrary, this is an absolutely different relation of the simple.[9]

And Koyré specifies in a striking note: "Different relation: *differente Beziehung*. We could say: differentiating relation." And on the following page, from another text of Hegel, we can read: *"Diese Beziehung ist Gegenwart, als eine differente Beziehung"* (This relation is [the] present, as a different relation). There is another note by Koyré: "The term '*different*' is taken here in an active sense."

Writing "differing" or "differance" (with an *a*) would have had the utility of making it possible to translate Hegel on precisely this point with no further qualifications—and it is a quite decisive point in his text. The translation would be, as it always should be, the transformation of one language by another. Naturally, I maintain that the word "differance" can be used in other ways, too; first of all, because it denotes not

9. Koyré, *Etudes d'histoire*, pp. 153–54. [The quotation from Hegel (my translation) comes from "Jenenser Logik, Metaphysik, und Naturphilosophie," *Sämtliche Werke* (Leipzig: F. Meiner, 1925), XVIII, 202. Koyré reproduces the original German text on pp. 153–54, note 2.—Translator.]

only the activity of primordial difference but also the temporalizing detour of deferring. It has, however, an even more important usage. Despite the very profound affinities that differance thus written has with Hegelian speech (as it should be read), it can, at a certain point, not exactly break with it, but rather work a sort of displacement with regard to it. A definite rupture with Hegelian language would make no sense, nor would it be at all likely; but this displacement is both infinitesimal and radical. I have tried to indicate the extent of this displacement elsewhere; it would be difficult to talk about it with any brevity at this point.

Differences are thus "produced"—differed—by differance. But *what* differs, or *who* differs? In other words, *what is* differance? With this question we attain another stage and another source of the problem.

What differs? Who differs? What is differance?

If we answered these questions even before examining them as questions, even before going back over them and questioning their form (even what seems to be most natural and necessary about them), we would fall below the level we have now reached. For if we accepted the form of the question in its own sense and syntax ("What?," "What is?," "Who is?"), we would have to admit that differance is derived, supervenient, controlled, and ordered from the starting point of a being-present, one capable of being something, a force, a state, or power in the world, to which we could give all kinds of names: a *what*, or being-present as a *subject*, a *who*. In the latter case, notably, we would implicitly admit that the being-present (for example, as a self-present being or consciousness) would eventually result in differing: in delaying or in diverting the fulfillment of a "need" or "desire," or in differing from itself. But in none of these cases would such a being-present be "constituted" by this differance.

Now if we once again refer to the semiological difference, what was it that Saussure in particular reminded us of? That "language [which consists only of differences] is not a function of the speaking subject." This implies that the subject (self-identical or even conscious of self-identity, self-conscious) is inscribed in the language, that he is a "function" of the language. He becomes a *speaking* subject only by conforming his speech—even in the aforesaid "creation," even in the aforesaid "transgression"—to the system of linguistic prescriptions taken as the system of differences, or at least to the general law of differance, by conforming to that law of language which Saussure calls "language without speech." "Language is necessary for the spoken word to be intelligible and so that it can produce all of its effects." [10]

If, by hypothesis, we maintain the strict opposition between speech and language, then differance will be not only the play of differences within the language but the relation of speech to language, the detour by which I must also pass in order to speak, the silent token I must give, which holds just as well for linguistics in the strict sense as it does for general semiology; it dictates all the relations between usage and the formal schema, between the message and the particular code, etc. Elsewhere I have tried to suggest that this differance within language, and in the relation between speech and language, forbids the essential dissociation between speech and writing that Saussure, in keeping with tradition, wanted to draw at another level of his presentation. The use of language or the employment of any code which implies a play of forms —with no determined or invariable substratum—also presupposes a retention and protention of differences, a spacing and temporalizing, a play of traces. This play must be a sort of inscription prior to writing, a protowriting without a present origin, without an *arché*. From this comes the systematic crossing-out of the *arché* and the transformation of general semiology into a grammatology, the latter performing a critical work upon everything within semiology—right down to its matrical concept of signs—that retains any metaphysical presuppositions incompatible with the theme of differance.

We might be tempted by an objection: to be sure, the subject becomes a *speaking* subject only by dealing with the system of linguistic differences; or again, he becomes a *signifying* subject (generally by speech or other signs) only by entering into the system of differences. In this sense, certainly, the speaking or signifying subject would not be self-present, insofar as he speaks or signifies, except for the play of linguistic or semiological differance. But can we not conceive of a presence and self-presence of the subject before speech or its signs, a subject's self-presence in a silent and intuitive consciousness?

Such a question therefore supposes that prior to signs and

10. De Saussure, *Course in General Linguistics*, p. 37.

outside them, and excluding every trace and differance, something such as consciousness is possible. It supposes, moreover, that, even before the distribution of its signs in space and in the world, consciousness can gather itself up in its own presence. What then is consciousness? What does "consciousness" mean? Most often in the very form of "meaning" ["*vouloir-dire*"], consciousness in all its modifications is conceivable only as self-presence, a self-perception of presence. And what holds for consciousness also holds here for what is called subjective existence in general. Just as the category of subject is not and never has been conceivable without reference to presence as *hypokeimenon* or *ousia,* etc., so the subject as consciousness has never been able to be evinced otherwise than as self-presence. The privilege accorded to consciousness thus means a privilege accorded to the present; and even if the transcendental temporality of consciousness is described in depth, as Husserl described it, the power of synthesis and of the incessant gathering-up of traces is always accorded to the "living present."

This privilege is the ether of metaphysics, the very element of our thought insofar as it is caught up in the language of metaphysics. We can only de-limit such a closure today by evoking this import of presence, which Heidegger has shown to be the onto-theological determination of being. Therefore, in evoking this import of presence, by an examination which would have to be of a quite peculiar nature, we question the absolute privilege of this form or epoch of presence in general, that is, consciousness as meaning [*vouloir-dire*] in self-presence.

We thus come to posit presence—and, in particular, consciousness, the being-next-to-itself of consciousness—no longer as the absolutely matrical form of being but as a "determination" and an "effect." Presence is a determination and effect within a system which is no longer that of presence but that of differance; it no more allows the opposition between activity and passivity than that between cause and effect or in-determination and determination, etc. This system is of such a kind that even to designate consciousness as an effect or determination—for strategic reasons, reasons that can be more or less clearly considered and systematically ascertained—is to continue to operate according to the vocabulary of that very thing to be de-limited.

Before being so radically and expressly Heideggerian, this was also Nietzsche's and Freud's move, both of whom, as we know, and often in a very similar way, questioned the self-assured certitude of consciousness. And is it not remarkable that both of them did this by starting out with the theme of differance?

This theme appears almost literally in their work, at the most crucial places. I shall not expand on this here; I shall only recall that for Nietzsche "the important main activity is unconscious" and that consciousness is the effect of forces whose essence, ways, and modalities are not peculiar to it. Now force itself is never present; it is only a play of differences and quantities. There would be no force in general without the difference between forces; and here the difference in quantity counts more than the content of quantity, more than the absolute magnitude itself.

Quantity itself therefore is not separable from the difference in quantity. The difference in quantity is the essence of force, the relation of force with force. To fancy two equal forces, even if we grant them opposing directions, is an approximate and crude illusion, a statistical dream in which life is immersed, but which chemistry dispels.[11]

Is not the whole thought of Nietzsche a critique of philosophy as active indifference to difference, as a system of reduction or adiaphoristic repression? Following the same logic—logic itself —this does not exclude the fact that philosophy lives *in* and *from* differance, that it thereby blinds itself to the *same*, which is not the identical. The same is precisely differance (with an *a*), as the diverted and equivocal passage from one difference to another, from one term of the opposition to the other. We could thus take up all the coupled oppositions on which philosophy is constructed, and from which our language lives, not in order to see opposition vanish but to see the emergence of a necessity such that one of the terms appears as the differance of the other, the other as "differed" within the systematic ordering of the same (e.g., the intelligible as differing from the sensible, as sensible differed; the concept as differed-differing intuition, life as differing-differed matter; mind as differed-differing life; culture as differed-differing

11. G. Deleuze, *Nietzsche et la philosophie* (Paris: Presses Universitaires de France, 1970), p. 49.

nature; and all the terms designating what is other than *physis*—*technē, nomos,* society, freedom, history, spirit, etc. —as *physis* differed or *physis* differing: *physis in differance*). It is out of the unfolding of this "same" as differance that the sameness of difference and of repetition is presented in the eternal return.

In Nietzsche, these are so many themes that can be related with the kind of symptomatology that always serves to diagnose the evasions and ruses of anything disguised in its differance. Or again, these terms can be related with the entire thematics of active interpretation, which substitutes an incessant deciphering for the disclosure of truth as a presentation of the thing itself in its presence, etc. What results is a cipher without truth, or at least a system of ciphers that is not dominated by truth value, which only then becomes a function that is understood, inscribed, and circumscribed.

We shall therefore call differance this "active" (in movement) discord of the different forces and of the differences between forces which Nietzsche opposes to the entire system of metaphysical grammar, wherever that system controls culture, philosophy, and science.

It is historically significant that this diaphoristics, understood as an energetics or an economy of forces, set up to question the primacy of presence qua consciousness, is also the major theme of Freud's thought; in his work we find another diaphoristics, both in the form of a theory of ciphers or traces and an energetics. The questioning of the authority of consciousness is first and always differential.

The two apparently different meanings of differance are tied together in Freudian theory: differing [*le différer*] as discernibility, distinction, deviation, diastem, *spacing;* and deferring [*le différer*] as detour, delay, relay, reserve, *temporalizing.* I shall recall only that:

1. The concept of trace (*Spur*), of facilitation (*Bahnung*), of forces of facilitation are, as early as the composition of the *Entwurf,* inseparable from the concept of difference. The origin of memory and of the psyche as a memory in general (conscious or unconscious) can only be described by taking into account the difference between the facilitation thresholds, as Freud says explicitly. There is no facilitation [*Bahnung*] without difference and no difference without a trace.

2. All the differences involved in the production of un-

conscious traces and in the process of inscription (*Nieder-schrift*) can also be interpreted as moments of differance, in the sense of "placing on reserve." Following a schema that continually guides Freud's thinking, the movement of the trace is described as an effort of life to protect itself *by deferring* the dangerous investment, by constituting a reserve (*Vorrat*). And all the conceptual oppositions that furrow Freudian thought relate each concept to the other like movements of a detour, within the economy of differance. The one is only the other deferred, the one differing from the other. The one is the other in differance, the one is the difference from the other. Every apparently rigorous and irreducible opposition (for example, that between the secondary and primary) is thus said to be, at one time or another, a "theoretical fiction." In this way again, for example (but such an example covers everything or communicates with everything), the difference between the pleasure principle and the reality principle is only difference as detour (*Aufschieben, Aufschub*). In *Beyond the Pleasure Principle*, Freud writes:

> Under the influence of the ego's instincts of self-preservation, the pleasure principle is replaced by the reality principle. This latter principle does not abandon the intention of ultimately obtaining pleasure, but it nevertheless demands and carries into effect the postponement of satisfaction, the abandonment of a number of possibilities of gaining satisfaction and the temporary toleration of unpleasure as a step on the long indirect road (*Aufschub*) to pleasure.[12]

Here we touch on the point of greatest obscurity, on the very enigma of differance, on how the concept we have of it is divided by a strange separation. We must not hasten to make a decision too quickly. How can we conceive of differance as a systematic detour which, within the element of the same, always aims at either finding again the pleasure or the presence that had been deferred by (conscious or unconscious) calculation, and, *at the same time,* how can we, on the other hand, conceive of differance as the relation to an impossible presence, as an expenditure without reserve, as an irreparable loss of presence, an irreversible wearing-down of energy, or indeed as a death instinct and a relation to the absolutely other that apparently breaks up any economy? It is evident—it is evidence

12. Freud, *Complete Psychological Works*, XVIII, 10.

itself—that system and nonsystem, the same and the absolutely other, etc., cannot be conceived *together*.

If differance is this inconceivable factor, must we not perhaps hasten to make it evident, to bring it into the philosophical element of evidence, and thus quickly dissipate its mirage character and illogicality, dissipate it with the infallibility of the calculus we know well—since we have recognized its place, necessity, and function within the structure of differance? What would be accounted for philosophically here has already been taken into account in the system of differance as it is here being calculated. I have tried elsewhere, in a reading of Bataille,[13] to indicate what might be the establishment of a rigorous, and in a new sense "scientific," *relating* of a "restricted economy"—one having nothing to do with an unreserved expenditure, with death, with being exposed to nonsense, etc.—to a "general economy" or system that, so to speak, *takes account of* what is unreserved. It is a relation between a differance that is accounted for and a differance that fails to be accounted for, where the establishment of a pure presence, without loss, is one with the occurrence of absolute loss, with death. By establishing this relation between a restricted and a general system, we shift and recommence the very project of philosophy under the privileged heading of Hegelianism.

The economic character of differance in no way implies that the deferred presence can always be recovered, that it simply amounts to an investment that only temporarily and without loss delays the presentation of presence, that is, the perception of gain or the gain of perception. Contrary to the metaphysical, dialectical, and "Hegelian" interpretation of the economic movement of differance, we must admit a game where whoever loses wins and where one wins and loses each time. If the diverted presentation continues to be somehow definitively and irreducibly withheld, this is not because a particular present remains hidden or absent, but because differance holds us in a relation with what exceeds (though we necessarily fail to recognize this) the alternative of presence or absence. A certain alterity—Freud gives it a metaphysical name, the unconscious—is definitively taken away from every process of presentation in which we would demand for it to be shown forth in person. In this context and under this heading,

13. Derrida, *L'Ecriture et la différence*, pp. 369–407.

the unconscious is not, as we know, a hidden, virtual, and potential self-presence. It is differed—which no doubt means that it is woven out of differences, but also that it sends out, that it delegates, representatives or proxies; but there is no chance that the mandating subject "exists" somewhere, that it is present or is "itself," and still less chance that it will become conscious. In this sense, contrary to the terms of an old debate, strongly symptomatic of the metaphysical investments it has always assumed, the "unconscious" can no more be classed as a "thing" than as anything else; it is no more of a thing than an implicit or masked consciousness. This radical alterity, removed from every possible mode of presence, is characterized by irreducible aftereffects, by delayed effects. In order to describe them, in order to read the traces of the "unconscious" traces (there are no "conscious" traces), the language of presence or absence, the metaphysical speech of phenomenology, is in principle inadequate.

The structure of delay (*retardement: Nachträglichkeit*) that Freud talks about indeed prohibits our taking temporalization (temporalizing) to be a simple dialectical complication of the present; rather, this is the style of transcendental phenomenology. It describes the living present as a primordial and incessant synthesis that is constantly led back upon itself, back upon its assembled and assembling self, by retentional traces and protentional openings. With the alterity of the "unconscious," we have to deal not with the horizons of modified presents—past or future—but with a "past" that has never been nor will ever be present, whose "future" will never be produced or reproduced in the form of presence. The concept of trace is therefore incommensurate with that of retention, that of the becoming-past of what had been present. The trace cannot be conceived—nor, therefore, can differance—on the basis of either the present or the presence of the present.

A past that has never been present: with this formula Emmanuel Levinas designates (in ways that are, to be sure, not those of psychoanalysis) the trace and the enigma of absolute alterity, that is, the Other [*autrui*]. At least within these limits, and from this point of view, the thought of differance implies the whole critique of classical ontology undertaken by Levinas. And the concept of trace, like that of differance, forms—across these different traces and through these differences between traces, as understood by Nietzsche, Freud, and Levinas (these "authors' names" serve only as indications)—the network that sums up and permeates our "epoch" as the de-limitation of ontology (of presence).

The ontology of presence is the ontology of beings and beingness. Everywhere, the dominance of beings is solicited by differance—in the sense that *sollicitare* means, in old Latin, to shake all over, to make the whole tremble. What is questioned by the thought of differance, therefore, is the determination of being in presence, or in beingness. Such a question could not arise and be understood without the difference between Being and beings opening up somewhere. The first consequence of this is that differance is not. It is not a being-present, however excellent, unique, principal, or transcendent one makes it. It commands nothing, rules over nothing, and nowhere does it exercise any authority. It is not marked by a capital letter. Not only is there no realm of differance, but differance is even the subversion of every realm. This is obviously what makes it threatening and necessarily dreaded by everything in us that desires a realm, the past or future presence of a realm. And it is always in the name of a realm that, believing one sees it ascend to the capital letter, one can reproach it for wanting to rule.

Does this mean, then, that differance finds its place within the spread of the ontic-ontological difference, as it is conceived, as the "epoch" conceives itself within it, and particularly "across" the Heideggerian meditation, which cannot be gotten around?

There is no simple answer to such a question.

In one particular respect, differance is, to be sure, but the historical and epochal *deployment* of Being or of the ontological difference. The *a* of differance marks the *movement* of this deployment.

And yet, is not the thought that conceives the *sense* or *truth* of Being, the determination of differance as ontic-ontological difference—difference conceived within the horizon of the question of *Being*—still an intrametaphysical effect of differance? Perhaps the deployment of differance is not only the truth or the epochality of Being. Perhaps we must try to think this *unheard-of* thought, this silent tracing, namely, that the history of Being (the thought of which is committed to the Greco-Western logos), as it is itself produced across the ontological difference, is only one epoch of the *diapherein*. Then we could no longer even call it an "epoch," for the concept of epochality belongs within history understood as the history of Being. Being has always made "sense," has always been conceived or spoken of as such, only by dissimulating itself in beings; thus, in a particular and very strange way, differance (is) "older" than the ontological difference or the truth of Being. In this age it can be called the play of traces. It is a trace that no longer belongs to the horizon of Being but one whose sense of Being is borne and bound by this play; it is a play of traces or differance that has no sense and is not, a play that does not belong. There is no support to be found and no depth to be had for this bottomless chessboard where being is set in play.

It is perhaps in this way that the Heraclitean play of the *hen diapheron heautōi*, of the one differing from itself, of what is in difference with itself, already becomes lost as a trace in determining the *diapherein* as ontological difference.

To think through the ontological difference doubtless remains a difficult task, a task whose statement has remained nearly inaudible. And to prepare ourselves for venturing beyond our own logos, that is, for a differance so violent that it refuses to be stopped and examined as the epochality of Being and ontological difference, is neither to give up this passage through the truth of Being, nor is it in any way to "criticize," "contest," or fail to recognize the incessant necessity for it. On the contrary, we must stay within the difficulty of this passage; we must repeat this passage in a rigorous reading of metaphysics, wherever metaphysics serves as the norm of Western speech, and not only in the texts of "the history of philosophy." Here we must allow the trace of whatever goes beyond the truth of Being to appear/disappear in its fully rigorous way. It is a trace of something that can never present itself; it is itself a trace that can never be presented, that is, can never appear and manifest itself as such in its phenomenon. It is a trace that lies beyond what profoundly ties fundamental ontology to phenomenology. Like differance, the trace is never presented as such. In presenting itself it becomes effaced; in being sounded it dies away, like the writing of the *a*, inscribing its pyramid in differance.

We can always reveal the precursive and secretive traces of this movement in metaphysical speech, especially in the contemporary talk about the closure of ontology, i.e., through the various attempts we have looked at (Nietzsche, Freud, Levinas)—and particularly in Heidegger's work.

The latter provokes us to question the essence of the present, the presence of the present.

What is the present? What is it to conceive the present in its presence?

Let us consider, for example, the 1946 text entitled "Der Spruch des Anaximander." Heidegger there recalls that the forgetting of Being forgets about the difference between Being and beings:

> But the point of Being (*die Sache des Seins*) is to be the Being *of* beings. The linguistic form of this enigmatic and multivalent genitive designates a genesis (*Genesis*), a provenance (*Herkunft*) of the pre*sent* from pre*sence* (*des Anwesenden aus dem Anwesen*). But with the unfolding of these two, the essence (*Wesen*) of this provenance remains hidden (*verborgen*). Not only is the essence of this provenance not thought out, but neither is the simple relation between pre*sence* and pre*sent* (*Anwesen und Anwesenden*). Since the dawn, it seems that pre*sence* and being-pre*sent* are each separately something. Imperceptibly, pre*sence* becomes itself a pre*sent*. . . . The essence of pre*sence* (*Das Wesen des Anwesens*), and thus the difference between pre*sence* and pre*sent*, is forgotten. *The forgetting of Being is the forgetting of the difference between Being and beings.*[14]

In recalling the difference between Being and beings (the ontological difference) as the difference between presence and present, Heidegger puts forward a proposition, indeed, a group of propositions; it is not our intention here to idly or hastily "criticize" them but rather to convey them with all their provocative force.

Let us then proceed slowly. What Heidegger wants to point out is that the difference between Being and beings, forgotten by metaphysics, has disappeared without leaving a trace. The very trace of difference has sunk from sight. If we admit that differance (is) (itself) something other than presence and absence, if it *traces*, then we are dealing with the forgetting of the difference (between Being and beings), and we now have to talk about a disappearance of the trace's trace. This is

14. Martin Heidegger, *Holzwege* (Frankfurt: V. Klostermann, 1957), pp. 335–36. [All translations of quotations from *Holzwege* are mine.—Translator.]

certainly what this passage from "Der Spruch des Anaximander" seems to imply:

> The forgetting of Being is a part of the very essence of Being, and is concealed by it. The forgetting belongs so essentially to the destination of Being that the dawn of this destination begins precisely as an unconcealment of the present in its presence. This means: the history of Being begins by the forgetting of Being, in that Being retains its essence, its difference from beings. Difference is wanting; it remains forgotten. Only what is differentiated —the present and presence (das Anwesende und das Anwesen)— becomes uncovered, but not insofar as it is differentiated. On the contrary, the matinal trace (die frühe Spur) of difference effaces itself from the moment that presence appears as a being-present (das Anwesen wie ein Anwesendes erscheint) and finds its provenance in a supreme (being)-present (in einem höchsten Anwesenden).[15]

The trace is not a presence but is rather the simulacrum of a presence that dislocates, displaces, and refers beyond itself. The trace has, properly speaking, no place, for effacement belongs to the very structure of the trace. Effacement must always be able to overtake the trace; otherwise it would not be a trace but an indestructible and monumental substance. In addition, and from the start, effacement constitutes it as a trace— effacement establishes the trace in a change of place and makes it disappear in its appearing, makes it issue forth from itself in its very position. The effacing of this early trace (die frühe Spur) of difference is therefore "the same" as its tracing within the text of metaphysics. This metaphysical text must have retained a mark of what it lost or put in reserve, set aside. In the language of metaphysics the paradox of such a structure is the inversion of the metaphysical concept which produces the following effect: the present becomes the sign of signs, the trace of traces. It is no longer what every reference refers to in the last instance; it becomes a function in a generalized referential structure. It is a trace, and a trace of the effacement of a trace.

In this way the metaphysical text is understood; it is still readable, and remains to be read. It proposes both the monument and the mirage of the trace, the trace as simultaneously traced and effaced, simultaneously alive and dead, alive as

15. Ibid., p. 336.

always to simulate even life in its preserved inscription; it is a pyramid.

Thus we think through, without contradiction, or at least without granting any pertinence to such contradiction, what is perceptible and imperceptible about the trace. The "matinal trace" of difference is lost in an irretrievable invisibility, and yet even its loss is covered, preserved, regarded, and retarded. This happens in a text, in the form of presence.

Having spoken about the effacement of the matinal trace, Heidegger can thus, in this contradiction without contradiction, consign or countersign the sealing of the trace. We read on a little further:

> The difference between Being and beings, however, can in turn be experienced as something forgotten only if it is already discovered with the presence of the present (*mit dem Anwesen des Anwesenden*) and if it is thus sealed in a trace (*so eine Spur geprägt hat*) that remains preserved (*gewahrt bleibt*) in the language which Being appropriates.[16]

Further on still, while meditating upon Anaximander's τὸ χρεών, translated as *Brauch* (sustaining use), Heidegger writes the following:

> Dispensing accord and deference (*Fug und Ruch verfügend*), our sustaining use frees the pre*sent* (*das Anwesende*) in its sojourn and sets it free every time for its sojourn. But by the same token the present is equally seen to be exposed to the constant danger of hardening in the insistence (*in das blosse Beharren verhärtet*) out of its sojourning duration. In this way sustaining use (*Brauch*) remains itself and at the same time an abandonment (*Aushändigung:* handing-over) of presence (*des Anwesens*) *in den Un-fug,* to discord (disjointedness). Sustaining use joins together the dis- (*Der Brauch fügt das Un-*).[17]

And it is at the point where Heidegger determines *sustaining use* as *trace* that the question must be asked: can we, and how far can we, think of this trace and the *dis-* of differance as *Wesen des Seins*? Doesn't the *dis* of differance refer us beyond the history of Being, beyond our language as well, and beyond everything that can be named by it? Doesn't it call for —in the language of being—the necessarily violent transforma-

16. *Ibid.*
17. *Ibid.*, pp. 339–40.

tion of this language by an entirely different language?

Let us be more precise here. In order to dislodge the "trace" from its cover (and whoever believes that one tracks down some *thing?*—one tracks down tracks), let us continue reading this passage:

> The translation of τὸ χρεών by "sustaining use" (*Brauch*) does not derive from cogitations of an etymologico-lexical nature. The choice of the word "sustaining use" derives from an antecedent *trans*lation (*Übersetzen*) of the thought that attempts to conceive difference in the deployment of Being (*im Wesen des Seins*) toward the historical beginning of the forgetting of Being. The word "sustaining use" is dictated to thought in the apprehension (*Erfahrung*) of the forgetting of Being. Τὸ χρεών properly names a trace (*Spur*) of what remains to be conceived in the word "sustaining use," a trace that quickly disappears (*alsbald verschwindet*) into the history of Being, in its world-historical unfolding as Western metaphysics.[18]

How do we conceive of the outside of a text? How, for example, do we conceive of what stands opposed to the text of Western metaphysics? To be sure, the "trace that quickly disappears into the history of Being, . . . as Western metaphysics," escapes all the determinations, all the names it might receive in the metaphysical text. The trace is sheltered and thus dissimulated in these names; it does not appear in the text as the trace "itself." But this is because the trace itself could never itself appear as such. Heidegger also says that difference can never appear *as such:* "Lichtung des Unterschiedes kann deshalb auch nicht bedeuten, dass der Unterschied als der Unterschied erscheint." There is no essence of differance; not only can it not allow itself to be taken up into the *as such* of its name or its appearing, but it threatens the authority of the *as such* in general, the thing's presence in its essence. That there is no essence of differance at this point also implies that there is neither Being nor truth to the play of writing, *insofar as it involves differance.*

For us, differance remains a metaphysical name; and all the names that it receives from our language are still, so far as they are names, metaphysical. This is particularly so when they speak of determining differance as the difference between presence and present (*Anwesen/Anwesend*), but already and

18. *Ibid.*, p. 340.

especially so when, in the most general way, they speak of determining difference as the difference between Being and
beings.

"Older" than Being itself, our language has no name for
such a differance. But we "already know" that if it is unnamable,
this is not simply provisional; it is not because our language has
still not found or received this *name*, or because we would
have to look for it in another language, outside the finite
system of our language. It is because there is no *name* for this,
not even essence or Being—not even the name "differance,"
which is not a name, which is not a pure nominal unity, and
continually breaks up in a chain of different substitutions.

"There is no name for this": we read this as a truism. What
is unnamable here is not some ineffable being that cannot be
approached by a name; like God, for example. What is unnamable is the play that brings about the nominal effects, the
relatively unitary or atomic structures we call names, or chains
of substitutions for names. In these, for example, the nominal
effect of "differance" is itself involved, carried off, and rein-
scribed, just as the false beginning or end of a game is still
part of the game, a function of the system.

What we do know, what we could know if it were simply a
question of knowing, is that there never has been and never
will be a unique word, a master name. This is why thinking
about the letter *a* of differance is not the primary prescription,
nor is it the prophetic announcement of some imminent and
still unheard-of designation. There is nothing kerygmatic about
this "word" so long as we can perceive its reduction to a lower-
case letter.

There will be no unique name, not even the name of Being.
It must be conceived without *nostalgia*; that is, it must be conceived outside the myth of the purely maternal or paternal
language belonging to the lost fatherland of thought. On the
contrary, we must *affirm* it—in the sense that Nietzsche
brings affirmation into play—with a certain laughter and with a
certain dance.

After this laughter and dance, after this affirmation that is
foreign to any dialectic, the question arises as to the other side
of nostalgia, which I will call Heideggerian *hope*. I am not un-
aware that this term may be somewhat shocking. I venture it
all the same, without excluding any of its implications, and
shall relate it to what seems to me to be retained of meta-

physics in "Der Spruch des Anaximander," namely, the quest for the proper word and the unique name. In talking about the "first word of Being" (*das frühe Wort des Seins:* τὸ χρεών), Heidegger writes,

> The relation to the pre*sent*, unfolding its order in the very essence of pre*sence*, is unique (*ist eine einzige*). It is pre-eminently incomparable to any other relation; it belongs to the uniqueness of Being itself (*Sie gehört zur Einzigkeit des Seins selbst*). Thus, in order to name what is deployed in Being (*das Wesende des Seins*), language will have to find a single word, the unique word (*ein einziges, das einzige Wort*). There we see how hazardous is every word of thought (every thoughtful word: *denkende Wort*) that addresses itself to Being (*das dem Sein zugesprochen wird*). What is hazarded here, however, is not something impossible, because Being speaks through every language; everywhere and always.[19]

Such is the question: the marriage between speech and Being in the unique word, in the finally proper name. Such is the question that enters into the affirmation put into play by differance. The question bears (upon) each of the words in this sentence: "Being / speaks / through every language; / everywhere and always /."

19. *Ibid.,* pp. 337–38.

Index of Passages
Cited from Husserl

[Page numbers refer to the present book.]

Logical Investigations

Ideas I

The Phenomenology of Internal Time-Consciousness

Index

[Italicized page numbers indicate major discussion.]